DESIRE, DIALECTIC, AND OTHERNESS

DESIRE, DIALECTIC, AND OTHERNESS
An Essay on Origins

WILLIAM DESMOND

Yale University Press
New Haven and London

Published with assistance from the Kingsley Trust
Association Publication Fund established by the Scroll
and Key Society of Yale College.

Designed by Nancy Ovedovitz and set in Baskerville type by
David E. Seham Associates Inc. Printed in the United States
of America by BookCrafters, Chelsea, Mich.

Library of Congress Cataloging-in-Publication Data
Desmond, William, 1951–
  Desire, dialectic, and otherness.
  Bibliography: p.
  Includes index.
  1. Dialectic. 2. Desire. 3. Beginning. 4. Philosophy.
I. Title.
B809.7.D45 1987   110   86–24632
ISBN 0–300–03789–9 (alk. paper)

The paper in this book meets the guidelines for permanence
and durability of the Committee on Production Guidelines
for Book Longevity of the Council on Library Resources.

10 9 8 7 6 5 4 3 2 1

For my Father and Mother

Is man no more than this? Consider him well. Thou ow'st the worm no silk, the beast no hide, the sheep no wool, the cat no perfume. Ha! here's three on's are sophisticated. Thou art the thing itself; unaccommodated man is no more but such a poor, bare, forked animal as thou art.

Shakespeare, *King Lear,* III. iv. 105–10.

Τίνες οὖν ἔφην ἐγώ, ὦ Διοτίμα, οἱ
φιλοσοφοῦντες, εἰ μήτε οἱ σοφοὶ μήτε οἱ ἀμαθεῖς;
Δῆλον, ἔφη, τοῦτό γε ἤδη καὶ παιδί, ὅτι οἱ
μεταξὺ τούτων ἀμφοτέρων, ὧν αὖ καὶ
ὁ Ἔρως.

Plato, *Symposium,* 204a8–b2.

Contents

Preface

Today one commonly comes across talk about philosophy's place in "the conversation of mankind," but the nature of that conversation is far from clear. Sometimes one senses that the professorial voice has usurped the voice of mankind. On occasion one overhears the unweary murmurings of different camp followers. Sometimes one fears that one has wandered into the vicinity of Babel full of the confusion of interminable tongues. But sometimes a singular voice rises above the clamor, almost to a shout— I think here of Nietzsche. Sometimes again the singular voice is swallowed up by the conversation of the commentators, and we hear only a carefully orchestrated symphony of echoes and repetitions. The avant-garde commentator resorts to the shock tactic of cacophony: the rhetoric is the rhetoric of difference, but the language tends to be the repetition of the same. The more cautious traditionalist, by contrast, dutifully reproduces a set of drab clones of the past.

There comes a point in philosophical reflection when one must risk saying something that neither merges with the past nor breaks with it violently. In this work I make no pretense of speaking some philosophical *Ursprache* that would gather together the many competing voices. But as I write, I hear two voices. The first is one of Nietzsche's many voices, which intones the skepticism, metaphysical distrust, even nihilism, of modernity. The second is the measured voice of Hegel, which serves as a reminder that fear of error may be the first error. Though we have been saturated with suspicion since Hegel, we are not condemned to a paralysis of silence forever. Metaphysical perplexity may prove to be the spur to constructive thought, not an excuse for perpetual philosophical procrastination. The time may never be ripe for philosophy; yet somehow the time is always right.

The voice of this work—if indeed it has a distinctive voice—derives mainly from what is thought of as the Continental tradition. By this I do not mean the set of philosophical attitudes struck since Nietzsche. It is true that some of the older voices have become strangely mute since Nietzsche; even so, if there is a conversation of philosophy, it did not start around the beginning of this century. Post-Hegelians may suspect me of being too Hegelian. Hegelians, if there still be any of pure pedigree, will convict me of not being Hegelian enough. Analytical philosophers will suspect the recrudescence of a form of metaphysics whose ghost they thought was laid to rest when G. E. Moore, gasping incredulously at the exotica of British idealism, wrung his hands in defense of what he took to be common sense. Be that as it may, if there *is* a conversation, I ask first the courtesy of a hearing.

I want to mention especially Carl Vaught and Stanley Rosen, whose voices ring in the views expressed here. I wish also to thank George Kline, whose meticulous reading of my manuscript greatly lightened the burden of revision, and Jeanne Ferris of Yale University Press, whose encouragement was the measure of editorial tact. The support of Maria, my wife, is incalculable. I thank William Óg and Pangur for frivolity, Hugh for a new beginning, and my father and mother for first showing me something of agapeic otherness.

Introduction

DIALECTIC AND OTHERNESS: THE HISTORICAL CONTEXT

This book is a philosophical effort to deal with the problem of otherness, particularly as it has been bequeathed to contemporary thought by the legacy of German idealism, whose most challenging, influential thinker was Hegel. The problem of otherness is not just a contemporary issue, of course; because of its intimate link with dialectic, it reverberates throughout the entire tradition of philosophy.[1] In the wake of Hegel, many thinkers have come to see the philosophical tradition as invariably favoring sameness over otherness, identity over difference, unity over plurality. Hegel's significance for Western philosophy in the last century and a half revolves around the suspicion that his dialectical system is the final apotheosis of this ontological bias. That is, dialectical philosophy, in Hegel's hands, completes and fulfills, but at the same time exhausts, the predilection of the Western tradition for sameness, unity, and identity. Not that Hegel simply rejected otherness, difference, and plurality, as less sophisticated monists tend to do. The metaphysical coup de grace was rather to subsume otherness within a dialectical *Aufhebung*, yielding diversity *within* unity, difference *within* identity, otherness *within* sameness. Otherness thus seems to be both saluted and domesticated within a larger, overarching totality.

Many thinkers, beginning with Feuerbach and continuing with Marx in his turn to revolutionary praxis, sought an alternative to the philosophical tradition that they saw as completed and exhausted by Hegel. Kierkegaard is one of the first in a line of philosophers who find otherness outside philosophical rationality as represented by Hegelian dialectics.[2] Closer to our own time, Nietzsche's dalliance with the artist, Heidegger, and post-Heideggerianism, as epitomized most recently by

1

Derrida's deconstruction, represent various efforts to explore an otherness on the margins or outside traditional philosophical reason.[3] Existentialist concern with concrete existence as resistant to categorical abstraction, psychoanalytic probing of desire and the elusive recesses beyond the threshold of self-possessed consciousness, continuing philosophical concern with the nonphilosophical, and the pervasive repudiation of the clarity and distinctness of the Cartesian *cogito* are all indications of movement into realms of otherness, seemingly resistant to philosophical dialectics.[4]

Instances could be multiplied,[5] but perhaps it will suffice for present purposes to put the many-sided problem of otherness in terms of the contemporary concern with finitude.[6] Since many of the crucial issues of contemporary thought can be articulated with reference to Hegel, I will take my bearings from him. Hegel is not only a towering thinker in the history of philosophy, but a continuing presence in contemporary thought, sometimes as a dragon to be slain with a myriad razor slashes of analysis, sometimes as a ghostly presence to be exorcised by the incantation of deconstructive chants.[7] Hegel challenges us both because of his profound historical self-consciousness regarding the philosophical tradition and because of the power of his systematic development of dialectical thought.[8] The problem of otherness in relation to man's finitude can be put in terms of what has been called Hegel's "panlogism." This is a reading of Hegel's thought as a philosophical system for which nothing but reason is actual; whatever is not rational is merely an evanescent, eventually self-canceling existence. Hegel's philosophy here becomes exclusively a logical doctrine, and even the absolute is identified entirely with the dialectical system of categories developed in Hegel's *Science of Logic*. Of course, we can evaluate panlogism in opposite ways. Erdmann, who coined the term originally, seems to have judged the matter positively and to have upheld Hegelianism as panlogism. More recent thinkers who have identified Hegel with panlogism have tended to evaluate him negatively on this basis, however. They have regarded panlogism as something to be rejected, and precisely on the grounds of man's historicity, finitude, and the experience of otherness that art, among other things, brings home to us. We find this repudiation of the tendency to panlogism in William James's denunciation of "the block universe," in Paul Tillich's claim that Hegel represents the essentialist tendency of modern philosophy, which has culminated in an account of reality as a system of logical essences, and in Russell's claim that Hegel reduced the richness of the real to something "thin and logical."[9]

Some thinkers after Heidegger have extended this charge, under the guise of "logocentrism," to the entire tradition of metaphysics. Hegel's panlogism is said to be evident in the seemingly hubristic claims he makes for his *Logic* as the thoughts of God before the creation of nature and finite spirit.[10] It appears that here we have the dissolution of finiteness into the infinite—indeed, Hegel's identification of himself, despite his limited humanity, with the absolute.[11] More generally, we have the seemingly totalitarian thrust of dialectical thinking, which seems to finally refuse to recognize anything other as other but reduces and subsumes all otherness within the overreaching development of dialectical thought itself.

Most of Hegel's critics take their stand somewhere here; which is to say that they refuse to accept what they see as the totalizing pretensions of dialectical thought and try to discover some knot of otherness or difference that resists the dialectic sufficiently to humble its purportedly hubristic aim.[12] Thus, the Marxist finds the knot of otherness "mystified" by Hegel's idealistic distortion and downplaying of the economic conditions of practical life. The Kierkegaardian finds unsurpassable otherness in the absolute, qualitative difference between man and the God of faith, a gap that can be bridged only by a leap of absurd faith, not by any mediations of dialectical reason. The Nietzschean finds what is other to logocentrism in art. "Plato versus Homer: this is life's great antagonism," Nietzsche claimed, and sided with Homer.[13] Much contemporary thought follows Nietzsche in this sense: logocentrism, the tradition of philosophy since Plato, is suspected of attempting to illegitimately privilege or absolutize the logical, thereby producing a systematic undervaluation of experiences of otherness, as encountered in the poetic and the aesthetic. A different kind of thinking is needed to contest this evaluation and to restore what is other than the abstractly logical to its rightful place. Once again, Hegel seems to carry the thrust of logocentrism to its extreme, not only in his dialectical reduction of difference to identity, but in making art, despite its revelation of otherness, subordinate to philosophy in his system of absolute spirit. Thus in our own time, it is no surprise to find successors of Nietzsche—Heideggerians and post-Heideggerians—seeing Hegel as coming to grief on the thought of a difference that is not a dialectical difference, one that cannot be subsumed within the self-developing identity of dialectical reason.

These are just a few indications of the problem of dialectic and otherness in historical context. Suffice it to say that we can agree with the contemporary suspicion of panlogism, if by this we mean a certain elevation of dialectical thought into a totalitarian absolute. We must also agree with the stress on human finitude and an appropriate sense of limits, though, as we shall see, this finitude coexists with a certain infinite restlessness in human desire. This restlessness, while it may feed man's totalitarian pretensions, can also be seen, I shall argue, as nurturing his continuing openness to otherness.[14] Thus we can support the contemporary emphasis on guarding the genuine openness of authentic thinking. On this score, the interpretation of Hegel's thought is not without important ambiguities; and, as I have argued elsewhere, specifically in relation to art, a more open reading of Hegel is possible.[15]

I also differ from many post-Hegelians in not being convinced that Hegel has exhausted the wealth of the philosophical tradition, for I find in the tradition as much reverence for otherness as violence toward it. I find there no simple unilinear tradition, but rather a plurality of streams, among them what is called logocentrism. It is not self-evident that the tradition can be totalized, either in a Hegelian way or in the way the anti-Hegelian, supposed antitotalizers appear to attempt, albeit for purposes of deconstruction. I find that dialectical thinking is often far richer than its antagonists are willing to grant.[16] I am not saying that dialectical thinking is adequate to all forms of otherness. Indeed, one of the chief aims of this book is to show the limits of dialectic in relation to certain forms of otherness and to develop a further possibility of thought. But a proper philosophical response to otherness does not mean that we jettison dialectic or leap outside it. It is rather to find within dialectic some further openness that will serve to break open any totalitarian pretension and then to develop it fully in a manner more faithful to irreducible otherness. The desire to "overcome" Hegel, the will to "overcome" the tradition, sometimes only gets beyond each by bypassing them both. But in the process we stand to lose what we might learn from them should we probe them with a more generous hermeneutic.

THE PROBLEM OF OTHERNESS: FOUR FUNDAMENTAL POSSIBILITIES

These remarks must suffice to indicate something of the issue in historical perspective. But this book is not a book on Hegel or on the history of philosophy or on post-Hegelianism, whether of a right-wing, a left-wing, or an anti-Hegelian sort. It is a book about otherness as a philosophical problem, a problem that in its origins is concretely human.

Man finds himself estranged from being, different from things and alien to himself. Otherness stuns us long before we even begin to think. For we are delivered over to this earth a raw, a wrinkled crease of flesh in need. Our first act is to cower; our second to cry out; our third to cast about for a breast to suckle; our fourth to suck feverishly; our fifth to sleep mindlessly. If there is to be a sixth waking day, much less a seventh of delight, a Sabbath, we must be reconciled to our furious fragility. I say reconciled, not resigned. We are bound to a finitude we cannot negate, though we may affirmatively transmute its hectic.

This, fundamentally, is the human context wherein the question of otherness arises, requiring a philosophical interpretation of its complexity and an attempt to see how its ambiguity may be variously mediated. Let me state the issue in terms of the notions of identity and difference. There is both a positive and a negative aspect to the matter. Negatively, one might assert one's identity by withdrawing from the fullness of otherness in such a way that the difference between human beings and the rest of being becomes a dualistic opposition. Then one might be tempted to one of two alternatives: to will to appropriate what is other and incorporate it within a horizon that subordinates being in its difference to us, as, say, in the Cartesian project of the mastery and possession of nature; or to disperse one's own difference in the manifoldness of the outer world in a manner that reduces one's identity to one finite thing among other finite things.[17] In connection with these alternatives, there are two extremes to be avoided: first, that of fixing difference in such a way that genuine mediation becomes impossible; second, that of allowing the notion of identity to dominate to such an extent that the mediation of difference becomes, instead, its reduction or disappearance. This allows us to state the problem positively. The question then is how, in avoiding these extremes, one can be affirmatively rooted in oneself, yet appropriately in relation to being other than oneself. The solution is not to disperse the center of selfhood within or to absorb the other without, but rather, to enter into a fitting relation with what is other and so come to proper wholeness within oneself. The issue, that is, involves the possibility of a *double* attainment: internal wholeness *of* being and external harmony *with* being.

In considering this matter, I find it helpful to think in terms of four fundamental relations between man and what is other. These are the univocal, the equivocal, the dialectical, and what I will call the *metaxological*. Since these relations and their diverse manifestations pervade this book, it will be useful if, at the outset, we try to delineate something of their essential character in terms of the notions of identity and difference.

The first relation, the univocal, defines the relation of self to other as one of immediate identity. It stresses their sameness, excluding any difference between them and asserting that their oneness precludes their manyness. It also excludes any internal differentiation in either the self or the other. The second relation is the equivocal, which, in contrast to the immediate identity of the univocal, conceives of the self and the other in terms of a simple, unmediated difference. It puts the accent on sheer difference, barring the possibility of conjunction. It underscores manyness without the possibility of oneness and, like the difference of recent deconstructive thought, tends to undermine the possibility of a grounded immanent identity of the self. Whereas the univocal relation sees the self and the other as absolutely the same and hence as having no unifying relation other than that of identity, the equivocal relation sees them as absolutely different and hence as having no relation whatsoever. Thus, they are both privative relations, one derived from a negative sense of union, the other from a negative sense of separation.

The third relation, the dialectical, takes us beyond this privative sphere, by claiming that self and other are neither entirely the same nor absolutely different. First, by contrast with the univocal, the very notion of relation implies some difference, however slight. Second, by contrast with the equivocal, every relation entails some mediation of this difference, however minimal. But most important, the dialectical relation claims that at least one of the terms of the dyad of self and other is *internally* differentiated and hence capable of effecting a mediating relation with its counterpart. The dialectical relation tends to put the stress on the *self* as such a reality: the self is not shut up within itself, as it were, but is capable of entering the space of external difference from its own side. Moreover, this mediating approach need not be a dispersion on an equivocal manyness. On the contrary, the self may try to appropriate such manyness and thus in some measure to circumscribe and internalize it. Hence the dialectical relation asserts that the self as a unity in itself is also able to encompass some degree of difference. It does not exclude difference and complexity from itself; nor does it define external difference as an absolute exclusion between irreconcilable opposites. Through its immanent power of differentiation, the self can traverse external difference; yet it can also return to itself and be self-possessed and so achieve some degree of self-identity, unity, and wholeness for which difference is immanent. And so, beyond mere unity and sheer manifoldness, it attains a certain manyness *within* a one.

The reader will recognize certain Hegelian overtones in this description of dialectic. Dialectic, as I have already suggested, must be given its due. But the matter does not stop with dialectic; nor need we step back from or behind dialectic, as some recent thinkers seem to try to do. Here I conceive of a fourth possible relation, one that tries to address the problematic, ambiguous status of otherness in an exclusively dialectical approach. Above, I called this fourth relation the metaxological relation. This neologism, despite its unpleasing sound, has a very specific significance for our purposes, for it is composed of the Greek words *metaxu* (in between, middle, intermediate) and *logos* (word, discourse, account, speech). The metaxological relation has to do with a logos of the metaxu, a discourse concerning the middle, of the middle, and in the middle. Thus it has a close affinity with the dialectical relation in as much as this may involve dialogue (dialectic as *dialegein*). For, like the dialectical relation, the metaxological relation affirms that the self and the other are neither absolutely the same nor absolutely different. But, unlike the dialectical, it does not confine the mediation of external difference to the side of the self. It asserts, rather, that external difference can be mediated from the side of the *other*, as well as from that of the self. For the other, as much as the self, may be internally differentiated, immanently intricate; hence, it too can enter the middle space between itself and the self and from there mediate, after its own manner, their external difference.

Thus, the metaxological may complete the dialectical by doing justice to the fact that from both directions a conjunction between self and other may be established that is more than an extrinsic juxtaposition. The metaxological is like the dialectical in seeking to overcome the tendency of the equivocal relation to fall away into dualism. But it is unlike the dialectical in having no propensity for the monism that arises when dualism is resolved from the side of the self; in this latter respect the dialectical resembles the univocal, but as having incorporated and interiorized equivocity. Because the metaxological relation allows the mediation of external difference from both sides, and because both sides are rich in their difference, not only in their mediation, it does not circumscribe their difference within an overarching monism. Thus it avoids the totalitarian propensity so rightly abhorred by many contemporary thinkers. Rather, it grounds a *positive plurality*, each of whose members is rich in its distinctive identity, and whose mediation is not only *self-*

mediation but also *inter*mediation. In sum, the intermediation of the metaxological relation grounds an open community of self and other. Beyond mere unity, beyond sheer manyness, beyond manyness within a single unity, it entails a community of full unities, each of which is inexhaustibly manifold within itself.[18]

These four relations, I believe, can help us develop an ordered approach to the self and otherness. In a sense, the four are bound together, for, if we isolate the first three from the last, they can easily become abstractions that generate certain contractions of our sense of being. In the first, self and other run absolutely together, so it is impossible to speak of a distinct other or a distinct self—indeed impossible to speak at all. In the second, self and other are split apart so absolutely that it becomes all but impossible to articulate their relation. In the third, we posit either the self or the other as the overarching totality, with the result that either the self tries to appropriate the external world absolutely, making it part of its total self-appropriation; or the external world becomes a whole of which the self is merely a subordinate part among other, indifferent parts. In the fourth case, however, we try to go beyond these inadequate possibilities: self and other are recognized as distinctive in themselves, neither of them a mere part or the only whole, since the plurality which, together, they constitute may be a community of wholes. Thus the metaxological also tries to preserve what is distinctive about the first three. It preserves the unity of the univocal in community, the self-mediation of the dialectical in the rich identity of its members, and the difference of the equivocal by qualifying this through communication between nonidentical members of its positive plurality.

This description of the four relations is highly schematic, of course. Their bare bones lack living flesh, and the animating spirit has yet to be breathed into them. This we will proceed to do in the main body of the work. For now, let us merely note that a logos of the intermediate, of the "between," is of crucial importance for contemporary thought. In one sense, the metaxological is as old as the Platonic metaxu in the *Symposium* through which the dynamism of human eros, culminating in philosophical vision, moves and unfolds. Yet it is deeply relevant to the thought of our own time, whether this takes a phenomenological or hermeneutical form, whether it be the recent "conversational" model of philosophy or the anti-Cartesian, antidualistic search for a new "holism" or, indeed, the post-Heideggerian concern with the problem of difference.[19] At its best, philosophy has always spoken out of "the middest,"[20] even when it has tried to speak about extremes and ultimates in its sometimes hubristic way. In this respect, the metaxological tries to renew the promise of an old possibility within the context of current pressing concerns.

DESIRE AND ORIGINS

Abstraction cannot be avoided in any philosophical venture. Yet the metaxological is not just an abstract concept that yields its full meaning only to the virtuosity of merely analytical thought. The metaxological points to a complex, concrete interplay between man and the otherness of being. Hence, to be faithful to it, our philosophical discourse must take its bearings from something dynamic in human experience. For this reason, my strategy is to focus on desire. Reflection on desire may yield philosophy a pathway of thought in the middle between the extremes of abstract analysis and an immediacy that is totally inarticulate. Desire erupts in experience; it does so spontaneously and, to that extent, is immediate. But beyond its initial, spontaneous upsurge, it may unfold in an articulated, mediated way. I want to plot a hermeneutic of desire that links its unfolding to the four fundamental possibilities outlined above. These four possibilities offer essential perspectives with respect to both human experience and the real itself. To interpret the metaxological properly, we must first dwell in, then move through and beyond the partiality of the first three. By sifting and moving through the univocal, the equivocal, and the dialectical, we must think our way toward the ultimate concreteness of the metaxological. This is not to deny the possibility of disorder, even chaos, in desire. Inevitably, too, in trying to let the line of articulation shine forth clearly for philosophical purposes, an element of formalization will be unavoidable. But driving even such formalization is the eros for intelligibility, the desire to discern order amid disorder and the need to illuminate and trace the contours of that order.

If the metaxological involves a dynamic interplay between self and other, it cannot be assigned a simple, stable fixity, as if the self and the other could be congealed into static, inert substances. On the contrary, they are original centers of active being, whose relations are relatings— dynamic bonds in the process of being constituted, rather than fixed structures already sedimented. Self and other are realities in the process of being defined and of defining themselves. Being dynamic, they are implicated in the movement through the complex middle, between origins and ends. If the four relations outlined above give a certain structure to such movement, it is the primordial intention of human desire, its thrust to what is ultimate, that gives it dynamism and matter. To explore this movement is to try to address the heart of our finitude, its frailty and its grandeur. For the point is not to baldly declare a series of propositions and then to demonstrate their validity with evidence extracted from elsewhere. It is to delve into the deepest aim of desire, to struggle with its initially amorphous goal, and to attempt to make both aim and goal visible through a progressive process of naming. It is to try to identify man imaginatively, to symbolize the earth, and to stumble toward a metaphysical metaphor of first and final things.

My concern with the question of origins must be briefly stated here. Some contemporary thinkers, after Nietzsche, treat the question of origins with the same distrust with which they treat any question of absolutes.[21] Questions of this type are suspected of being merely residues of the now supposedly dead religious tradition of the West. Like the quest for an absolute, the search for origins is seen as either an ontological cowardice before the indifferent face of bare becoming or a totalitarian will to power, traditionally disguised as the eros for eternity, over the same becoming. Plato's eros for eternity seems to be indicted by Nietzscheans and post-Nietzscheans as *the* grandiose lie of the philosopher. Philosophy yoked to dissimulated religious sources is branded, charged with being secretly "ontotheology," to put it more strongly. Today this charge is identified primarily with the successors of Heidegger, but, in fact, it simply repeats in a new context the accusation of Left Hegelians such as Marx against the so-called religious "mystifications" of their appropriated—some would say usurped—father, namely Hegel himself.[22] Put very simply, the accusation is that nostalgia for God poisons traditional philosophy, which should make us suspicious of the apparent purity of its devotion to reason and logos.

This nostalgia, the charge continues, often disguises itself as the search for origins. The more theologically inclined philosopher may direct his search to a philosophical surrogate for the religious absolute, the originating ground of all being. On the other hand, moderns who take seriously the Kantian critique of metaphysics may transfer the search for origins to a transcendental subject who serves as the originating, primordial synthesis in human efforts to render experience meaningful. What we have witnessed in contemporary philosophy since Kant and Hegel is, first, the progressive dismantling of the religious absolute and its purportedly philosophical surrogates, metaphorically exclaimed in Nietzsche's "God is dead" (though, in fact, Hegel and his contemporaries had already traveled a long way down this road). Second, we have witnessed the deconstruction of the transcendental subject as but another version of the quest for an absolute origin. The outcome seems to be the historicization of the transcendental realm and the temporal relativization of all supposedly eternal and unconditional absolutes, culminating in recent proclamations of even the "death of man." There appears to be no divine absolute, as sought by traditional metaphysics and the Hegelians; no human absolute, as believed by humanists, Marxists, or some Left Hegelians; and no transcendental absolute, as held by Kantians and Husserlians. This leaves nothing absolute at all, and any search for a radical original is judged a philosophical wild goose chase. Even Heidegger, seemingly the most radical critic of ontotheology in his destruction of the history of metaphysics, finds himself the object of a similar dismantling by his successors. These decry a similar tabooed nostalgia in his "archaism" and longing for a pristine beginning in the pre-Socratics, undefiled by the forgetfulness of being perpetuated by ontotheology or traditional metaphysics after Plato.[23]

A full discussion of this problem would require a number of volumes and would involve hermeneutical studies of contemporary thought and the tradition of metaphysics. While not wishing to downplay such studies, I am here trying, within certain limits, to wrestle with the problem of origins in relation to dialectic, desire, and otherness and to defend the emergence in desire of man's search for origins as among his most basic, metaphysical perplexities.[24] I am trying to turn to "the thing itself," as it were, reminded of both Hegel's requirement of philosophical abandonment to the life of *die Sache selbst* and the phenomenologist's cry of *zu den Sachen selbst*. Again, not forgetting that our approaches are always mediated to some degree by our historical situation, I believe this effort to be absolutely essential, for only by attending to the thing itself is it possible to discriminate among the different views presented by recent philosophical debate. Attention to essential landmarks in the tradition of philosophy is not lacking in this work, but because of the need to impose limits on discussion and facilitate some direct address to the issues themselves, I have sometimes presented these landmarks as essential possibilities, rather than historical contingencies, reluctantly foregoing more extended scholarly, historical exposition.

I have tried to offer as uncluttered a philosophical discourse as possible. Yet I think one can both direct oneself philosophically to the thing itself and not be devoid of sophisticated self-consciousness regarding the tradition of philosophy. I regard that tradition as a plurality of complex efforts, some more successful than others, to think the thing itself, and not as a set of historical curiosities or dead monumental abstractions. While my primary focus is on the direct philosophical address, I hope that there will be some fruitful interplay between this and the historical self-consciousness of philosophy. Hegel's dictum that philosophy is its own time comprehended in thought is often quoted, sometimes against the spirit of Hegel, in justification of a dissolving historicism. But least of all should the philosopher simply drown in his time. The philosopher's sense of time should have something of the span of millennia, not to mention an openness to recurring essentials that may emerge in time. Here I intend as much constructive appropriation as critical reflection on essential philosophical possibilities.

I do not deny that certain legitimate questions need to be put to traditional views; but the question of origins is not, I believe, just a historical contingency foisted on us by certain metaphysical presuppositions of Western thought. A metaxological understanding of desire and otherness, I will try to show, brings out and illuminates its inherent necessity. Indeed, the charge of ontotheology may be seen as a two-edged sword. Against the Nietzschean charge of ontological cowardice, it is perhaps one of the great strengths of traditional philosophy that it drew positively from other sources, religious sources in particular, though often not properly acknowledging this debt or even criticizing these sources that fed it.[25] The term *ontotheology* sometimes strikes one as a kind of intellectual bogeyman conjured up to frighten philosophical thought away from origins, a menacing effigy to be burned on ritual occasions. Ironically, there was a time when the effigy *atheist* served a similar function. Then the threat of fires was physically real; now the power of the taboo is metaphorical or spiritual. The bogeyman role has been reversed: it is now the ontotheologian who has to go in hiding, looking over his shoulder, anxious lest he be unmasked.

The act of philosophical naming defining the overall development of this work can be set forth in three stages. Some remarks on the work's structure may be helpful. Part 1 deals with the restlessness of human desire and its search for immanent wholeness. This restlessness reveals what we might call a certain intentional infinitude marking the human self; but this by no means precludes the self's actual finitude, as will become clear in parts 2 and 3. In fact, finitude would not be a problem at all, properly speaking, were human desire not marked by this ambiguous and powerful restlessness. In chapter 1, I discuss the emergence of this restlessness and its temptation to seek wholeness in what I have called the absorbing god. In chapter 2, I try to develop a view of original selfhood, in the process contrasting this view with both the empirical and the transcendental ego. In chapter 3, I try to develop an intermediate view of human wholeness that avoids a fixed closure on the one hand and sheer indefinite openness on the other. Overall in part 1, we move through the univocal and the equivocal toward an understanding of human desire as capable of dialectical self-mediation.

No final closure emerges from this dialectical self-mediation. Part 2 develops further the absence of closure in desire in terms of its radical openness to otherness. Here we are concerned primarily with man's metaxological intermediation with otherness and the affirmative finitude that may emerge. In chapter 4, I explore a misleading account of transcendence in terms of the notion of static eternity. In chapter 5, I develop the metaxological in relation to our knowledge of otherness, and in chapter 6, the sense of concrete being revealed by man's metaxological intermediation with otherness. In chapter 7, I discuss the sense of infinitude that has emerged and offer two significant exemplifications of the metaxological sense of being—namely, the sublime as an aesthetic infinitude, and what I call agapeic otherness, as instancing a rich sense of the community of being.

Finally, in part 3, on the basis of the metaxological sense of being that has emerged in parts 1 and 2, I try to offer a metaphysical metaphor for the ground of being, what I will call the absolute original. The view I am proposing does not see desire in terms of a simple, horizontal progression from finite thing to finite thing. It reveals a sense of human becoming as, horizontally, desire's extension to what finitely is, but, vertically, as capable of a certain metaphysical ascent to the ground of what is. I am not talking about some leap outside experience, but rather the emergence from within experience itself of its own ultimate dimension. Human desire is not only a horizontal exigence for wholeness, but also a vertical openness through otherness to what is ultimate.[26]

Overall we will follow an itinerary reminiscent of St. Augustine's description of the double movement of his own thought, which proceeded, he said, *ab exterioribus ad interiora, ab inferioribus ad superiora.* "Exterior" and "interior," "inferior" and "superior" are not to be taken as kinds of beings, but rather as modes of being.[27] Because of my wish to do justice to the self-knowledge of desire and its openness to otherness, without falling into an unacceptable dualism, this work exhibits aspects of what might be called an Augustinian odyssey, embarked on in the wake of Hegel. Part 1 is roughly analogous to the first kind of movement, from exterior to interior, while parts 2 and 3 correspond to a version of the second, from inferior to superior. The importance of desire here is again that it makes it possible to give proper weight to self-knowledge, without sacrificing openness to otherness. Desire need not be some vague psychological feeling but may reveal a metaphysical openness to being that is twofold: an eros for immanent wholeness and a reaching out to being other than itself. Then we may know ourselves without being catatonically contracted into ourselves, cut off in monadic inwardness. We may be like a glass that in one light gives us back our own reflection, but which, in another light, and if we swivel slightly, becomes diaphanous, and we open out into the other's world.

PART I
INTENTIONAL INFINITUDE

Chapter One
Desire, Lack, and the Absorbing God

Man is the active animal, intensely restless and forever questing.[1] Living on the move, no sooner do human beings settle in a place but its limits become manifest to them, and their restlessness reappears within its borders. As marked by desire, their being often sends them bustling over the globe to gain a habitation and a home. As temporal beings, their present slips away into the past, while the future they anticipate shows them not to be self-same, not to be coincident with themselves. Behind themselves in a past, in front of themselves in a future, in the present, humans are not absolutely self-identical.[2]

Desire's restlessness reveals in us a certain protean power, and not surprisingly, its ambiguous fluidity calls forth myriad interpretations, ranging from Plato's eros to contemporary Freudian views.[3] Our interest lies more with Plato, perhaps, in that we want to explore the sense in which human desire is metaphysical, not just psychological in a manner abstracted from its ontological matrix. I will start with something minimal—namely, the sense of lack and need that all human beings experience—and ask how we might be led by a progressive, immanent unfolding to some glimpse of the ontological power, the power of being, inherent in desire. Such a power need not be explicitly grasped for it, nonetheless, to be active all along. Understood dialectically, desire may give us access to a certain power of active difference that is internal to the self's identity, an inherent power of self-differentiation. This power, in turn, may point to a certain character of being: the ability to be self-articulating, and to be so in openness to what is other. Beginning with finite desire and the sense of lack that permeates it, I want to look at

17

various responses to human restlessness; self-frustrating efforts to fulfill it finitely, equally self-frustrating flight from it into an absorbing god, and, finally, a genuine turn toward the tension of one's own nature and the challenge of self-knowledge it poses.

FINITE DESIRE AND LACK

As Socrates reminds us in the *Symposium,* when we desire something, we experience the lack of that thing. The first point we should make about this lack is that it shows that desire cannot be completely self-enclosed. Desire is desire *for* something and so already reaches beyond itself. For this reason, lack is not solely negative: it attests to the stirring of an impetuous power through which desire begins to be more than itself. Negatively understood, it is a witness to unfulfillment; positively understood, it may make desire aware of itself and so awaken it to what is more than itself. Consider the case of hunger, for example. The lack's intensification here brings a correspondingly acute sharpening of the sense of what is needed to requite the lack, the negative soliciting its opposite positive. And this importunate sense of the opposite positive is not just an external superposition on desire; it is an internal development that arises from its own negative factor. Thus, when hunger is aggravated in the extreme, when we become ravenous, the emptiness inside is matched by an obsession with food outside. Colloquially, we then say that we could eat a horse. This means that if the negative of hunger is sharpened to the extreme, then the concomitant imperative of the positive of food will spring up so urgently that we contemplate the limit possibility of eating anything at all, as long as it appeases the cavernous gap within. Even here (a point whose full significance we will see later), something, no matter what, is better than nothing. We might describe this as desire's tenacious witness to the primordial power of the "yes."

We see, then, that there is a dynamism within the lack expressed by desire, the deepening of which engenders a correlative need that the demand of life be met. This is because what desire wants, needs, and is committed to is fulfilling life. Put more directly, desire is desire for life, a dynamic expression of life and a restless reaching out to larger life. Moreover, this conversion of lack into an affirmative expression of life is the process whereby desire puts itself in a suitable position to thrust out to life beyond itself. Thus, desire is not determined solely by what is initially beyond it; rather, it overcomes its seemingly null character through its own self-expansion. It reveals the *immanent* exigence to invert its own lack.

Suppose we now look at desire from the standpoint of its possible end, or goal. We cannot here undertake a full discussion of the teleological view of desire, its strengths and its difficulties. As will become clear later, I do not think we can avoid a certain teleological view of human desire (see chapter 3 below). But this is not to imply any Cartesian clarity and distinctness with respect to that teleology. Nor is it to deny the paradoxical power of desire to try to thwart any teleology (see chapter 3 on equivocal desire), as, for instance, when someone knowingly "drifts" through life—that is, paradoxically purposes to be without purpose and makes it his aim to be aimless. Nor does a teleology of desire necessitate a totalitarian tyranny of the self over otherness.[4] Granting provisionally that desire seeks fulfillment in some end, the difficulty with finite desire is that it comes up against the obstruction of external life. In reaching beyond itself, it is faced with what seems, at least initially, to be not fully congruent with an immanent process of self-development. We must explore briefly how some sense of an end enters desire at all stages of its development, and how this makes desire possible in the first place. Just as desire inverts lack, so also, it may reverse its goal's absence into an anterior presence.

The initial absence of an end reveals desire's precariousness, for it opens a rift within desire, which, in turn, may threaten to collapse and issue in nothing. Divergent courses become possible: either desire may become party to deepening this absence, thereby losing itself in its own progressive impoverishment; or it may seize on a different possibility. If desire is to be sustained *as* desire, however, the second course is unavoidable. For if we take the first course, we become immersed in a spreading despair, one that absolutizes the absence of an end. But where desire lives on, absence can never be total. Desire is a form of life which, while originating in lack, wars with lack, seeking thereby to keep despair at bay. For this reason, we cannot say that despair is another form of desire. It takes itself out of desire's sphere, not simply by forsaking the goal, but also by willing to annihilate desire totally. It perverts desire by inverting it; by not seeking its fulfillment, it becomes totally averse to it. Despair finds desire as such repulsive.[5]

By contrast, desire looks forward, keeping its prospect alive even when it is suspended in the middle of an uncertain, though for it not absolute, absence. Far from being some simplistic exclusion of despair, desire is the adventure of action, which braves and puts to the test any hope. We may be perpetually aware of the absence of the end, but even in this, some sense of the end is apparent *within* desire. Anticipation is a relation which, in being dissatisfied with the gulf between a desire and its goal, refuses sheer absence. Even though we may not possess an end, that end may intrude on desire; and the more hope triumphs over despair, the more importunate this intrusion becomes. It may be so insistent at times that we become confused as to whether we have yet to possess the end or have already in fact enjoyed it. In the act of sexual congress, for instance, the end inserts itself in desire prior to the climax of the deed. And it can do this with such *puissance* that desire reaches a level of lively excitation not far short of the outburst of consummation. Under such circumstances, desire may even lose sight of the upshot yet to be attained and lose itself in the fever with which its hope infects it.

Thus, through anticipation, the end penetrates the course of desire, not only from without but also from within. In the absence of an immanent end—and the presence of such can range from the vaguest of hunches to the most self-conscious of purposes—desire is not properly desire at all, but random motion without direction. Such purposeless motion is not even groping, for groping casts about for direction and has an obscure sense of seeking a goal. Without the presence of an end, however dimly apprehended, desire would never be precipitated in the first place, much less be specified with respect to a determinate bearing or tendency. There would be but purely inert being, wanting nothing, absolutely immobile. Within inert being, desire opens up a space in which active forms of life may come to emergence. The fact that we are not completely self-same testifies to such a disruptive power. The end does not lie solely beyond desire, as a dim, distant future easily postponed while the present remains undisturbed. On the contrary, it disquiets the present, deposits desire within it, and issues in a relation to what is beyond inert thereness. It is an ingredient in the origination of desire, giving birth to it and forcing it to seek some consummation. It is not merely a disruptive power that subverts the fixity of immobile being; it is, rather, a generative power in refashioning in active form what, in passive form, it dissolves, excites, and animates.

In sum, we find here the first unfurling of the power of self-articulation. As it emerges, this power will help shape the forms of activity that will subsequently develop as desire moves from first precipitation to possible consummation. It will transform the space between beginning and end into an articulated middle ground through which desire passes on its adventure. It will seek to bind together a beginning and an end, while at the same time setting them apart and interposing between them a sequence of passing stages that may constitute a way to fulfillment.

This is no reduction of human desire to pure bodily urge. The picture is far more complex. With the eruption of the sense of lack and the intrusion of the end in anticipation, the experience of desire reveals, rather, something of the self-articulation of man's bodily being. It testifies to the emergence from homogeneous bodily being of a sense of a determinate self. In the initial stages of human development, a determinate self can hardly be said to exist, being, as it were, submerged in its body.[6] Desire introduces disjunction into this submersion and sows the seed of a determinate self through the sense of difference and dissatisfaction. We begin to come to ourselves as different in our lack and our want; this sense of need is connected with the initial articulation of human identity in its peculiar paradoxical character (well known to Augustine, Hegel, and Sartre, among others) as aware of itself as not being fully identical with itself.[7] The paradox of human identity is that, because its origin is linked with desire, it is also nonidentity—that is, the space where the sense of difference enters the world. Desire discomfits us, thrusts our bodies out of themselves, as it were, out of the womb of the world's body, and stirs our first sense of naked difference and identity.

Desire expels the body from itself and through the body's self-differentiation begins to disclose the difference between self and what is other by differentiating between the "in-here" and the "out-there." It is to be found at the origin of self-consciousness in necessitating our presence to ourselves as lacking. Hence it is tied up with the differentiation of the body into a corporeal and conscious intentionality.[8] At a certain point in the development of self-consciousness it transforms the body by converting its impulses into intentions. This emergent sense of self may be seen, for instance, in the experience of nakedness, where we clearly differentiate not only between the inner and outer, but also between our own bodies and a larger sense of self-identity which is not exhausted by our immediate exteriority. In the experience of nakedness, as the myth of the Fall perhaps indicates, we find some first intimations of the import of human difference. Of course, our reaction may well be an impulse to overcome difference, to destroy it even, though, as the myth also tells us, the path back is forever barred to us.

PARTICULAR POSSESSIONS AND THE INFINITUDE OF DESIRE

Let us now consider desire's relation to difference in its efforts to possess its end. The question now bears more directly on the divorce of desire from an external end that may rebuff it as it reaches out to life beyond itself. In speaking of desire's end, we must distinguish two senses. The first refers to the termination of the act of desire itself: thus the end of hunger is no longer to feel hungry; the end of hunger is the *activity of eating*. The second sense does not designate the activity but the *object* possessed: thus *food* is the end of hunger in this sense; the end of hunger is not just eating, but the eating of food. To avoid confusion we will speak of end in this second sense as the telos.[9]

But we must be more specific about the type of telos involved, for desire is specified by its telos being thereby articulated as a desire for this or a desire for that. We desire, but not altogether amorphously. The development of desire gives rise to a particular appetite for this or that. In coming forth from the sluggishness of the inert body, desire not only lifts the body to a specific act in localizing and articulating it, but is itself particularized into a number of specific desires, each with a commensurate objective. It is the resistance of such a telos—one that is limited, particular, and finite—that is of interest here.

Finite desire meets with frustration when its particular *telos* remains beyond its reach in recalcitrant externality. It has to broach the break between itself and its telos. Should this split be unsurpassable, desire will continue to lack self-identity within, and its self-development will be cheated of full unfolding. What we discover is that finite desire, though implicated in the articulation of this or that thing as a specific objective, refuses to allow the finite telos to subsist in its merely external particularity. This particular appetite seeks this particular thing. It grapples with the disjunction between itself and its telos, is not curbed by it, and tries to appropriate to itself the resistant externality of the finite thing. By going over the gap outside, it seeks to alleviate the gap within and constrain the possessed telos to contribute to its own self-identity. Thus, hunger undermines its sunderance from food by effecting in eating an identity with it; and in achieving an identity with food, the body, now full, attains identity with itself and rounds itself off in a renewed return to self-sameness. Desire tries to complete itself through the interiorization of the particular external telos. Possession is this process of interiorization by which, via the mediation of the external telos, desire becomes capable of a self-possessed self-appropriation.

The significance of this appropriation need not be, I emphasize, merely negative. It need not be tyranny over the external thing, on the one hand, or crass selfishness, on the other. Though these consequences are possible, they are not necessary. Rather, the positive outcome is the impossibility of an interpretation of desire as merely reactive. Desire shows itself to be increasingly active within itself. Least of all is it a mechanical response to some stimulus, since the mediation between desire and telos is constituted by the series of complex articulations adumbrated in our discussion so far. Most important, it becomes clear that in possession, desire interposes between the stimulus and the response the power of its own activity.

If we speak of nothing but stimulus and response, as behaviorists tend to do, we cannot account for the positive power of desire to mediate between the interior and the exterior and bind them together. We have only a dualism of inner and outer to which we react by attempting to define the interior solely by the exterior or, alternatively, the exterior solely by the interior. Desire's possession of particular objects points more properly to a *dialectic* between inner and outer, one that is grounded in desire's power of activity, which cannot be confined to either the inner or the outer exclusively, but which moves restlessly between them. For the experience of desire, which reveals the advance of the human self toward articulate identity, exteriorizes the interior and interiorizes the exterior and is the dialectical movement between them. The difference internal to the self that appears with desire not only images the difference between the self and the external thing, but also thrusts the self outside itself into the space between the interior and the exterior. In plunging the self into the space of external difference, thereby exposing it to the risk of dissolution, and in surmounting this, the thrust of internal difference grounds the dialectical interplay between desire and the external thing.

This dialectical interplay manifests, establishes, and confirms the possibility of human power. When we face down the friction of the external thing, in our not stumbling or being blocked, in our being submitted to the trial of internal and external difference, something emerges of the power of being that defines us human beings. We cannot simply say that human desire is impoverished in itself and hence seeks enrichment elsewhere. We must say, rather, that it directs us to an inherent richness that is already there in the one in whom desire erupts. This is the paradox of desire. It rears up first as lack, but as it gathers momentum, it is increasingly shown not to be mere privation. Instead, it reveals a rich power, which, as the ground of a process of articulation, transports us beyond the apathy of inactive "thereness." The course of desire is not reducible to simple remedial compensation in reaction to poverty. Indeed, any palliative redress presupposes what desire more deeply designates—namely, the inherence in man of self-articulating power.

However, the most significant consequence of particular possession is the *infinitude* of desire. Here we run across desire's paradoxical nature in another form. For the fulfillment that brings consummation also consumes this particular desire, thereby bringing it to an end; the climax thus mingles life and death, the highest consummating moment being also a commitment to extinction. We enjoy the object of our desire, but in satisfying this particular appetite, we reduce it to nothing. I reach; I pluck; I eat. The apple I crush fills me, top to toe, with the taste of godlike repletion. But in my brief divinity I am deluded. I fall from fullness. The gnawing sense of my nothingness returns, with the re-doubled hunger of ever dissatisfied desire: lack again, only endless now.

Possession puts a seal on this particular desire, but it is at just this juncture that desire generates desire. This or that appetite may be quietened, but this is not to do away with desire altogether, but rather to heighten its power and to elicit its further excitation. It is to activate and awaken the infinitude of desire as such. Though we may have an appetite for this thing or that, we are not identical with what we have or confined to the level of particulars. Even the satisfaction of a particular desire shows it to be more than the specific limit of a finite telos: such a telos fails to constrain absolutely the full sweep of human eros. By proving itself never to be entirely quelled by this or that limited satisfaction, the infinity of desire rises above these limitations of particularity. We are always oriented to something more.

In terms of the distinction we made at the beginning of this section, the appearance of desire's infinitude consists precisely in the subordination of the end in the second sense (object) to the first sense (activity): the second end, as the particular limited thing, proves incommensurate with the activity that desire generates. Activity and object, desire and end, must be commensurate for final consummation. Insofar as we cannot escape a disjunction between desire and the finite particular thing, we are precipitated into an incessant process of going beyond limited satisfactions. The infinitude of our desire is more than this or that desire, this or that satisfaction, more than the limits imposed by this or that external telos, more than all these taken together. The possibility of its emergence is woven into the fabric of our most qualified satisfactions, outliving this bounded ease and remaining, in despite of this, at our core.

I do not intend to deny what we might term "the drag of the finite." The finite is a drag on desire in two ways, one positive and one negative. On the one hand, we are attracted and drawn to the particular; on the other, the merely particular to which we are drawn does not ultimately satisfy us. We are caught in this tension: we seek gratification in particular goods; yet the outcome of such satisfactions is desire for what is more—that is, renewed dissatisfaction. Thus, desire is infinite, yet bound to the finite at the same time. It is driven to unity at the point of satiety, but the then renewed craving reopens the gulf, driving it apart again to infinity. The power it expresses is thus taut, its intent of a limited objective coexisting in uneasy equilibrium with its infinitude, as simply desire. Desire desires everything, but it also desires this thing. It springs up in the tense space between limitation and transcendence. Its determinate gratification is merely a prelude to a deeper indeterminate restlessness. And the moment it possesses the particular thing is the moment it is dispossessed of the merely finite and its odyssey into the infinite is instituted.

Are we, then, visited with a dissolute desire, whose infinitude robs purpose of any specificity and once again disperses desire in the amorphousness of inchoate feeling? In fact, I imply no regression to capricious, orderless immediacy. The realization that desire has an infinite dimension, far from being a dull undeveloped impulse, is one of complex sophistication. For it presupposes the articulations so far explicated. In overcoming lack and becoming positive power, desire ceases to be merely immediate impulse and proves to be the possibility of freedom. The self breaks with simple naturalness, its existence as one external particular thing among other particular things. Desire becomes distinctively human in not being an instinctual inundation of the self by compulsive passion. The self is power over its immediate, natural passions because it is not merely immediate: as free, it acts and purposes, thereby mediating with itself. This is another way of saying that the appearance of infinite desire in human beings is also an emergence of the exigence to be *whole*, insofar as this is implied by self-mediation.

The paradox inherent in desire is here given another, but this time most fundamental, formulation, in the dialectical tension between wholeness and infinitude. And again, the consequence is not negative, but is instead a heightening of the problem. From the side of desire's infinitude, we discern the human spirit's upsurge, which is not quietened by this or that desire, satisfaction, or external telos, and which shows itself as the power to undermine the partial peace afforded by this or that gratification. From the other side of the desire for wholeness, we discover that the power that underpins, permeates, and outlives any particular upsurgence of the human spirit is also self-mediating and self-relating, a will to appropriate itself and be centered within itself. The unfolding to the finish of finite desire opens the way for infinite desire, which it also prompts toward the goal of being whole. With this broadening of finite orientations toward a more fundamental infinitude and deepening of limited satisfactions toward a more basic wholeness, our problem now must be the dialectical stress of this tension. For the search for wholeness threatens to bound desire's infinitude, while the latter risks the breakup of any possibility of wholeness. Yet these two, man's search for wholeness and his infinitely restless desire, both offspring of the same power in man, desire must attempt to reconcile.[10]

THE DIFFICULTY OF DISCOURSE ABOUT DESIRE

How can one be philosophically adequate to desire's infinitude? Discourse inevitably takes a finite and particularized form, whereas desire, as we have seen, resonates with the sense of something more. All our discursive categories, to the extent that they are finite, might seem to be inadequate. Since, I think, we cannot settle philosophically for silence, what we must find is a mode of discourse that itself reverberates with this sense of more. We require what might perhaps be called "speculative categories" or, better, "metaphysical metaphors." This requirement is related to the sense of difference that emerges in desire. Traditionally, speculative thinking has tried to direct itself philosophically to a sense of identity and difference that is more metaphysically ultimate than the distinctions present on the surface of ordinary language, and which a certain kind of external analysis may help us to tidy up.[11] But the articulate difference that issues forth with desire cannot be reduced to formal, "logical" distinctions: it is living, existent difference, alive with the original power of being. A difference reducible to formal logic would be derivative and tend easily to sedimentation, whereas this living difference is original and, only by contradicting its own nature, can it be anything other than dynamic. Traditionally, speculative thinking has sought to philosophically identify and reflectively articulate the dynamism of this difference.

It is impossible, given present limitations, to address fully all the relevant controversies. In the discussion that follows, I hope to indicate, in part by way of exemplification, that we can speak philosophical sense about what seem to be boundary questions through the mediation of metaphysical metaphors. Infinite desire provokes us to ponder the possibility of an intelligibility that is beyond that of finite objects. It seems to call for a mode of discourse that, from the standpoint of finite intelligibility, must strike some thinkers as, at best, indirect mediation, and others as, at worst, mystery mongering and mystification. To those who refuse to consider anything except finite intelligibility, our discussion may appear to be nonsense. Yet, I would maintain, we visit ourselves with absurdity if we restrict consideration to this finite level. Though it might seem prudent and moderate to limit self-knowledge to finite determinations of the self, the danger here is a false modesty that reneges on the real problem. Finite determinations of the self are always strained by desire's infinitude. We ourselves are infinite desire, and the real problem is how to remain true to the deeper reaches of our being and its philosophical eros. Here we need philosophical imagination.[12] We must ponder, no doubt with failing instruments always becoming blunt, what a more ultimate sense of intelligibility might be.

The problem is that, while limited to the finite, we are always finding the infinite opening up. In our being, desire is where the struggle between our finiteness and infinitude is fought. We are defined in the strife between the particularization of our finite desires and our transcendence of any such specification. We cannot assert that desire is *either* finite *or* infinite, for it seems to be both. It must necessarily determine itself in a particular way, and yet it is never fully expended by any such determination. Its dynamism transcends the exclusiveness of an either/or in the direction of the inclusiveness of a both/and. And if it is deemed unacceptable to assent to the finite and the infinite at one and the same time, this is due to the phenomenon itself. To express this tension in discourse, we require categories which, although determinate, do not solidify into petrified particularity, but which, while transcending simple determinacy, do not evaporate into sheer indefiniteness. What I have called metaphysical metaphors are an attempt to meet this requirement.

There are those, on the one hand, who relish sheer indefiniteness, and those, on the other hand, who abhor it. There are those, too, who are obsessed with inflexible determinacy and those who turn away from any kind of determinacy with disgust. Among the first group are thinkers who idolize a certain technicist rationality; among the second, irrationalists who reject all reason as narrowly technicist. These two possibilities are, I believe, complementary sides of the same contraction of concerns, one narrowing reason to a rigid univocal logic, the other dissolving this univocal logic in favor of an equivocal illogic. We need to stand in the middle between these extremes, seeking there an open determinacy and a sense of the indeterminate which is nevertheless articulate.[13] Inevitably a certain *strain* must be put on language. This is not a perverse refusal to speak common sense, but, rather, a necessity of philosophical honesty. We sometimes need to tax language because philosophical reflection stretches common sense, and because we ourselves, as desire, are subject to the strain engendered by the coexistence of finitude and infinitude. Finite desire extends beyond itself into the infinite, and philosophical eros, in reflecting this reach of desire, and giving rise to reflection on it, cannot exclude a more radical extension of its own quest for intelligibility. Moreover, one must ask: What is ordinary anyway? Given what has already been said, we have difficulty isolating any merely ordinary desire: for in all desire we seem to detect, sometimes sleeping, sometimes vigilant, the coil of infinity.

INFINITE LACK AND THE ABSORBING GOD

Let us now consider an important reaction to desire's restlessness, one that has been a recurring metaphysical response to the experience of lack. Human beings have often been regarded—by Cusanus and Bruno and other Renaissance thinkers, for instance—as microcosms, each a world within itself opening on to the space of a kind of inner galaxy. This opening may not be comforting. For the space of infinity can strike us with such shock that we reel away from it, as does Pascal, for example, in a vertigo or dread. For it seems to implicate not only the particularized difference found in the lack of finite desire, but also an infinite sense of difference, which can readily shift its shape into a sentiment of infinite *estrangement*. I now wish to probe this negative reaction in terms of this metaphysical metaphor, what we might call the absorbing god.

What might be at issue here? When desire's infinitude is awakened, it must seek a commensurate telos with corresponding absoluteness; otherwise desire would search for satisfaction in vain below its own level and so find itself inane. The absorbing god names one typical attempt to supply such a telos. It tries to supply a sense of absoluteness by claiming to be the epitome of *wholeness,* while allocating to desire the negative role of infinity, now interpreted as estrangement from the whole. It thereby addresses the tension in desire between wholeness and infinity. The absorbing god interprets desire's infinitude in terms of an external telos, whose absoluteness is imputed to its enveloping wholeness. Just as finite desire searches for spontaneous relief from lack in the bounded wholeness of things, seeking to alleviate the pain of internal difference and thereby return to self-sameness; so, too, infinite desire sometimes looks to an absolute whole that would heal the shock of estrangement and abolish difference by enclosing within itself whatever is otherwise partial. In brief, by the term *the absorbing god* is meant a principle of completion which, purporting to be absolute wholeness, subsumes all parts within itself and in this engulfment absorbs their distinctiveness.

When the negative aspects of desire are isolated and emphasized, resort to something like an absorbing god is not unusual. We come across it in quietistic religious and monistic philosophical systems, where the end is the utter abnegation of desire as such, no distinction being made between worthwhile and worthless desire. Thus, the Parmenidean view of being as a dense, homogeneous sphere is reminiscent of the absorbing god. Ascetic religious traditions that try to undermine what they see as an exaggerated sense of isolated selfhood often harbor a hidden desire for an absorbing god. Eastern pantheisms that seem to imply the extinction of the finite individual would seem to be another expression of the same desire. The Hegelian Absolute is sometimes criticized as an absorbing god that purportedly "swallows up" all difference, finitude, and individuality. Hegel's views are always richly ambiguous, and his elusive language sometimes indicates a tendency toward an absorbing god; yet his stated intentions were always to preserve difference and not to dissolve finiteness. Indeed, his criticism of Spinoza's one Substance (which has overtones of an absorbing god) is that it lacks the self-consciousness that his own Absolute *Geist* is said to preserve. As we shall see, the intention to preserve difference is laudable. The larger question, beyond the present stage of our discussion, is whether the dialectical view that preserves difference *within* identity is adequate. As I shall argue later, when we consider the metaxological view, there is a sense of otherness and difference in tension with such a dialectical preservation of difference.

Traces of a sense of an absorbing god can even be detected in thinkers commonly regarded as the antithesis of Hegel. Thus, Nietzsche's defense of the Dionysian is often couched in language that implies an intoxicated dissolution of the self in its Apollonian individuation. Perhaps this is not surprising, given the early influence of Schopenhauer on Nietzsche and the influence of oriental religions on Schopenhauer. Whereas Schopenhauer wants to resign his willful individuality and his desiring being Nietzsche wants to express desire actively. Yet the paradox is that, if we push Dionysian intoxication to the extreme, willful desire and the sense of difference vanish, and the Nietzschean individual surrenders himself to *amor fati.* The difficulty is that this surrender to fate, although not a resignation à la Schopenhauer, becomes an active identification with the divine such that the self ceases to distinguish itself from the absorbing god in Dionysian form, as perhaps some of the megalomaniac utterances of the later Nietzsche seem to indicate.[14]

Let us look in more general terms at why unsatisfactory consequences follow from any version of the absorbing god. But first we should ask why such a notion might be plausible at all. There seems to be a natural propensity to duplicate and intensify finite need on the infinite level. Hence, one might argue, if finite desire is evidence of a limited lack, infinite desire must be evidence of an infinite lack. The human being thereby becomes defined as infinitely impotent, reaching beyond itself as infinite lack, only to be thrown back upon its own want and weakness. Moreover, since we spontaneously seek a particularized objective and no particularized objective can quiet an infinite desire, we might be inclined to say that nothing can satisfy it and that, as a result, infinite desire is itself sheer nothingness. Caught in the collision between inner and outer and narrowing down the outer to a collection of particular items, none of which can fill the expansiveness of the inner, we are tempted not merely to pare the infinity of desire down to particularity, but to dismiss it as an utter nullity to which nothing can correspond as telos. This abnegation of desire may reveal itself in a progressive process of divestment that presents itself in the guise of desire's fulfillment. On the one hand, desire seems to be the badge of our tainted disablement, the stain that darkens us with unregenerate imperfection; on the other, it remains inexorably impelled to reach beyond itself. It is no accident, then, that the desiring self should be tempted to take flight in a direction away from itself, toward an absorbing god, who, taking all power into itself in aloof disdain, maintains itself as a whole, uncontaminated by the powerlessness of any self. The dissolving disability of desire breeds its opposite positive: absolute, assimilating power, the absorbing god.

This swing from dissolving desire to absolute assimilating power is persuasive, however, only when the negative aspects of desire are given extreme emphasis. For this recourse yields a new dissolution, more extreme than the one it sought to avoid. For a moment, let us take this flight to the absorbing god on its own terms. Desire then becomes absolutely unintelligible in itself: what seems intelligible about it is only the external bright surface, but the internal, inmost, dark core of desire is utterly indigent and null. Moreover, cut off from the absorbing god, the self is unmitigated nothingness; for, only as a part of this whole can it have even minimal significance. The self is diverted from any intrinsic good in its own nature; at the same time, it is pitched back into its own privation because, as part of this whole, it is nothing in and through itself. Thus the human self is trammeled by two extremes: it is in thrall to the nothingness within and is mesmerized by the whole that would overwhelm it from without. Should the self attempt to assert a significance of its own, it will be dwarfed by one of these extremes and undone. In short, appeal to an absorbing god is conditional on a sense of the intractable insecurity of existence; but its effect is to produce a more radical, deeper instability.

While we must acknowledge the precariousness of our existence, the real rub concerns how we make this acknowledgment. If we accept the idea of an absorbing god, we are led from man's insecurity to a deeper disintegration, and this, paradoxically, we discern most clearly when we consider what completion here would mean. One might think that completion would prove victorious over instability. But what we find is a blotting out of internal unsteadiness, accomplished by an obliteration of everything, inside and out. To remedy its infinite lack, the self must surrender itself to the assimilating whole, but in doing so, it forfeits the partiality of its distinct existence. Because the self, as part, is not commensurate with the telos, as whole, a person as a person cannot be whole, and hence, to be whole, must forsake all humanness. We cannot approach completion without putting ourselves in jeopardy of certain death: we must disintegrate, so that the absorbing god can retain its unity, die that it may live. The absorbing god reminds us slightly of Sartre's contradictory god, who reverses the passion of Christ, through which God died so that we might live. Indeed, it seems to will to reverse any passion whatsoever. For passion brings only the curse of need, and our goal must be the absolute termination of desire, its absolute effacement. The absorbing god thus fails to surpass instability; or rather, it may indeed set insecurity aside, but only at the price of expunging the self. In the eventuality of this not even Pyrrhic win, we lose our lack but in no way regain ourselves.

The absorbing god, then, signifies a flight that aims to do away with the distinct identity of the self and hence is based on the paradoxical desire to escape desire. The notion of such a being issues in the absolute self-contradiction of desire, which yearns for refuge from what it takes to be the tedious futility of endless lack. It anticipates, as rest from desire's travail, a comforting closure wherein, by our cession to blank oblivion in a homogeneous whole, our suffering and separation from ourselves and things is alleviated. Desire disturbs us within, disturbs us infinitely, but the absorbing god seems to allay this agitation and soothe us to sleep. At the level of the infinite, it calls for the suppression of difference, thereby mirroring the attempt to cancel disjunction at the finite level; and both movements endeavor to return us to the undisturbed quiet of inert self-sameness.

We are dealing here with a self-denial that seeks the total reversal of desire through the dissolution of its inner tension. For infinite desire testifies to a certain indeterminacy in the self. And though the absorbing god seems to answer to this indeterminacy, it substitutes what in essence is a cosmic void, within which all distinctions vanish. Void calls to void; or rather, void is lost in void, and we are left with nothing; or rather still, if we could only say it, *we* are not even left. Properly speaking, we are not even left with recourse to silence, even less to a silence that would chatter incoherently in order to justify and excuse itself; for to be silent we would have *to be,* and again, could we but say it, we are said *not* really to be.

Since all distinction is erased in absolute assimilation, there is a sense in which the disappearance of the self is also the vanishing of any distinct meaning to the absorbing god. For if we, as infinite lack, are said to be *within* the assimilating whole, we then visit *it* with a nothingness and an internal instability. The absorbing god makes these latter facts absolutely unintelligible, yet the notion must acknowledge the real problem they present, for it is defined in reaction to them. What we wish to negate or would rather not be, we must first admit to be. The absolute positive wholeness imputed to the absorbing god makes unintelligible, as it too is made unintelligible by, the nothingness of desire supposedly present within one of its parts, namely, the human self. A truly absorbing god would not, properly speaking be an absorbing god at all; for if it were the absolute whole, it would already have assimilated all its parts, in a manner that would make it inert and inarticulate in itself. Put differently, radical absorbing power, taken alone as absolute, is indistinguishable from indifferent, inactive inertia. We might consider here how

Parmenides, when asserting that being was the One, likened being to a dense, immobile, homogeneous sphere. Why there should be parts in the first place is hard to say. And why there should be the radical eruption of difference and lack within desire is even more difficult. The absorbing god ultimately drives us to dismiss all partiality and to abandon desire. We are driven to delete ourselves; and though this solves the problem in a certain sense, it also dissolves difference and brings the cancelation of articulateness.

Because it is an extreme negative solution to the problem of infinite desire, the absorbing god cannot in the end prevent self-destruction. For with our disappearance into the absorbing god, it disappears too. In this, its blank invisibility, it becomes indistinguishable from nothing. To the extent that ascetic religions resort to an absorbing god of this type, the Nietzschean criticism of their implicit nihilism finds some justification. We might think here too of Nietzsche's repudiation of Schopenhauer's pessimism as expressed in the motto: it is better not to be. The absorbing god is based on an infinite abnegation of desire, which means that it is not unrelated to infinite despair; for despair, as we saw on the finite level, finds desire as such repulsive. We render finite frustration infinite, find ourselves courting the unbounded vanity of desire, and in desperation of its inanity perceive no recourse except oblivion. For to be in despair is to have recourse to nothing. And this is what we discover here. We cannot avoid a nugatory conclusion on two fronts. On the side of the self, the absorbing god begets nothing, precipitates no origination, fructifies in no creation, affords no fruition; for what might create and fructify and be fulfilled ("we") has been stifled and has suffered elision. On the side of what is more metaphysically ultimate, the nugatory inarticulateness of the absorbing god empties of content the ultimate end of infinite desire. We cannot here slake our thirst with the water of life, as it were, and still enjoy our desire, but must extinguish this thirst and eliminate its delight.

Despite all this, desire's infinitude continues to haunt us, and we are forced to ask if we can look at it with eyes other than the "evil eye" of negation.[15] The annihilation of desire just examined manifests the power of negation, manifests the *power of being*, even in negation, albeit directed against the self and its sense of difference. We cannot sustain this response in the long run. We must forfeit the false security of the absorbing god. But then we become burdened once more with the weight of our difference and its possible nothingness. The self must again face its fragility, in relation to both its own being and what is beyond it. Were it absorbed, this fragility might be set at nought; since it cannot be, desire must make a different trial of its own possible nullity. We must return again to the primordial power of the "yes," to which, as we have already seen, desire is a tenacious witness.

For the yes inherent in desire is implicitly the self's affirmation of being, despite its partiality, its precariousness, and its frailty. Here is manifest a self-distinguishing power of being outside absorption, one that possesses the power to be other than any absorbing god. If we fail to tackle the nostalgia for assimilation, we will no doubt be nagged by the suspicion that the self is straw. This misgiving arises from the sense of infinite lack but fails to fashion a corrective. Yet the overall drift of our discussion in this chapter indicates that desire brings to articulation certain immanent resources of power in human beings. Even if humans are mere "parts," they are most peculiar ones, since no assimilating whole seems capable of incorporating them without residue. Without cutting one off from being other than oneself, the active exigence of one's being is to be one's own whole. No mere part rebuffs its assimilating whole. The fact that humans can counter and stand against this whole shows that they are more than mere parts. The defect of the absorbing god is its failure to do justice to this "more."

Here, however, there is no question of willful, tyrannical self-assertion. Rather, a correct understanding of our difference determines how we approach what is more ultimate metaphysically. The absorbing god is not an adequate metaphysical name for what is ultimate because, in undermining the sense of difference accompanying desire, it screens what may be properly ultimate about the self. This cannot be entirely suppressed. The restlessness of desire and its sometimes divine discontent breaks open the closure that, rather than being absolute, was rather an absolution from the dare of difference. The power we ourselves are, the power that is our burden and our grandeur, breaks out in desire and cries out for a positive accounting.

Chapter Two
Desire and Original Selfness

The search for origins is a recurrent theme in the tradition of philosophy. It tends to be approached in terms of either an origin that is other than human, in traditional transcendent metaphysics, or in terms of a source of meaning immanent in selfhood itself, as in modern transcendental philosophies. The search for origins has been criticized recently on both these scores, the first as so-called ontotheology, the second as in essence a nostalgic continuation of the same ontotheology, only now relocated and hidden within transcendental subjectivity (see Introduction). What these criticisms largely amount to is the accusation that the search for origins wrongly looks for some fixed, static, thinglike foundation. If origins are conceived in such terms, such criticisms may well be justified. However, the issue need not be posed in terms of some immobile, frozen ground. The dynamism of desire provides, I believe, a richer base from which to explore a complex sense of self that is other than mere static substance.

We must return, then, to the tension in desire between infinitude and wholeness (see chapter 1) and dwell with it more deeply. Resort to an absorbing god involves an immediate denial of this tension and a premature flight from desire's infinite restlessness into a false wholeness. If the quest for wholeness is at the expense of desire's infinity, then we will give neither its full due. We need an affirmative sense of the second if we are to have a genuine form of the first. For this reason we must enter more radically the experience of lack to consider the original power of being that is disclosed by desire. The search for articulate wholeness, if it is to be commensurate with desire's infinity, requires that this infinity itself be centered in the unity of a prior originative source.

We need not enforce an either/or between beginning and end; we must insist on both, for the end need not leave the beginning behind or outside itself. A proper end may span, from its eventual reposed prospect, the beginning that breeds it, however obscure and perplexing this beginning may be.

A metaphysical consideration of what it means *to be* a self is unavoidable, in light of the power of being that comes to articulation in desire. I will address this question in stages. First, I will situate the problem historically. Second, I will discuss difficulties that confront philosophical discourse concerning the self considered as an origin. Third, I will develop a view of what I will call *the original self*, a view that is internally complex and differentiated, but one that avoids the trap of falsely substantializing the self, I believe. Finally, I will further clarify this view by comparing it with two of the most important traditional conceptions—namely, the empirical self and the transcendental ego.

THE ISSUE IN HISTORICAL CONTEXT

The search for an origin within the self may be viewed in terms of the contrast between ancient and modern concerns. We might say, for example, that classical Greek eros was not always as strongly marked by the sense of individuality—indeed, willful individuality—that tends to mark modern consciousness. Thus, some commentators have pointed to the absence of the will in Greek thought. We here find a strong sense of the metaphysical dimension of desire, but a less insistent sense of self-consciousness than we find in modern, post-Cartesian philosophy. In what follows I will try to speak to the problem of modern self-consciousness without jettisoning the ancient emphasis on the metaphysical sense of desire. I will try to find some balance between modern transcendental consciousness and the traditional metaphysical sense of transcendence, by taking seriously the dynamism inherent in human desire.

Of course, some thinkers claim that individual selfhood is itself part of the problem of modernity. Thus, Cartesian subjectivity is attacked as being an excessively inwardized self that, in turn, tends to tyrannically overlord an objectified nature. Contemporary attacks on selfhood often imply that the Cartesian understanding of the self is the only one available. And undoubtedly it has been dominant in the modern age. I do not think, however, that we can erase the modern sense of self, of inwardness, and the self-consciousness it brings to light. The problem is not solved by pretending that we can get behind self-consciousness.[1] Rather than trying to dissolve the self, we should be attempting to do justice to the greater complexity that appears with modern self-consciousness. We must grant the sense of the infinite worth—indeed the inviolable being—of the self that the religious and moral traditions of the West have brought to the fore. We may agree with Hegel in seeing this sense as a fundamental advance. The problem, of course, is how to do justice to this infinite inwardness. The Cartesian solution abstracts the self from being other than itself, creating dualism, disunion, and fragmentation, which in turn leads to man's rationalized will to power over the rest of being. I believe that we must develop the self's infinitude in a different direction to this will to power, which has been ably criticized by many contemporary thinkers. We need some dialectical balance between the modern sense of infinite inwardness and the classical sense of harmony and wholeness of being.

I grant, then, that the modern self has been excessively subjectivized. On this point, contemporary criticisms of Cartesianism are not without justice. But the Cartesian view has the merit that it brings out the inescapability of the problem of self and self-consciousness. We do not address the issue adequately if our strategy is simply to dissolve the Cartesian problem, to show that there is really no problem at all. We may criticize the answer of Cartesianism, the presuppositions of its whole approach, even the adequacy of the way it formulates the problem, but we can still hold that the problem of the self is one of the fundamental problems. We must acknowledge modern self-consciousness, preserving what is genuine in its emphasis; yet we must try to see if the human self can be anchored once again in being, without the excessive subjectivization of Cartesianism, but preserving infinite inwardness. Only by such anchoring does it seem possible to overcome the vacuity of empty inwardness and thereby allow once more some approach to human wholeness.[2]

Let me add that this problem is not only philosophical; it invades the whole of modern culture. It is not possible to develop this point here,[3] but in the area of art, the problem of the Romantics, which is still our problem today[4] and which involves the same issue of the self's infinite inwardness, is crucial: how might such a self be grounded in some rich sense of nature, exteriority, or being other? In the view that I will develop below, I will try to do justice to the sense of "originality" that is given strong expression in the modern aesthetic. The problem, of course, is to develop a sense of the self as original that does not uproot it from being other than self. Undoubtedly, the modern emphasis on "origination," or "originality," is often debased. But this debasement is a distortion of something essential, not evidence that this essential does not exist at all. It is the unanchoring of originality, the uprooting of the self as origin, from the richness of being that has generated this seeming mania for debased originality. Simple classical mimesis tends to see what is other than human as the original, and the human being as, ideally, a submissive image. The excessive "creativity" of modernism tends to see the human person as the absolute original, and other being as merely an image thereof. We need to find a middle between these extremes, in which the self as originating is balanced by being in its genuine otherness, in which the self as originating is itself a participant in the original power of being itself.

THE BEING OF SELF AND THE DIFFICULTY OF DISCURSIVE ACCESS

Let us now look at some of the difficulties we face. Consider this initial, provisional view: *selfhood is original self-articulating power to be*. We cannot be content, however, with this preliminary assertion. What it asserts and its very status are problematical. Our difficulty relates to how we might approach selfhood in the first place, much less express what we grasp, should we successfully close with it. On the level of *our* discourse, we seem restricted to a limited utterance that must specify a finite determinate something. Yet the assertion above seems not to specify anything in particular and therefore appears vacuous of particularized content. If our discourse must exhibit determinate content,[5] are we enmeshed in nonsense from the outset, liable to be accused of—suppose we name the crime—metaphysical cacology? Are we to conclude not only that we cannot speak about the self, but that there is no self at all?

Such a judgment would be off center, I think. We must rotate this judgment on its own axis, so to speak, for it is like a prism which now refracts the light dully but which, should we swivel it slightly, will break it up brilliantly. We must grant the fact but modulate the interpretation. First, selfhood might indeed be nothing in the sense of no thing; but now the real question emerges, for selfhood might somehow be no thing, yet without being merely nothing. Second, what is no thing without being utterly nothing might rather be positive original power that is not empty of content but a ground of the determination of content.

That is, selfhood need not be sheer particularity, but neither need it be nothingness pure and simple; it may be original power to be, in excess of determined particularity. Still, we must try to give some more positive account of this peculiar indeterminate power. It does not suffice to say that selfhood is *not* this, *not* that, and so on, ad nauseam. This yields only an empty, indefinite characterization, which may in fact lead to Sartrean nausea before the nothingness of desire,[6] which, in turn, can easily lure us back to something like the refuge of the absorbing god or confine us to the merely negative freedom of resistance. The self is not this particular thing, not that particular thing; but this is so because it is *more* than any particular thing, not because it is less. It is this more that insists on being positively formulated.

Thus we come back to difficulties already touched on in connection with the absorbing god as a metaphysical metaphor. The more, the excess of the power of being of self, requires language adequate to its possible inexhaustibility. There may not be an absolutely determinate concept of selfhood, but there may be a metaphysical metaphor perhaps. For metaphor and the metaphysical might be said to have this in common: both share a root in the word *meta,* which means both "in the midst of, in between," and also "beyond, over and above." Exploiting this double sense, we see that a metaphysical metaphor may not be a fully determinable concept in any limited, finite sense. Yet neither need it be wholly indefinite. It is more like an articulated image, which points to a meaning that cannot be pinned down or fixed absolutely, but which nevertheless manages to genuinely articulate what is more than any particularized determination. It is an index of this more, as something that is not exclusively beyond or over and above determinate things but is also manifest in the midst of such determinacy. Below we will consider the *original self* as such a metaphysical metaphor.

We must still address the question of how can we reach this more, this meta, while claiming that it is not simply beyond determinate things but also in their midst. How can it be both? If we begin with the determinate and yet say that the real origin is more than the determinate, how can we be said to really "begin" with the determinate? Moreover, how can we get from there to what is then said to be the true "beginning," the true origin that is more than the determinate? It would seem that the original self (here using this notion in a preliminary fashion) cannot be derived from determinate experience in any immediate, or even mediately synthetic, way. The original self would appear to lay claim to a priority that it seems impossible to uphold from the perspective of determinate experience. How, then, can we speak of this priority at all?

To respond to this perplexity, we must draw on our treatment of desire and also on certain lines of argument drawn from the tradition of transcendental thought. It will become clear later that there are difficulties with that tradition, especially in relation to the concreteness of its concept of self. Nevertheless, there is great persuasiveness in some of its reflections concerning the problem of synthesis in experience.[7] Here we find ourselves having to distinguish two senses of *synthesis:* synthesis as a *prior power* of uniting, discriminating, and relating and synthesis as a *posterior result* issuing from this prior, active unifying.

Let us first examine the synthesis of a manifold of determinate experience. As opposed to its determinate elements, this synthesis might seem at best to be just another (if more extensive) determinate experience, one that merely widens the scope of the determinate. The more that this synthesis gives us is the more of quantitative extension—that is, more of the *same* determinate experience—not the more that is also beyond the determinate. There is an element of truth in this analysis, but it is not the whole truth. For we have confined ourselves to synthesis as an end product, a result, and have forgotten the activity of synthesizing that (to make synthesis as an end product possible at all) must be presupposed to have qualitatively extended itself within the interstices of the manifold of determinate experiences and to have held them together. Now this activity cannot be characterized as exclusively determinate, for if it were, it would be one more item among an aggregate of others, and there would be no synthesis in the sense of a resultant unity, much less any synthesizing in the sense of an activity of unification. Synthesis as product is grounded in the prior active power of synthesis, which is twofold: power to delimit the determinate and power to bind together the multiplicity of what is delimited.

This prior power must be more than the determinate; otherwise it could neither stand in the gaps between finite items nor span their dispersion and bring them into relation. Relation as resultant is conditional on the activity of relating, just as the delimitation of *relata* as fixed terms is contingent on the activity of discrimination. But the activities of relating and discriminating and their *compresence* in the comprehensive act of articulate relating are themselves grounded in a more primordial power. This primordial power is the power of active synthesis but is not identical with synthesis as a resultant. Synthesis as a resultant presupposes elements already distinguished which it then unites and to that extent is not identical with this primordial power. Nor is it discrimination that is primordial: for the act of distinguishing presupposes the power to differentiate. Original power here is precisely what is more primordial than differentiation and unification; indeed, these latter manifest this prior power and point us back to the source they express.

The activities of differentiation and unification, then, can orient us toward this primordial power that is not either one of them but that can manifest itself as and be both of them. They point toward the power that in its original unity—not merely in the derived unity of resultant synthesis—can enter the space between distinct items and hold them together without denying their difference. This power cannot be simply determinate because, given the activities of relation and discrimination, it must be both itself and not itself. It must be in itself and beyond itself, capable, as it were, of entering the skin of what is other. In order to identify and bring into association determinate others, it must possess a dimension of indeterminacy. From the standpoint of synthesis, then, consideration of any determinate experience pushes us back behind the achieved synthesis of distinct elements requiring unification, behind the discriminating and relating of these distinct elements, to a more primordial power to set apart and bind together, which, though it may manifest itself determinately, must have a core indeterminacy to enable it to identify and connect other determinate things.

What this consideration of synthesis reveals is not merely beyond the determinate but in the midst of it. Hence we can approach it in a number of different ways—for instance, through the mediation between self and externality that we find in knowledge. But it is in human desire especially that we find a freedom of experience from the merely finite and determinate. For desire is a determinate form of experience within which we perceive the seeds of indeterminacy and original power, and through which we may gain our bearings vis-à-vis the underpinning, permeating power to be of selfhood. Through it we are opened to something prior (the source of original power) and something posterior (the goal of active wholeness), both of which are more than finite determinations. The crucial point is that here we have a genuine approach to this more. Moreover, this access is not something we demand of desire, a requirement that we impose on it from outside; desire itself seems to press this opening on us. To that extent we do not even need access, for that would suppose that we were at present cut off from our goal and only hereafter in touch with it; whereas the trajectory of desire is always in advance through the opening. Our difficulty seems to be one of recognizing what is the case and articulating it explicitly. It is not that our richness has yet to be created. We are already deep, deep beyond present measure. The point is to bring to expression this profound plenitude.

Desire, then, can be said to insistently prompt us toward the active ground of synthesis because it emphatically exhibits some of the features required of this ground. It is both itself and yet not completely coincident with itself, in itself and yet beyond itself, more than, yet less than, itself. It is internally differentiated; yet, in entering the space of external difference between itself and things, it is the power to bring the inner and outer into relation. We have here the integration in process of the prior and the posterior, because we have the middle between the beginning and the end and the dialectical mediation between them. This middle allows us to look in both directions, toward originality and toward wholeness; moreover, its nature is such that we are not barred from bringing to expression the extremes that bound it. Because, with desire, it makes no sense to set the beginning outside the middle or the end outside either of these two; because beginning and end are interwoven; because beginning and end converge on the articulate middle; there is a sense in which *we can start from wherever we are,* let us say in the middle, and speak from there to both the beginning and the end. For wherever we are—and there is a sense in which we are always in the middle—the end and the beginning repeatedly erupt in our eros. Nor does it seem fully correct to say that we are *in* the middle, for we *are* this middle.[8]

THE ORIGINAL SELF AS FACT

When I speak of the original self, I am trying to find a philosophical name for this middle: the mediating and articulating power of being that emerges with and gives determinate form to human desire. I admit the risk of naming here—that is, of wrong substantialization. This warning has been sounded by contemporary thought, from both analytical and Continental camps, against the tradition of metaphysics. Yet we must still try to name what cannot be frozen or hypostatized into static substance. The original self need not elude discourse entirely. In what follows I will consider two of its manifest forms: as realized and as idealized selfhood. In this section I will consider the self as fact; in the following section I will look at the self as ideal; then I will consider the dialectical interplay between the real and the ideal by speaking of the original self as concrete ideality. But again I remind the reader that I am not talking about a plurality of "selves," completely different from each other and the original self, but rather about what we might perhaps call "selfscapes" of the original self—that is, formations of its self-unfolding that help us interpret its power of being.

First, then, let us consider the self as fact. We sometimes come across the view that there exists no self at all, a view tied to the above-mentioned charge of false substantialization or, alternatively, to an excessive emphasis on process and becoming such that the self tends to dissolve into sheer flux. The dynamic view of self defended here tries to avoid these extremes of frozen thinghood and formless flux. In speaking of the self as fact, we first need to affirm a real form of existence, but then we must interpret its inherent intricacy. That the self is, is both basic and compellingly insistent: starting wherever we are, it can only be "we" who begin, even if our intent is to dodge the self. But no dodge is possible, for we carry with us what we are determined to avoid.

Suppose we recollect our reflections to this point: we are struck by a sequence of relevant facts. For "we," in fact, locate ourselves through the specification of our bodies which desire effects. Again, "we," in fact, begin to be selves when we are hit with the shock of difference that breaks forth from desire. Once again, it was "we," in fact, who pondered, but did not falter before, the flight from difference; "we," in fact, who balked at suppression of self in the absorbing god. To try to exorcise the self is only to redouble it. Were the self not, all this would be nonsense. The jolt of difference that startles and jars us, our grappling with its sometimes violent impact, the dynamic but not always guaranteed interplay between desire and externality—these would be coagulated again into a kind of ooze of inertia. That they are and are as articulated: this is the rock of fact on which a denial of self founders and to which we must anchor our understanding.[9]

The peculiarity of this fact, however, is that it is always internally complex. Its affirmation is no bare assertion but is necessarily fraught with an immanent intricacy. Existence riddled by desire cannot be merely a ready-made fact, present in uncomplicated givenness: this follows directly from desire's relation to lack; lack is given yes, but what is given is not only the presence of something, but, paradoxically, its compresent absence. The inherent intricacy of the self is that it is not a finished fact, but an open, self-making fact. Keats calls this world a "vale of soul-making," and the human self is a fact in that sense. It is, and it is a reality both made and being made.

Given the self as fact in an internally complex sense, a kind of energy of internal difference springs up in it as a driving, dynamic force. This internal difference might seem to be a fissure within the self as fact, but it is not a splitting of the self into two substances whose dualism makes relation impossible. Rather it is related to a double directionality within desire. In one direction, it has to do with human orientation toward an active self-identity. In the other, it points us back to the primordial power of being, relative to which the human person is not a dualism of two substances, but an internally self-differentiating identity. These two directions always coexist, the tension between them grounding the emergence of the self's internal complexity. That is, a person's original power to be exists in tension with its determinate realizations. Though this protopower of selfness actualizes itself, its self-surpassing sweep can also reshape any such concretization and instigate a new form. Thus the dynamism of human becoming exists together with its resting in stable nodes, but the tension engendered thereby augurs something profoundly positive. Immanent differentiating power makes visible the power of the original self as present, though not absolutely, in the sedimented realization of the self as fact. This present power of internal difference initiates the dynamic process that would bring back, in the shape of articulated existence, the self from its division.

Desire manifests the infringement on bland passivity of a certain dynamic power of being that interjects a rift into dead self-identity. The arousal of disquiet that occurs here is essentially originative: an active form of existence germinates in the dislocation we experience when desire disconcerts our dormancy. Desire reveals a power that disrupts any simple self-identity, yet one that can also become the cradle for a new opening. Relative to dormant self-identity, it might be seen as the constructive destruction of the seed of selfhood which, as the old religious wisdom has it, must die before it can quicken. Put differently, it reveals the death of the human being as merely a natural substance, as but one indifferent thing among other indifferent things, and its rebirth as free activity.

Likewise, we are not talking of a self subsisting in a kind of monadic solitude. The impact and pressure of external difference are necessary for the actualization of self. Yet this actualization cannot be reduced, as it is in behaviorism, to a simple stimulation of reactive response from the outside. The self is active in forming the pattern of its own progression. We are immanently and spontaneously disjoined from our existence merely as a particularized fact; yet we endeavor to heal inward disjunction through the powers of origination. Nor is it the case that at first we are totally in possession of ourselves and that only thereafter do we *will* to be internally articulated. As facts we are already realizations of the original power of being. Initially we do not will to be internally articulated; for this will is itself an articulation derived from the original energy of our being. We are between the total freedom of untrammeled will and the vanishing of freedom into the indifference of inert being. The original self points to a middle between these extremes, from which the power of freedom begins to emerge.

Thus, against Cartesianism and certain forms of idealism, we cannot divorce the self from externality, either its own or that of other things. If we do so, we invite atrophy and emptiness. But if we fail to acknowledge the difference between self and externality, as does a reductive materialism, we risk a related outcome, namely dispersion. A distance that is simply alienated and a dispossession that is utterly lost are neither of them appropriate relations between the self and externality. Indeed, the internal complexity of the self as fact seems to render impossible any merely extrinsic relation to externality; for sheer separation seems to be indistinguishable from pure dispersion, insofar as both fail to ground an articulate relation between man and being in its otherness.

The human self as fact is an embodied being, an articulated exteriorization of the power of being. This articulated exteriorization, our embodiment, issues forth into form only through man's dialectical, reciprocal interplay with external things. From the moment of its beginning, the human self conceives a world within itself that it must bear within its own inwardness. At the same time it must carry the weight of externality. This is the order of its nature: to be outside itself but still to be in tension with its own exigence for self-relation, self-unification. The human being's caliber is tested by its capacity to give the head to these two requirements of its being, while proving able to stand the strain of their tension and yet to hold them together. The narcissist who retreats into the privacy of his own inward theater, there to posture before his own eyes and disport himself in self-absorption, defeats himself in this trial by missing the mark of externality. The braggart of the public realm who, in advertising his surface, captures the limelight, wins the world but squanders his own soul, fails this test from the side of centered inwardness. Both desert the tension of human doubleness, which demands both facing the heterogeneous universe and succeeding to some steadfast soul.

THE ORIGINAL SELF AS IDEAL

We cannot confine ourselves to the self as fact or model the self on the external thing. The terror and promise of human selfhood is precisely its nonconformity to the external thing as a passive image conforms to an extrinsic original. There is something that is itself original about human beings.[10] Our being shows a spontaneous power that articulates itself in terms of both what we are and what we are yet to be. In this latter light let us now look at the self as ideal.

The complexity of our exterior embodiment is inwardly matched by an immanent depth of being that cannot be reduced to simple substantival unity. This is clear if we consider how we set before ourselves an image of ideal selfhood,[11] a goal we constitute by way of anticipation and by way of wanting to realize more fully the power we find welling up within our own depths. Though such an ideal is an anticipated goal, initially it is not fully realized or executed in fact, and in this sense the ideal self is not absolutely determinate. Yet we throw ourselves forward toward the ideal we project, and in the process the ideal becomes more concretely determinate. The more definite anticipation is, the more oriented becomes the bearing of desire with respect to it. Thus the self as ideal is neither sheerly determinate nor absolutely indefinite. It is an intentionally realized, but not fully executed, determination of selfhood, and hence it is midway between determinacy and indeterminacy. Out of an indeterminate beginning, it discloses the exigency for self-determination and mediates an approximation to it through the ideal it projects.

We indicate this, for instance, when we sometimes say, "I am this, but I might be *other* than I am."[12] We are the possibility of being other. We are not simple facts, but possible worlds, possibly other worlds, which is to say counterfactuals. We counter the present fact of self and its lack of assured identity by intending a form of future selfhood which, though not identical with what we are, gives expression to the deeper identity that we are, since it answers by anticipation the want of our desire. Escaping from mere givenness, the self proceeds to something more. We give content to this advance through the mediating foresight of ideal selfhood. In a sense, we are both in advance of ourselves and yet at the same time gaining ground on ourselves, such that it becomes difficult

to say which comes first and which last; an interesting case of the prov-
erbial hen and egg. We aim beyond ourselves and are shot forth like
an arrow. But then, rather than expiring on the target, we begin to come
to ourselves and traverse a circle in return. Standing outside ourselves,
it is *we* who are outside, and so we are returned within ourselves. But
which comes first: what we presently are or what we purpose yet to be?
It seems difficult to answer this question as a disjunctive either/or. We
seem to require a more inclusive both/and. What we find is always mixture: a complex ambiguous middle in which we have to find direction
through indirection. We seem to be driven to the light in front of us
by the shadow thrown over our shoulder by the same light behind us.

Transcending mere givenness, we may, of course, proceed to something less. Our reach exceeds our grasp, but the gulf between aspiration
and attainment may precipitate flight from the ideal. Then we settle for
less than our peculiar givenness demands and stifle desire's infinitude
in the anonymous particularity of finite things. To settle thus is to embrace an uneasy ease, for, despite our flight, intimations of something
more ultimate will inevitably flare up and even invade our anticipation
against the grain of its willingness. The self in flight divides itself from
the ideal only to be dissociated and in retreat from itself. Identifying
its own facticity with the facticity of particular things, it disowns the call
of the original power of its being. This flight thereby disowns what
cannot be disowned, except as a literally self-frustrating regress into the
inert facticity that obtained prior to desire's appearance. But this re-
version can be effected only *because* of the original power of being that
appears with desire. The self in flight thus turns its life against its own
urge and direction and, like a house divided, it cannot stand. Should
it succeed, it finds itself a failure, with a victory that is defeat and an
ease that is absolutely anxious. The self in flight is disquieted by its
original power, controverted by its ideal, and called to confront and
convert the unease of its internal division into a self-relation that is truer
to the original power of its being.[13]

Thus, the ideal self need not be a foreign norm superimposed on
human desire *ab extra*. Through desire of the ideal, we counter our own
limited facticity, thereby awaking to the emergent freedom that, though
realized now in a specific way, might still be otherwise. The ideal self
is the insistent charge, issuing from self-awakened desire, that our original power be answered for and actualized in ways more qualitatively
adequate than those provided by the self as a given fact. The ideal gives
expression to our way of intending, approaching, and trying to consti-

tute human wholeness. Through the ideal we bring to manifestation a measure by which we appraise ourselves. We are in advance of, but never fully coincident with, ourselves; but without an exacting measure, we would never advance to ourselves. The self as ideal is necessary to the internal orientation of desire, a guiding telic principle that regulates its direction. It provides a teleological exemplar corresponding to the protopower of being that we find in the depth of self. Such a regulatory ideal need not be, I repeat, an extrinsic end, adventitiously superimposed on desire, nor one that, because we have not reached it, must be indefinitely postponed. This regulatory ideal is simply the immanent standard of self-regulation, a norm that, though we fail to live up to it and fall short, is already present and operative in our being. In this respect it is not merely regulative: it is both regulative and constitutive at once.[14]

Human becoming is not blind movement but steadies and gives aim to its own dynamism. Through the power of the ideal we try to guide, regulate, and correct ourselves. Man reveals himself as both an end in himself and as an orientation to an end that he is not.[15] The positive power of the ideal makes the demand on us that we be genuinely true to ourselves. Of course, there is a cynical response that wants to debunk all ideals as illusory fantasies. And undoubtedly some particular ideals may indeed prove to be empty, just as some people who claim simply to be true to themselves fester with self-deception. What we are talking about here, however, is the impossibility of evading completely the call of the ideal as such, regardless of the specific ideals we might accept, sometimes perhaps falsely. The self as ideal in this sense can be said to be something intimate to the reality of the self as fact. This ideal is insistently real, since it issues in the summons that the self be genuinely true to itself. We are a certain form of being that is haunted by the ideal, and whose qualitatively highest activity is conditional on, and in some sense constituted by, truthfulness to self. Thus the ideal, far from being an empty abstraction, can be the absolute call of truthfulness that erupts in desire. It may be fundamentally concrete because it charges us with the task to be and become the original power we are.

THE ORIGINAL SELF AS CONCRETE IDEALITY

Having looked at these two selfscapes, the self as fact and as ideal, let us now try to bring the two together. In actuality we never find one without the other, but always a complex, dialectical interplay between the two. Selfhood reveals a certain concrete ideality. What this means will become more clear as we proceed. But first, let us be clear that concrete ideality is not to be thought of as a self-subsistent essence that resides in substantial permanence behind the flux of consciousness. As suggested previously, the original self tries to name what cannot be a simple principle of unity but, as an origin of difference, is a unity of power that differentiates itself. Moreover, this unity of power cannot be said to be merely possible; it is an actual power—which is not to say, of course, that it is realized absolutely. Even when it does not realize the possibility of its power, it is real power. Thus, the original power of selfhood is not like a simple transition from the possible to the actual, the second not yet existing while the first does, and the first being left behind when the second is realized. Instead we find a dialectical interplay of extremes that might normally be regarded as exclusive.

We must not reduce the original self to a determinate category for this or that particular unity or, indeed, even for its universal form. Consistent with the metaphysical understanding of desire, the primary accent of our account falls on the being (the "isness") of the self, rather than on determinate characteristics of being such as, for instance, universality or particularity, form and matter, ideality and reality. Yet no exclusion of these determinate characteristics is implied by this emphasis. For this isness of the self reveals itself to be not just blank being, but something dialectically self-articulating. It transcends any merely extrinsic antithesis of the ideal and the fact. The original self is not a static determinate essence, form, or structure; these last are originated, not original; derived, not primordial. They are original only to the extent that they manifest and participate in the source whence they issue. Nor is the original self an atomistic, infinitesimal point that floats on the void. It is a still, but active center; positionless, yet capable of informing any position; not a form, not a body, yet the power to originate form and to inform a body. It erupts outward from the center of this positionless position, making the body its circle, being the body as an embodiment of the power of being. Appropriating an environment, it makes a world for itself out of a material sphere. Moreover, its self-articulation grounds the differentiation between the mind and the body, between "lower" and "higher" desires. Each form of consciousness, such as sensation, understanding, reason, and so on, is a determinate specification of this original power to be, rather than a subsistent whole or part comprising a substantial self. And since the originative power of differentiation approximates its epitome in the ideal self, which, as we saw, is active truthfulness to self, we might say that one of desire's highest possibilities reveals itself in the love of truth. This is an acme of desire, in that, here, being in man opens itself up to being other than man with no ulterior motivation beyond that of establishing, as an end in itself, an articulate relation between one form of being and another.[16]

The "what" of the original self is the power to produce a unity in process of fact and ideal. Selfhood cannot be reduced to either slow materiality or wistful ideality, each of these being antithetical vanishing points of concreteness. Consider again why we cannot sustain the normal antithesis of fact and ideal. Selfhood is their synthesis, not primarily in terms of their derived unity (though it may be this too), not primarily in terms of their being set apart as distinguishable terms of an antithesis (though this may also be true), but rather in terms of the original power out of which division and reunifiction spring. Here we must say that concrete ideality is not only an anticipated goal in the process of being achieved; it is already actual as a real power, though not, of course, fully actual in the form of explicit actualization. We are both in possession of and in process toward concrete ideality, which, as antecedent and consequent, can be original, purposive, and mediating all at once.

Desire's movement exhibits this concrete ideality in that its passage to an end need not be the degeneration of a whole into fragments, but can be the generation of the self's internal complexity. Fact and ideal need not fall away from a rich beginning, but can specify self in raising its power to be to appropriate articulateness. We can converge on a *subsequent* unity of fact and ideal only because we are *already* the power of concrete ideality. This is manifested sensuously in the body's self-articulation and reflectively in the mind's conscious self-relation. But in itself, concrete ideality is a root of articulation more pristine than its sensuous and reflective stems, one that transcends the antithesis of form and matter.[17] It is not exclusively sensuous, not exclusively reflective; not structure, not matter; yet it is all these, while being beyond them at their source. We should say that concrete ideality is closer to active intelligence than to structured intelligibility, where being closer to the first does not entail the exclusion of the last, however.

Original selfhood is concrete ideality because it exists as, but is not simply identical with, fact, when this is taken to refer to bare existence.[18] Here we have concrete fact, which, through the mediation of ideality, awakens to existence and affirms itself. Concrete ideality, then, is the power of being reaching out to being, not blindly, but in awareness of itself, and hence, in its institution of relations, capable of procession to-

ward some self-appropriation. It is fact, but not merely fact; it is immanently articulated, but this and more; it is fact, immanently
articulated, and yet open to the affirmation of being in the fullness of
its otherness. Concrete being, always active but not always awakened to
itself, ceases with the original self to be a chrysalis; restlessly shaking
off slumber and shattering the cocoon crust of mute substance, it takes
wing above silent nature into the open space of speech.

It might be objected that we are verging on something totally indeterminate, thereby running the risk of undermining all claims to intelligibility. This objection has some validity with respect to the necessary
strain put on language. But though the original self has no "whatness"
in the sense of being sheerly identical with a determinate essence, this
is not to deny the importance of intelligible structure. On the contrary,
we discern structure in its self-articulation when we approach it through
desire. There we have found the coexistence of self-structuring and infinite restlessness, the tension between which makes it impossible for the
self to be merely a formless abyss. This tension, indeed, powers the self
to form itself into a dynamic unity, in which it need neither disperse
itself outward nor disappear inward. Put differently, original selfhood
is not simply a translation of the absorbing god into the depths of man.
As an assimilating whole, the absorbing god is pure centripetal incorporation that, in drawing all into itself, vanishes along with every particular thing. Selfhood is marked by some assimilating power certainly,
but this is balanced by centrifugal self-articulation. It is this that gives
it an embodied, yet open, external determination. We might thus say
that selfhood entails an integrated outwardness that is appropriate to
its inherent power of being, and that the negation it must overcome is
either of two different deaths, each in the end the same: on the one
hand, the scattering of the self which the center cannot hold; on the
other hand, the collapse of the center on itself, the sphere of selfhood
caving in.

Because of this peculiar doubleness, this coexistence of the centripetal
and the centrifugal, as we have metaphorically put it, human selfhood
offers a recalcitrance to direct encapsulation and strains discourse to the
point of paradox. Here, perhaps, is the point of the objection cited
above. Yet, though this recalcitrance would seem to stand in our way
and make selfhood what is furthest away from us, there is a vital sense
in which it is closest to us. For we bear within us an intimate sense of
selfhood, which suffuses our being and radiates outward through our
action.[19] This is not a particular thing that can be circumscribed deter-

minately. It is more like a light, which, though it seems like nothing in particular, illuminates nevertheless; like the Platonic sun, as a very ground of visibility. Even if we should manage to find the source of light, we would not find a particular thing, but rather a presence, a power; nor do we know this source except as it manifests itself as radiation. Selfhood is like this source, this power, this radiation, this light that we cannot pin down absolutely or localize statically.

Action emanates from selfhood; we know ourselves to be its source; we emanate from ourselves; we do our action. And though we may compare this emanation to light, it still cannot be reduced to pure transparency or be captured in the clear Cartesian glitter of some shadowless language.[20] Here one must agree with many of the contemporary criticisms of Cartesian clarity and distinctness as applied to the self. There is kernel opaqueness at the heart of this rich light, which might justifiably be called rich darkness, for it exceeds any determinate clarification of it. To those who object to the obscurity of this, one can only reply that such obscurity is not merely symptomatic of some deep defect that mars and undoes our philosophical language; rather, it mirrors the mystery of selfhood itself. One cannot but concur with Augustine when, in perplexity and celebration, he exclaimed: *grande profundum est ipse homo.*[21]

We should not attempt, therefore, to give a determinate explanation of selfhood. Such an explanation would have to be grounded in a determinate relation of already delimited terms; but man's desire seems to push us beyond finite determinacy toward, not explanation of that kind, but a certain kind of *acknowledgment*. Yet this acknowledgment is not mute; for its sense is situated in and mediated by a context of open intelligibility. In such a context, the discourse of a metaphysical metaphor is not a finite explanation, but a philosophical acknowledgment of what determinate explanation points to at its limit. No finite conceptual objectification, by the nature of the case, can fully encapsulate the original self. The metaphorical dimension of our expression acknowledges the necessity of images as well as concepts to preserve the truth of its real concreteness. As a metaphysical metaphor, the original self strains toward the root of any metaphor or concept, toward the power to be at the root.[22]

The paradox that makes selfhood at once both foreign and intimate, present and fugitive, might be put this way. In eluding the structural fixity of conceptual objectifications, there is a certain incommunicability to the self; yet original selfhood appears to be communicability itself:

it is the original power to be that expresses itself externally in order to bring itself to articulate realization. Thus we are not trapped, as it were, in a centerless shuttle between night and day. Sometimes, indeed, we do decompose in the night. We lose our composure when the mask of finalized determinacy falls away. Moreover, we are inundated, if but briefly, by the unexpected, the surpassing, the unsolicited power of being that overflows any finite self we fix, and that does not cease to await another awakening, even while we, forgetful and unwatching, sleep on. We can speak about the original self, although, in doing so, we tax language in the manner already indicated and just now displayed. We are caught, as it were, on the spokes of a still, but rotating, wheel; our discourse traces radii of selfhood, traversing the line of their direction, inward to the wheel's axis and center and outward to its periphery and definition. We must try to grasp what we can neither encapsulate nor avoid. The paradox of original selfhood is that we are pointed to what is at once both prior and consequent. We cannot stand outside the communicability of this yet incommunicable power of self-articulation. Our place is not outside it, for we are placed in it; we *are* it, this mysterious moving station of communicability. We are only outside it because this intimate power of articulation takes place outside itself. But from this outside place, we are *again* pitched into this mysterious space of communicability, within whose amplitude we live and move and have our being.

THE ORIGINAL SELF AND THE EMPIRICAL EGO

We will now look at two important traditional conceptions, namely the empirical and the transcendental ego. There is always the temptation to cover over the grounding power to be of selfhood and to contract our sense of its concreteness. We confuse what is derivative with what is original and then confine attention to the former. This may occur from the side of either content or form, or, in the language used above, from the side of the self as fact or as ideal. These two sides broadly correspond to certain emphases in the empirical and transcendental conceptions. Let us first turn to the empirical ego and examine some of the relevant essentials of a classical philosophical position. The reader will recognize references to classical empiricism as, say, it moves toward a culmination and dissolution in Hume. But my remarks also have application to more contemporary views, which substitute for the classical doctrine of sense impressions the stimulus-response model of behaviorism.

Given the self as fact, one must agree with the empiricist's commitment to concrete experience. Despite this, however, one cannot identify the original self with the psychological ego of the empiricist. This follows from the restricted manner in which classical empiricism interprets the nature of experience.[23] For this interpretation is initially governed by a rigid sense of determinacy; hence, the empiricist expects the self to be just like any other particular substance. He is surprised, often shocked, when he finds (rightly) that no such thing exists. Assuming that the identity of the particular thing is the obvious paradigm of concreteness, he is confounded when the self fails to show itself with the same obvious concreteness (as he is also when, on deeper reflection, the particular thing itself loses its obviousness).

The empiricist's failure here might be called the fallacy of univocity: the reduction to unmediated sameness or identity of different kinds of beings. Solid substances, like rocks, provide paradigms of the kind of univocal concreteness for which he is searching. Not surprisingly, he fails to find any self of this sort. At first he is dismayed, for his expectation has been defeated; instead of the rock of substance he seems to peer into an abyss of nothingness. His second response is one of vexation, for this "nothing" looks like nonsense. His third move is dismissal: instead of confronting a univocal particular, he has been forced to wander in a labyrinth, which, for an empiricist, is nebulousness itself. And, as we know, the empiricist, priding himself on his no-nonsense common sense, shrinks in horror from what his technical jargon calls "woolliness." Eventually the empiricist shakes off this vague fog to return to his initial univocal sense of the concrete.[24] Only now, like a sightseer who has returned unharmed from the cave of the Minotaur, he is emboldened to proclaim of the self that there is no such thing.

The empiricist, then, swings from his starting point in the determinacy of the particular thing, through a brief, but quickly abandoned, confrontation with something different (appearing in the negative guise of "a something that is nothing in particular"), and ends by returning to his beginning, his circumscribed sense of the concrete. Given his propensity to univocity, the empiricist is perhaps right to reject the self as something different. For a something that is nothing in particular is, of course, paradoxical, and this is the deep dread of any univocal logic. But this does not end the matter. The empiricist must still derive some selfhood; he must find some substitute sense of unity, even if this is not an absolutely determinate identity. For he has to account for the *psy-chological feeling* that, after all, there is some selfhood. Hence he proceeds to construct a self (or, more accurately, some hazy psychological feeling of a kind of inner sense) from what he takes to be the elementary "atoms," rudimentary units of internal experience. He constructs the self as an aggregate of such units, whose principle of integration is, on the one hand, derivation from external impressions and, on the other hand, their customary connections over a period through which they cluster together to form a "complex." But because their connections have to be sustained over a passage of time, these elementary atoms of psychic feeling and their aggregation have to be set in motion. The psychological self then becomes, as classically in Hume, a flow of rapidly succeeding internal impressions, which give the impression of identity, but which mask the underlying fact that there is no unity to the succession of psychic states beyond the flux of particular impression following particular impression.[25]

What is the outcome of this? Again, it is not quite what the empiricist had expected. Because the self lacks the determinacy that the empiricist anticipates, he reinterprets the sense of selfhood through both a reduction and a remaking that eventually leads to the opposite extreme of rigid particularized determinacy. That is, the self is reduced to a kind of dissolute substance in which psychic state succeeds psychic state in a pure flux of consciousness. We come across a significant paradox. For the empiricist wishes to discover a *univocal identity* for the self. But in pursuit of this and in terms of the dissolute flux of psychic states, he is driven in the end toward an *absolutely equivocal self-identity*. Rather than fixed, definite, unambiguous unity, we end up with equivocal manyness and no unity beyond the adventitiously connected bundle of indefinite psychic states. To avoid paradox, the empiricist clings to univocity. But in doing so, he cannot avoid the paradox that, at some stage, he will be forced to the opposite extreme, where, with no self to cling to, he is lost to the indefinite equivocalness of a centerless tumult of inner impressions.

The empiricist duplicates in inward impressions his constricted notion of externality but is thereby led to a loss of centered inwardness. He is, if he is consistent, also led to a loss of externality. For nothing then exists by which this could be grasped articulately. We are not even allowed the view that the self consists of a series of *perspectives* on externality. A perspective (from *perspicere*) necessitates an act of looking (*specere*) through (*per*). But if there is no center of selfhood, there is nothing that could look through anything, and hence no perspective is possible.[26] A series of inward impressions cannot be perspectival until it possesses within itself some organizing center. The most the psychological ego has by way of center or synthesis is an aggregate of psychic atoms in flux. The inadequacy of this is that, as a derived synthesis, it has no integration beyond the extraneous link of one particular psychological item with another. The connection of psychic atoms is purely adventitious.

As we have already seen, any derived synthesis, however minimal, not only presupposes the discrimination of differentiated elements, but, more important, the prior integral power of differentiation and unification. A series of psychic atoms may indeed coalesce and associate into some loose "congeries." But if our sense of the concrete is too narrow, we conceal the self's power of being, which makes association and aggregation themselves powers and not merely products. Though the self is not univocally the same as the particularized thing, this is no ground for claiming that they must be absolutely different, and hence that the self lacks its appropriate concreteness. Nor is it grounds for patching together bits of inward experience and then supplanting the self with this scissors-and-paste makeshift, this proxy mosaic. The self, rather, possesses its own concreteness. The original power of our being is an immanent ground of determinate differentiation and unification, which is never, as power, univocally identical with these determinations but is nonetheless mediately immanent within them as product.

The moves made by the empiricist—fixating the self in petrified particularity, letting it disintegrate into a dispersed drift of discrete psychic atoms, and then repairing it into a collage of extrinsically conjoined fragments—do not answer fully to the *worlds* that we are. Original selfhood tries to name the rich power of the human being to be an entire world unto itself. By contrast with the empirical ego, the original self is not a stream of awareness or one act or even a series of acts. It is the source of a series of acts, without being exhausted by any particular one. The power to be a world cannot be reduced to a series of states related only by fluctuating and free-floating association. So, too, the original self is not an entity that "has" various states in the way that an object like a rock is sometimes said to have different properties and attributes. It cannot be equated with essence in the sense of being univocally identical with a determinate form or with a sequence of properties that would fix such a form. Its "essence" is original self-articulating power to be. And its self-differentiation is not the division of a thing into parts or exclusively the appearance of a form by means of its properties. We are here dealing with neither an exhaustive determinate form nor an indefinite sequence of determinate appearances, but with indeterminate original power whose determinate manifestation is its own internal differentiation as self-articulating activity.

As a flux of psychic states, the empirical ego sinks downward into the anonymity of silent and ultimately decomposing substance. But we might salvage something from the empiricist's failure to fix the self to univocal determinacy. The dissolution of psychic substance gives us an opening to something more, an opening that the empiricist tends not to utilize. A significant example of such an opening of the psychological self is the notion of the unconscious. This topic is beyond our present scope, but a few remarks may be relevant. Here we have an opening up of the self in a genuinely rich and immensely suggestive way. The force of the unconscious may offer us challenging images for the original power of the self. But the present approach has a different emphasis from any psychological conception, however deeply expanded, since its concern is to reflect metaphysically on human desire.[27] The unconscious tends to remain within the ambit of psychological considerations; though, of course, it might be reinterpreted as giving expression to the ontological power of being characteristic of man. Though it gives us an expanded psychological sense of something more than the surfaces of empirical selfhood, it does not necessarily give us a proper metaphysical sense of this more. The unconscious tends to be specified with respect to a particular dimension of selfhood, which is defined by contrast with other dimensions, often as that extremely complex and elusive transitional realm between the somatic and the incipiently self-aware. Original selfhood, by contrast, cannot be confined to this. For it tries to point not simply to what is specified but, more deeply, to what does the specifying. Thus, it may be said to pervade all dimensions of selfhood, being the grounding power to be that fills the whole from crown to toe. Though it specifies itself as the somatic, the unconscious, the conscious, we cannot assert its simple identity with these. It is beyond them as, if you like, their surplus source, while it is immanent in them as the ground of their differentiation.

Like the unconscious, the notion of the original self tries to avoid the dualistic bifurcation of the body and consciousness into sundered Cartesian substances. Its power of being not only grounds an immanent transition between body and consciousness but, beyond this, sends the self in search of articulate wholeness.[28] This immanent self-articulation reveals the human self as a center of being that reaches out to being beyond itself. A metaphysical difficulty with the unconscious is that it can lend itself to a purely immanent, even if very rich, consideration of the self. By contrast, we find in the immanent ontological power of being of the original self the space of infinite desire, which necessarily opens out to what is other and what is more ultimate metaphysically. The power of being that makes the self an origin guides us to an origin and power of being more absolute than the self. The intelligibility of these assertions rests, one must add, on the fuller framework that will be adumbrated in due course.

THE ORIGINAL SELF AND THE TRANSCENDENTAL EGO: BEING AND THE "I THINK"

I now want to compare original selfhood with the transcendental ego. This, of course, is a large issue, extremely important in contemporary thought.[29] But again, I must confine myself to a few relevant remarks. I will consider features of an essential philosophical position, not any one historical figure, though I will allude to figures here and there. There is a strong affinity between the original self and the transcendental ego, particularly with respect to the problem of primary synthesis. But difficulties tend to arise on the issue of form. In transcendental philosophies, in Kantian and Husserlian views, for example, one sometimes finds a significant tension between the emphasis on primary synthesis and the transcendental self considered as a formal universal ego. This tends to create a gap between the self and being. That is, in being immediately directed to the epistemological question of knowing, the transcendental ego does not always make it clear how we are again to deal with the metaphysical question of being. Of course, this has been a recurrent problem in modern philosophy, haunting the German idealists in the aftermath of Kant's so-called Copernican revolution and, in our time, confronting Heideggerian thought and existential philosophy in the wake of Husserl's transcendental phenomenology.[30] In the following, we will confine ourselves to the problem of formalism and the issue of the self's grounding in being.

Difficulties with the empirical ego (as, for example, in Hume) tend to lead us toward a concept of the transcendental ego (as, say, in Kant).[31] For the empirical ego itself forces us to give some account of the relation between elements of a manifold of experience. At some point we have to ask about the unity of this manifold and its form. The empiricist's answer, as we saw, tends to be that it is an aggregation of atoms of

psychic feeling connected by extrinsic association. Now the defender of
the transcendental ego rightly sees that the form of such a unity is that
of derived synthesis. He also discerns that this derived synthesis can just
as easily fall apart again, thereby failing to provide an *intrinsic* principle
of unity. Rightly, too, he sees that we can possess an intrinsic principle
of unity only by means of a prior and not merely derived synthesis, what
he sometimes calls a "synthetic a priori." This notion of course, is unintelligible to the empiricist, for whom the synthetic cannot be defined
except in derivative, a posteriori terms. The empiricist fails to see that
a derived synthesis is possible only on condition of a prior synthesis,
which is, in this respect, the condition of its possibility. On this point,
of course, there is a clear-cut connection between the original self and
the transcendental ego.

They differ, however, in terms of their respective relations to the
concrete. Though the defender of the transcendental ego demands
more than the merely empirical, he tends to share with the empiricist
the view that the concrete is just the particular thing.[32] The fact that
he sometimes speaks of the "merely" empirical is perhaps indicative of
this point. That is, the empiricist and the transcendentalist tend to have
a similar sense of the concrete, but with this difference: where the first
regards this concreteness as positive, the second views it somewhat negatively, because it cannot provide the a priori unity he demands.
Whereas the empiricist states that the concrete is the empirical alone,
the transcendentalist claims that it is merely the empirical and proceeds
to seek something other than the concrete. Thus he defines his difference from the empiricist not in terms of the concrete itself, but in terms
of the form of its unity. The thrust of his reflection is not to expand
the concrete, for this would yield (and here again he agrees with the
empiricist) only another, albeit possibly broader derived synthesis. And
no such synthesis can be entirely adequate. To attain the prior synthesis
he genuinely seeks, he appeals to a domain other than the concrete:
namely, a transcendental sphere.[33] The transcendental ego then becomes
the prior form of unity that cannot be equated with anything concrete
or anything derived from the concrete. Reacting to the particularity and
free-floating fluctuations of the empirical ego, disgruntled by its lack of
primordial unity, and alarmed by the permanent threat of a downward
dissolution into anonymous substance, the transcendentalist invokes a
universal ego that, as it were, floats above the flux of all merely phenomenal egos, a transcendental self that escapes the contingency of
particularity.

The transcendental ego arises from an immediate concern with the conditions of the possibility of knowledge. But the original self arises only mediately with respect to knowing. More immediately, it arises from consideration of the actuality of desire's infinite restlessness, relative to which the desire to know is just one specification (see chapters 5 and 6 below). Just as desire is not only a form of being, but being reaching out to being beyond itself, so the original self is a metaphysical opening to what is and hence points to original power that grounds an actuality. As metaphysical, original selfhood points to the power of being, whereas the transcendental ego tends to be a set of logical conditions for the possibility of knowing. The original self manifests the actual power of being whose articulation may become the occasion of the knowledge of being. In that sense, it signifies the ontological unity of the self in which the metaphysical and the cognitive, the order of being and knowing, need not be bifurcated.

We might pursue this point by briefly discussing the Cartesian formulation "I think therefore I am." I am not suggesting that we can reduce transcendental philosophy to Cartesianism per se, though some thinkers like Husserl grant a continuity in the very act of giving a more complex interpretation to the original Cartesian inspiration. There is an affinity between them in that the transcendental ego is sometimes characterized as the pure "I think" that is prior to all determinate contents.[34] In looking at the Cartesian formulation, we will also gain some perspective on some of the anti-Cartesian currents of contemporary thought. Both the Cartesian "I think" and the transcendental ego are in themselves empty of determinate content. Without sensuous intuition and the determination of the particular, empirical item (which is here, as with the empiricist, our only contact with the concrete), the pure "I think" tends to be devoid of content. (Here again the transcendentalist and the empiricist, like form and matter, glove and hand, tend to be made for one another.) Now if we grant transcendental priority to the "I think," then not only is the "I am" something we derive subsequently, but our whole metaphysical sense of the concrete is defined relative to this priority. The notion of being is then narrowed and on two fronts: it becomes constricted metaphysically relative to the existence in the midst of which we are, and it becomes closed metaphysically to existence that is more than, beyond, that of determinate things. Or, to put it more strongly, this second possibility may be ruled out of court completely; for the concrete existent seems to be nothing beyond determinate particularity. Then the temptation is for the "I think" to close in upon itself in formal self-identity. The only interruption it will subsequently allow is that of sensuous particularity, and the "I am" and the whole metaphysical notion of being relative to it are subjected to a similar limitation.

In crucial respects, original selfhood reverses the priority of the purely formal "I think" and relieves the metaphysical cramp to which it gives rise. Though, in the order of knowing, the "I think" has a certain cognitive priority, in the order of being, the "I am" has ultimate ontological priority. This involves no egotism, in the sense that the "I" is then the absolute arbiter of the universe. This view is found in some debased versions of the transcendental ego—in the untrammeled egotism of a Young Hegelian like Max Stirner, for example, and in our own century in some vulgarized versions of Sartrean existentialism.[35] With original selfhood, on the contrary, we find no such view. Since this conception emerges from a metaphysical concern with desire, we are driven to ask after the condition of being, the nature of the "is," which makes desiring existence possible and out of it the desire to know (the "I think"). A metaphysical analysis of desire breaks with any determinately limited sense of the existent, because it provides us with a form of being, the self, which is always in the midst of and beyond any such delimited, determinate concreteness. Desire is at bottom metaphysical, because it makes us consider not only being from the side of self-consciousness (the "I am" from the side of the "I think"), but also self-consciousness from the side of being (the "I think" from the side of the "I am").

If we simply stay with the "I think," we fail to reach this added complexity—namely, that between the "I" and the "thinking" is desire. We must rewrite the "I think" as "I desire to think," where desire is not first an act of deliberate will, but a spontaneous upsurgence into awareness of immanent articulation. Thus selfhood is internally complex in a way which demands that we consider differently what it means metaphysically to be a self. The objection that desire is not relevant because it is merely psychological, a merely empirical feeling, the objection sometimes summarized as "psychologism," quite misses the point. For the point is that desire is not merely psychological in this sense. Rather, it is metaphysical openness to being. And the desire to know is the manifestation of this metaphysical openness in an articulate self-conscious mode. This perhaps is one reason why the "is" is called the copula; for is never a merely external connection between dead entities. Knowledge is articulate self-conscious desire. Being is the ground and objective of knowing, in that knowledge is the articulate self-conscious eros of a being that, in coupling with being other than itself, does not splice together two utter strangers but expresses, affirms, and consolidates its primordial bond with being.[36]

Hence, the original self cannot be fully identified with self-consciousness, whether conceived transcendentally or psychologically. Rather, self-consciousness specifies a determinate, albeit fundamental, mode of the original self without exhausting its core as power to be. Desire, self-consciousness, and original power are all intimately related, but we cannot assert a univocal identity between any two of them. We can say that finite desire mediates the emergence into self-consciousness of the original power of our being, whereas infinite desire is mediately the self-consciousness of this original power in its proper ultimacy (see chapter 1). The close relation of these three terms, the lack of univocal identity among them (which does not exclude the necessity of each in a fuller, active identity of self), reflects the complexity that is added when desire inserts itself between the "I" and "thinking." Instead of the dyadic structure of the "I think," we have a double triad of terms: "I (1) desire (2) to think (3)" corresponds with original power to be (1), desire (2), self-consciousness (3). Desire appears in both triads and in both as the mediating term. This should not surprise us. For desire is always mediating internally; here, its commonality to the two triads provides us with the binding link between them—that is, with the mediating access to the original power to be, not only from the side of thinking and self-consciousness, but, most important, from the side of the "I" that is.

There is no special metaphysical magic in the number three, though thinkers like Hegel have sometimes been made the object of derision on this score, often wrongly.[37] But there are serious philosophical issues at stake here, particularly with respect to the multifaceted problem of dualism. For the triads set out above take us beyond dyadic structure, both in the knower and in the knower's relation to what is other. They also take us beyond structure as such to the power and process out of which structure comes into being. The ingression of desire into the space intermediate between the ego and thought calls for a more than formal self, just as its dynamic mediation between self-consciousness and original power calls for selfhood that is metaphysically rooted in being. Such a self is not the unity of form and matter as a posterior derived synthesis, nor yet the prior possibility of synthesis from the side of form, but the actual original unity out of which form and matter can subsequently be derived as distinct terms and subsequently be unified again in a posterior synthesis.

Thus, any affirmation that "we are" cannot be confined to saying solely *that* we are. Indeed, any such assertion already begins to tell us *how*, and mediately *what*, we are. Our mode of actuality is self-articulating power, because the "I am" that grounds the "I think" is qualitatively articulate. Even bare self-assertion, though only just distinguishable from silence and on the verge of vanishing therein, must not be looked at solely in terms of *that:* for its truth is not that it is a minimal assertion, but that it is actually an affirmation and hence irretrievably in the domain of the articulate. Moreover, in this domain we *appear*—which is not the same as saying that we are mere appearance. We *are* what we appear, even if we are not exhausted by the forms of determinate appearances. Even if we have no access to self except through appearance, this is still something genuine: for the original appears *in* the image. Just as no image can be a mere image but must in some degree be an original image, so no appearance is mere counterfeit but must in some respects be the making present of what appears.

Accordingly, the original self cannot be a mere unknown, *x*, as is the Kantian noumenal self. There can be no absolute disjunction between the "I" and the "think"; hence, too, the hiatus between appearance and what appears cannot be total. It is not that we must simply deny disjunction, but rather, that we must cease describing it as an unsurpassable external dualism. In this instance, the disjunction we witness is the internal difference of a process of integration. We find that discontinuity, as well as mediation, between the "I" and its "thinking" is necessary to the whole process of self-identification, if the resultant identity is to be articulate. The "I am," as it were, is the thoughtful power to interiorize the energy of activity whereby, through a dialectic of desire, it articulately finds itself in the interplay between its own finiteness and its infinite restlessness.

But perhaps the fundamental point about original selfness that needs to be made here is that, whether we start with the "I am" or with the "I think," we are brought back by desire to being and, from the side of existence, to thinking and desire, to our prior affinity with it.[38] This affinity is primarily ontological, because our existence, thinking, and desire are grounded in the articulating power of being that they manifest. We think because, first, we are; and we are in that certain way revealed by thought and desire. But though this prior affinity is ontological, it is also cognitive, because our being is essentially characterized by the power to know, the ontological power of being awaking to itself in the self. Our primordial ontological affinity with being is a necessarily, awakened, self-present affinity, precisely because the self's power of being, as implicated in this affinity, is articulately open to itself. Being and knowing here exist in original affinity because, with the self, the ontological power of being can know and affirm itself, not simply as a knower, but also as being. This affinity is not derivative, not something that is subsequently added to being and self as two delimited, fixed terms. Knowing is an articulate self-presence of being; or put somewhat differently, being becomes articulately present to itself in knowledge.[39]

The focus of the transcendental ego is, as we have seen, conditions of the possibility of knowledge, which are treated initially in abstraction from the power of being.[40] This, of course, is in line with its implicit agreement with the constricted concreteness of the empiricist. Any such abstraction or constriction, we now see, is impossible in terms of the original self, for this requires a qualitative expansion of the notion of the concrete, one, moreover, that discloses the fundamental affinity between concrete being and cognition, thereby making even abstraction possible. The transcendental ego does not always qualitatively extend the concrete in this way. Though the transcendental ego may introduce a formal universal principle over and above the concrete and is to this extent an expansion, this expansion does not regard what must also be necessarily in the midst of the concrete. Here again, the empirical and transcendental egos are not unrelated: the former, as psychic flux, becomes a kind of nothing by vanishing downward, even below the level of particular entities; the latter becomes a kind of nothing by disappearing upward into an abiding universality cut off from everything empirical. The transcendental ego seems to learn as little from the richness of the concrete as does the ego of the empiricist: the first seems to be denied this lesson by a pure apriorism, the second by a pinched aposteriorism.

The superficiality of the empirical tends to be matched by the purity of the transcendental in such a way that we risk setting up an opposition between the ideal and the concrete and defining their relation by the dominance of one or the other. If we take the transcendental position in which the ideal dominates, as many post-Kantian philosophers do, then at most the real becomes so much dead content to be formed by the active self. Henceforth it is said that what is real is what is real *for me*. Then the real is one-sidedly redefined in its relativity to the active self, while we omit the real's definition of the self as existent by virtue of the ontological power of being. All the embarrassments of a faulty idealism rear their heads before us. And we continue to evade these if we intransigently refuse to revise *our redefinition* of the real as what is simply for us. The real is, no doubt, for us; but the tedious reiteration of this trivial proposition becomes an epistemological hocus pocus that tells us nothing if we do not specify *how* it is for us. In terms of the original self, the real is being that must be recognized and affirmed for what *it is;* and it is not what it is merely for us; rather, it is for us to be open to the acknowledgment of its being as coordinate with, but not necessarily subordinate to, the self.

What I am arguing against is what follows when we define the transcendental ego negatively, as *not* the empirical.[41] For then, its transcendence tends to become set in a dualistic opposition with the empirical. Thus, it tends to become formal even in its purported act of synthesis: for to give it content in itself would again risk reduction to the empirical. To avoid this, the transcendental is again said *not* to be the empirical, and this endlessly repeated "not" becomes the sign of their radical discontinuity. Hence, difference ceases to be internal to the self as a primordial unity of original power to be: it becomes the void that rends the transcendental and the empirical absolutely apart. Thus, in a peculiar way, the transcendental ego turns out to be a kind of Parmenidean One,[42] which maintains itself in its own pure, uncontaminated unity while prohibiting any effort to confront the intelligibility of the "not" that divides it from the empirical. Having sloughed off the merely empirical and ascended from it by a process of negation, it seems to negate its own ascension and cannot find a way to descend again. For descent would be its own internal diremption, and the pure transcendental ego shuns this, lest it again fall foul of the dissolute flux of the empirical. By contrast, the original self, free of the absorbing god, refuses any prohibition against facing the "not," whether from the side of ascent or descent. The act that distinguished the transcendental from the empirical is itself possible only because the self is original in itself, is the very act of setting itself apart into different determinations. It is ascent above particularity and descent into the concrete. It is not the empirical as a fixed particular starting point or the transcendental as a fixed universal term that transcends particularity. It is the movement between fixed beginnings and ends and, in the middle between them, is an end and a beginning, more radically moving, powerfully positive, and indeterminably rich.[43]

Relative to the problem of dualistic opposition, the situation is even more complex. At a certain point we become defenseless to preclude the very consequence we sought to avoid by resorting to the transcendental ego. For, should the transcendental ego cut itself off from the empirical, our sense of the concrete can easily topple over into a void, with the transcendental ego soon following suit. The transcendental ego might seem, as it were, to stiffen with skeletal form the vicissitudes of the experiential realm through its a priori categories; but when it is not actually inherent there, we find ourselves denied a real principle of concrete discrimination. Similarly, any principle of unity that is not actually inherent in the concrete is not really a principle at all and so tends to create once again an unoccupied space for any form of misplaced concreteness. And we do not find a lack of those ready to gladly, even blindly, rush in to take up residence in this vacancy; we see this in many strands of nineteenth-century thought that take their bearings from what was perceived to be the decomposition of idealism after Hegel, and we witness it today in those forms of thought that seem to mass under the flag of post-Heideggerian deconstruction.[44]

In this way the purity of the transcendental ego easily becomes its impure, perhaps more brutal, opposite, while the ardency of its uncontaminated idealism engenders a more cunning realism or a more skeptical historicism or even a grosser irrationalism.[45] For the transcendental flight into this pure ether quickly breeds contempt for the emptiness it seems to gain, and what ensues can be a realistic recoil, one that is not always deeply discriminating, for any content, no matter what, seems better than no content at all. The formalism of the transcendental ego produces a kind of ontological undernourishment that may seek alleviation in anything at all. In this way, too, the transcendental and empirical egos might be seen as opposite symptoms of a common predicament that links them together, defines them in their difference, and makes them necessary for each other. The predicament is how to define *originative movement* between the sensuous and the spiritual, between the real and the ideal, between the nonrational and the rational. But since each of these opposites, in asserting itself in abstraction from the other, forgets the power of being that this movement displays in desire, each tends to lose the rich center of actual original selfhood. In becoming ontologically unballasted, they cannot safeguard themselves sufficiently against the imbalance of the opposing philosophical extremes that they may eventually precipitate.

Let us now recapitulate. The original self is not identical with particularity or form, and its rootedness in being does not turn it into an existential void. It shares with the transcendental ego its transcendence of limited particularity, but shares with the empirical ego its determi-

nation as fact. But its determination is self-determination, and its transcendence is the inexhaustibility of indeterminate original power. Fact
and ideal do not sunder into dualistic opposition, for the original self
is concrete ideality. This does not dematerialize into nothingness either
upward or downward, but discloses the positive power of being that
overcomes nothing, considered as lack. Again, it may bring the one and
the many into relation. The ego of the empiricist, by contrast, disin-
tegrates into dissolute multiplicity and, losing the positive power of desire's infinitude, decays into an infinite succession of psychic states. The
pure ego of the idealist tends to disappear into an indefinite, empty unity, which is, in some respects, not unlike the absorbing god, insofar as
it seeks to stand substitute for individual indefiniteness. The night of
dissolute multiplicity and the night of absorbing unity are not altogether
dissimilar, in that they both turn away from original selfhood, albeit in
different directions. But our choice is not exhausted by that between
absolving universality and dissolving particularity. For original selfhood
is concreteness articulating itself: as uttered into desire, it manifests the
power to be a centered unity and to reach out to being beyond itself.
Its response to difference and identity is not to turn fugitive from difference toward the identity of either a particularized substance or a
nonindividualized universal. Anchored in being, participating in the
power of being, it is the quest of its own possible wholeness.

Chapter Three
Desire's Infinitude and Wholeness

Man's quest for wholeness matches his quest for origins both as an essential human desideratum and as a recurrent philosophical theme. Whereas in the last chapter we addressed the question of what it means to be a self, in this chapter we will address the question of what it might mean for a self to be whole. In what follows, I want first to consider the desire for wholeness as it gets expressed in terms of either a univocal or an equivocal sense of being. The former tends to yield a sense of wholeness in terms of simple self-identity, the latter to undermine wholeness in a search for difference that dissolves simple identity. Second, I will consider a positive notion of man's infinite restlessness—what I will call his *intentional infinitude*—relative to which an open, dialectical sense of wholeness is possible. Third, I will explore how such a sense of wholeness tries to find a balance in tension between a person's sense of unity and of plurality, the desire to hold in a nonunivocal way to one's own integrity and yet sustain one's openness, beyond mere vacillating equivocalness, to the manyness in experience. My point here is that this requires the effort to embody wholeness in acts or works, such as ethical acts that incarnate noble ideals or great works of art. Finally, I will briefly recollect the circuit of desire that we have traversed since the beginning of chapter 1 and indicate how wholeness need not be a closure, completion, or immanent totality entirely folded in upon itself, but may open beyond dialectical self-relation to a metaxological relation with otherness. This will bring us to part 2.

UNIVOCAL AND EQUIVOCAL DESIRE: WHOLENESS SHORT-CIRCUITED

Perhaps the most obvious way to understand the search for wholeness might be in terms of what can be called univocal desire. By this I refer to a tendency found in various hedonistic treatments of human satis-faction. Very broadly, the hedonist tends to reduce desire to finite par-ticular, immediate satisfactions, since, in common with the empiricist and the nominalist, he sees being or the world as comprised of a collection of finite, univocal particulars. A contemporary version of this kind of thinking is seen in the commodity mentality, which seeks wholeness through the unceasing acquisition and accumulation of material things. Initially, such univocal desire is governed by one particular objective, as, say, animal hunger is directed univocally to food. Overall, however, the effect is a minimizing of the scope of desire, which becomes fixated exclusively on particular objects. Constraining its own openness, univocal desire becomes mesmerized by this contracted thing before it. It seeks an immediate discharge and, because its sense of inner and outer dif-ference is often minimal, often lacks any mediated self-appropriation. There is a certain parallel here with the contracted concreteness of the empirical ego, as also with the stimulus-response model of the behav-iorist.

Of course, this seemingly obvious, immediate satisfaction turns out to be fraught with ambiguity. Traditional hedonism itself points out the paradoxes of immediate satisfaction, in which satiation breeds not de-light but disgust, where excess satisfaction generates dissatisfaction, re-quiring the mediating intervention of the calculative intellect to sift desire's ambiguity and often restrain its immediacy.[1] Thus, it ultimately proves to be impossible to determine human desire solely in univocal terms. Human desire "lifts off" the univocity of animal impulse, so to speak, and as Kant saw (related to the limits of univocal desire) moral wholeness is impossible at the level of such impulses.[2] This lift-off tes-tifies to the deeper freedom of human desire and to the fact that we never know unambiguously what will confer fullness on it. Here, even what we seem to be able to separate and delimit as specific appetites often twine together into dense, bewildering complexes. Apropos of the commodity mentality mentioned above,[3] we see a conjunction of this lift-off with univocal desire in the phenomenon of the fetish: desire in-vesting an object, finite in itself, with its own fascinating infinity, as in the idolatry that worships inanimate things or the modern romance with the machine.

It is this ambiguity of immediate desire that tends to generate a sense of the equivocalness of desire. Instead of being unidirectionally extra-verted onto external things, the astonishing fluidity of human desire forces us to face a kind of inner labyrinth that, by contrast with the fixed univocal identity of external things, may seem to possess no unity at all.

Univocal self-sameness is a travesty of the freedom of human desire, and so we might be inclined to deny any center at all to desire. Desire's density may then be said to be sheerly equivocal, ultimately devoid of all specificity, or, as the phrase goes, "polymorphously perverse." Again, the parallel with the empirical ego is clear: this, as we have seen, flows away into an endless succession of psychic states when its fixed particularity becomes unstuck. Thus, what I am here calling equivocal desire is often just univocal desire run wild. That is, both decline to defer their immediate gratification: where one is a unidirectional immediacy, the other is a promiscuous immediacy.

A metaphor for equivocal desire might be the figure of Don Juan, whose endless search for immediate gratification and its relationship to boredom and despair both fascinated and offended Kierkegaard, and whose apotheosis we find in Camus's efforts at a so-called ethics of quantity.[4] Viewed in this light, equivocal desire is a very common condition in the modern age, for Don Juan as epitomizing the insatiable spirit in quest of particular conquests is not unrelated to the Faustian restlessness of the modern self in its refusal to be stayed by any one definite, finite satisfaction.[5] So perhaps it is appropriate to dwell further on it, since in the end, it undermines the possibility of wholeness.

For it is a common modern confusion to mistake the person of equivocal desire for one who is genuinely free. When someone says, "Not by this am I satisfied, nor by that, nor yet by this other . . . and so on *ad infinitum*," we seem to encounter someone who really knows what he wants and hence is master of his fate. How else, we wonder, could one be so sure of what fails to gratify one? The issue is never completely clear-cut, but in the present case this freedom seems to be merely negative. If nothing at all satisfies one, then one is hardly distinguishable from the malcontent. Just as the bovine contentment of univocal desire is the inverted form of desire's finiteness, so the freedom to grumble and gripe might be said to be the perverse form of its infinitude. Here we might think of the infinite discontent of the Beautiful Soul (*die schöne Seele*), so well attacked by Hegel, or the pining, infinite inwardness of some Romantic selves. When it grows tired of itself, of course, such inward discontent can easily flip over into the raging violence of the political revolutionary, who now vehemently directs outward the previously merely inward discontent. The unrepentant malcontent and, more extremely, the smoldering iconoclast often harbor souls of wistful infinity but in other dress—namely, in the brooding refusal to wear the limited dross of this present earth.[6]

The infinitude of equivocal desire is a sheer succession, in which it flits from one particular object to the next. Here it is often proclaimed, after the fashion of Lessing, that desiring itself is the thing, never mind the goal.[7] Then we are told to crave ceaseless movement, to give ourselves up to restless transition, disdaining the destination. The goal becomes inherently indifferent; it seems merely the external occasion of ferment and arousal. Then it is said that the pursuit of happiness is preferable to happiness itself. We hunt the quarry but refuse to corner it, relish the excitement but loathe the climax. Now this attitude may seem to make desiring the whole thing, but in effect it robs desire of the very possibility of being whole. Desire without some end is not desire at all (see chapter 1). If the goal is indifferent, so, likewise, the pursuit of it straightaway alters in character and itself is made indifferent. At most it manifests a rush of enthusiasm for everything and anything (the goal does not matter), in which intense self-absorption is indistinguishable from self-distraction in sheer immediacy. We can chase every and any bauble, for, after all, it is the chase, not the catch, that matters.

The self caught in equivocal desire rebuffs all placation and hurries on from this thing to that, that situation to this. At each stop it must be adjusted to the circumstances and so be disappointed by their limits. But rather than acknowledge this, at every new turn, it tries to remake itself entirely and, like Hegel's "bad infinity" that *ought* to be but never actually can be, this self never *is* itself. Moreover, it makes itself over anew, not because it is positively originative, but because it cannot tolerate anything that exists determinately. Disdaining every resting point, it ends up disowning not only transition, but itself too. For it is not whole, much less a whole that would overflow itself creatively, but rather, a disjointed sequence of fragments that, to relieve the pressure of the past and the present, must race off into an endless future. This phenomenon is not unrelated to the mania for unanchored originality mentioned in the last chapter or to the modern cult of novelty, with its endless clamor for new stimulation. We choose this course, and then, because we despise any outcome, we shrink from commitment to its consequences. Finally, we take the outlet of an incessant repudiation of our earlier choice. But there is no improvement here; for at each turn, this self lacks courage to confess its prior foolishness and humble humor to profit from its blunders. Every outlay is rashly absolute, though heretofore, in previous ventures, no return has ever been won.

In sum, this self of equivocal desire revels in its predicament when it should be rebuked and deeply disquieted by it. Its counsel "Be true to desire!" seems to be, in effect, a subtle evasion of desire. This is a dodge masking itself as deep dedication, as a devotion to desire that is really a revulsion from its necessity, namely, that we direct ourselves to a proper goal. On the outside, a frenetic eagerness sometimes clothes an anxious discontent; and, no different from malingering, it may block, on the inside, the resolution that would search out wholeness. It is as if the love that drives one to union really longs for fruit only in a future divorce. The self of equivocal desire makes it a point of pride to be the perennially lost soul, the hero in unhappiness, a kind of swooning, liquid subjectivity that is so dazed by its fluctuating depths that it never ventures beyond the shallows. It is of no importance to him whether desire regards a happy objective, whether it be foolish or sensible, as long as it is intense; for though it be intensely foolish, it is still intense, and there's the rub.[8]

The real outcome, however, is sadness after every sally, disenchantment succeeding every air-blown honeymoon. In the aftermath of this, we might expect more discrimination. But for one for whom the goal is indifferent, this outcome is short-circuited and, despite desire's undoing, such a one remains unruffled. Desire's infinitude need not be just blind zest for wanton, vehement living. But in this case, the repeated undeceiving of desire proves to be but another pretext for flinging oneself further into a fresh infatuation, only this time with a redoubled fury, masquerading as indomitability. Thus disillusion breeds explosiveness to indemnify its vacuity; and equivocal desire, a centerless infinite succession, swings loosely to and fro between lusterless apathy and violent instability. It is hurried from tedium to delirium, and its lethargy follows its frenzy, as the night does the day. Borrowing from Oscar Wilde's witticism about fox-hunting: equivocal desire is the unspeakable in full pursuit of the uneatable.

INTENTIONAL INFINITUDE AND WHOLENESS

Let us now consider a more positive conception of desire's infinitude than is to be found in equivocal desire. A univocal drive to particular objects alone involves an inflexible finiteness, lacking in infinity; equivocal maundering after nothing in particular is a slack infinity that sags and is finally sapped for want of a determinate, definite tendency. Over against rude finitude and wispy infinity alike, we require an infinity that is grounded and a concentrated finitude that is originative and unclotted. Desire may be densely ambiguous, but it need not be sheerly equivocal. Of course, because of the free indeterminacy inherent in human desire, we are here exposed to many possibilities of deformation and failure. At its best, however, desire exhibits an equilibrium between finiteness and infinitude, allowing a dialectical interplay and tension between the determinate and the indeterminate, the specific and the ambiguous, the grounded and the originative, the open and the whole. Likewise from the direction of the end of desire, it must strike a similar balance, a wholeness that both uncloses a rigidly fixed determinacy and avoids an irresolute wistfulness for the merely indefinite.

This more positive conception I will term *intentional infinitude*.[9] We may clarify it by contrasting it with equivocal desire. The latter, as already implied, has to do with a limitless number of particular appetites, an infinite succession of cravings for this, that, and the other particular thing. On the one hand, it fosters demand for greater and greater satisfaction, where this means having numerically more of this and that, ad nauseam, in an infinite, quantitative succession of covetings. On the other hand, it hatches a hypertrophy of discontent, in that it is always the *next* item that is coveted, and so on, indefinitely. Now the positive sense of desire's infinitude is not this greed for endless gratification or, alternatively, this distended discontentment. Endlessness need not be the primary paradigm of the infinite as it is, say, in Schopenhauer's and Hobbes's understanding of desire. Man, says Hobbes, exhibits "the restless desire for power after power that ceaseth only in death."[10] What we are here calling intentional infinitude is an attempt to elucidate a qualitative sense of desire's dynamism, as marked from within by a principle of centered continuity over a period of time.

Intentional infinitude reveals desire's openness to the appropriation of the original power of selfhood, which it understands to underpin each particular desire and to pervade the very process of going beyond particularity that allows an endless sequence of appetites. If we are restricted to the sense of infinity as endlessness, there can be no reconciliation between desire's restlessness and wholeness. But intentional infinitude helps ground this latter possibility: for it sees both the unlimited procession of desire and its will for wholeness as issuing from a common source—namely, the self's original power to be. This exacts a centered sense of self-identity such that we come to ourselves in the course of our self-differentiation and free becoming. Intentional infinitude is antecedently the possibility of an accord of wholeness and infinity, circularity and linearity, because by it, the self always circles around and returns to itself, even when in motion along the line of limitless passage.

We might think here of Pascal's diagnosis of the human predicament as the incapacity to sit still, alone in one's room, instead of seeking distraction from boredom in endless diversion. We might think, too of Augustine's response, namely, the recollection of desire from its dispersion in an unending sequence of limited things. Beyond univocal impulse and equivocal discontent, our desire is self-mediating, capable of self-relation and recollection, since it is mediated through the self-knowledge of our own being.[11] The notion of intentional infinitude tries to name this twofoldness of our being: as something that is both present to itself and, in fulfilling its deepest desire, reaches out to being beyond itself. Thus, intentional infinitude is not to be narrowed simply to the epistemic position that all consciousness is bent on something, as in some doctrines of intentionality.[12] It points, rather, to the primordial eros of the human spirit, which, indeed, is determinately revealed by, but has greater amplitude than, the orientation of epistemic consciousness to specific objects. Its primordiality is precisely its not being spent by any such direction of consciousness. If we circumscribe its intentionality to the determinate epistemic role, that there be no subject without an object, we encircle its primordiality in a way that robs it of its proper absoluteness. Original selfhood unfolds a primordial intentionality that transcends any particular intention, any determinate specification of desire. As grounding man's self-relation and his openness to being, we can call intentional infinitude the *first intentionality* of primordial desire, by contrast with which particularized intentions are secondary and derivative. This first intentionality is elaborated in the mediation of desire, which, through memory and anticipation, tries to span a sequential passage and weave it into an ordered time. But in spreading itself thus, it is still capable of being recollected and gathered into itself, because of its self-mediating power.

Intentional infinitude tries to name the original prolepsis of human desire, unrestricted in breadth and scope. Selfhood extends itself, is self-extension over dispersed succession, but need not thereby be mere self-distraction. In its intentional extension to being beyond itself, it is the repudiation of enclosed and closed self-transparency.[13] It defines us as intermediate between inwardness and things and mediates the space in which the world is set forth as articulate for us. It upholds this space as a balance in tension between self-relation and heed to what the self is not. This infinitude is so fundamental that desire goes beyond not only the particular objective, but beyond desire itself. But, like original selfhood, it can be said to stand in a prior affinity with being. What human desire lacks initially is not this affinity with being, but the appropriate explication of it. First this prior affinity is operative, but desire lacks its express elaboration; desire requires the self-knowledge of our being as existence in the midst of this affinity. This last statement, coupled with what was said in chapter 2, helps us to this further characterization of selfhood: *Selfhood is the internal difference of our intricate identity which, as original self-articulating power to be a world, is intentionally infinite existence (now more or less tacit, now more or less articulated, but always the interplay between these) in the midst of its primordial affinity with being beyond itself.* In the light of this complex characterization, human desire can be ontologically grounded without betraying its inherent dynamism, even in its infinite restlessness.

We will see more fully later that this affinity with being reflects our metaxological placement in being, within which our own dialectical self-mediation is effected. Here we might say that our extension to being, in intentional infinitude, is not exhausted by either an extraversion onto finite things or an introversion onto a merely formal self. Mere extraversion tends to lack proper self-mediation and ultimately dissipates desire's dynamism. Formal introversion, by contrast, often fails to get beyond self-mediation or settles for such an excessive self-mediation that wholeness is reduced to a game of solitaire, the play all revolving around the one player. Whereas the first easily ends up in inward distraction, the second tends to atrophy into alienated voyeurism, the abstracted self trying to fill up the empty form of idle time. Something more is demanded when desire is properly submissive to the deeper *anankē* of intentional infinitude. Then, the human person is viewed as the open intention of the infinite, not *the* infinite, and human desire is seen as the exigence of the unconditioned, but without making humanity the absolute; moreover, it is recognized that the quest for wholeness cannot make one into *the* whole. Since human desire is free, it can lift off its specification to the particularized objective and become implicitly a desire for everything. This ascendant potency is perhaps the source of human self-assurance, but it is also the source of human folly, when one thinks oneself actually *to be* everything.[14] Then the intention of the whole is confounded with the whole, and the possibility of human wholeness is perverted. For this, though impossible without dialectical self-mediation, also attests to a sense of being more ultimate than human being.

That is, there is an inevitable tension between the wholeness we seek via dialectical self-mediation and the unrestricted openness to otherness engendered by our intentional infinitude. To give ballast to desire's infinite restlessness and openness to human wholeness, we must accept this tension, dwell with it. Insofar as intentional infinitude seeks to be comprehensive and all-embracing, its reach is the real universe, its drive an unreserved desire for what is absolute. Here the issue cannot be a matter of refusing *simpliciter* to assent to the finite. What is required is discriminating acceptance of finitude. It is rather a question of not assenting absolutely to what itself is less than absolute. Finiteness is not repugnant; but an unquenchable insistence carries human desire beyond it. Finiteness is not all vanity, even if all finiteness cannot be absolute.[15] To see finiteness as it is—namely, finite and not absolute—may yield some determinate fulfillment.

Thus, too, we can avoid the harried futility of inconstant, ceaseless change. For we can find ourselves in our becoming. We might use the image of a journey. On a journey one is not at home; yet, while traveling, one can still be at home with oneself. What we might call qualitative restlessness does not escape frigid fixity only to fall into dissolute fluidity; it is evidence, rather, of a creative interchange between determinacy and indeterminacy. For we are not endlessly striving to be selves; we are always selves, but not always adequately. Put in the language of an earlier discussion (chapter 2), intentional infinitude is grounded in the prior unity of original selfhood; but this groundedness makes possible, through essential self-mediation, the subsequent synthesis of wholeness. The movement here is not from an imperfect potency to its perfected actualization, but from one kind of perfection to another. This may sound strange. However, if the original self is indeterminate in the positive sense of being overdetermined, its movement to subsequent wholeness need not involve simply the complete determination of an imperfect potency which, in completing itself, also exhausts itself, all its possibilities spent. It may yield a determinate wholeness that overflows itself, testifying thereby to the continued immanence of the dynamism or original power that shapes its being. In the human self, I suggest, we may find the embodiment of such an open wholeness, which, in its inexhaustibility, contains the suggestion of something infinite.

So, although intentional infinitude reveals our unreserved reach to being, we inevitably find here also a certain necessary reserve. Since intentional infinitude cannot be actual infinitude, and since human wholeness cannot be determined in an absolute, finalized way, we encounter a certain absence even in the presence of wholeness. For internal to human identity is a certain difference, a lacuna, or openness, that holds us back from being identified without reservation with this or that particular presence. The human self is more than simple presence. Its open affinity with being cannot be reduced to univocal identity. If it could be, we would have to turn a blind eye to desire's sense of lack and make our self-identity indistinguishable from inert "thereness"; and ultimately, our search for wholeness would culminate in the absorbing god. Our metaxological affinity with being is also a measure of our finiteness.

In human beings we have a peculiar coexistence of absence and presence, which brings to mind the nothingness in Plato's *Sophist,* which is not the opposite but the other of being (being here taken in the sense of determinate being).[16] Thus there is some truth in talking about the self as negativity, as Hegel does, and as nothingness, as does Sartre. Here we might also locate the emphasis on absence and the attack on univocal identity in much recent post-Heideggerian thought. But we should avoid too rigid a sense of determinate being, in terms of which the self becomes parasitically defined as "nothing." For then, as seems to have happened in some forms of deconstructionist thought, the self becomes an absolute absence, and no mediation between it and being proves possible. A sense of being as sheer presence leads to the dissolving of the self into sheer absence, and these opposites play back and forth in a game of mutual definition. But these opposites offer us excessively limited options, if the present perspective has any merit. The position I have been advocating entails a less rigid view of determinate being, such that the human self may be other than, but not necessarily the opposite of, determinate being; this allows for a more dialectical interplay between absence and presence, the indeterminate and the manifest.[17] If the human self is overdetermined in the positive sense indicated above, it can be more than the manifold of its determinate appearances; yet it can also overflow itself and appear in its embodiments. Ultimately, we must grant that there is a reserve here that we cannot entirely dispel, an abyss we can sound but never entirely plumb. We find ourselves at a verge between a perplexing enigma and its articulation. Arrested at this edge, we again find the space before us filled with the continuing call of desire.

BETWEEN INCOMPLETENESS AND ABSOLUTE CLOSURE: ART AND THE DIALECTICAL TENSION OF WHOLENESS

Let me state, as clearly as I can, what I take to be a basic dilemma here. No man can be absolutely whole, as we have already seen. So in some sense wholeness is always an ideal desired but never absolutely attained. Does this mean, then, that wholeness will always be indefinitely postponed and that the human self may never attain to such fullness of being? We might respond to this dilemma by distinguishing two senses of wholeness: first, wholeness as a projected ideal; second, wholeness as an actuality having to do with our being. In relation to the first sense, obviously our reach exceeds our grasp, and we are never identical with absolute wholeness. In relation to the second sense, however, we can say that, even when we project an ideal wholeness (in the first sense), our anticipation can still be grounded in a prior ontological wholeness or integrity of being. In that sense, the power of being always revealed in human desire indicates that we exhibit an already rich wholeness or integrity of being, even though we be still ineradicably finite. The power of this prior integrity that is already at work drives desire forward to its projected ideal. Its solicitation is already imperiously active in our being. Because of this prior sense of integrity of being, human desire can come to possess, through the mediation of its own self-knowledge, a sense of being properly centered on itself, which provides a balance to its efforts to realize any projected ideal of wholeness.

There is inevitably a tension between our approximation to an ideal wholeness and this prior integral ground. Yet we can genuinely approximate the ideal and exemplify the integrity of our being in acts or forms of life in which a sense of wholeness and absoluteness may emerge. Certain ethical deeds might perhaps be exemplary in this regard. Indeed, the integrity of the acting moral person, in his faithfulness to ethical ideals, might be a crucial case of this exemplification of human wholeness with all its tensions.[18] We might also mention the great work of art as manifesting the presence of wholeness, an issue I have discussed elsewhere,[19] but concerning which a few remarks may be helpful here.

Art has always been one of humankind's chief weapons in its war with decay and its fight with the fragmentation of being that time brings. It tries to be a gathering together of human power, wrested from time's scattering, to be a concentration of intense attention that tries to survive the disintegration of the day. The imaginative formation of art reveals human efforts to shape originative activity. It tries to ground self-knowledge concretely in a sensible work, which, if it is great, is full of a certain inexhaustible wholeness. The work of art gives shape to the inner formlessness of the self such that it comes to genuine expression. This externalization of the self coincides with an inward articulation such that the inward now shines outward. In the work of art we thus come to attain some sensuous self-relation. Nor does this necessarily mean that the artist, by sheer will to power, imposes his own form on externality or being other than himself. What is other may often seem alien and opposed, but the great work of art gathers this foreignness of existence.

The imaginative formation of art may help embrace what is alien by returning us to the point at which the distinction between interiority and exteriority has no absolutely fixed shape. At this point the sense of difference has not congealed into dualistic opposition; it is in the process of emergence, rather than a stable product already sedimented. Art may serve to articulate a double emergence, in which both the self and what is other are creatively coaxed out of anonymous thereness. Imaginative formation may be an original identification of significant difference. It need not be the work of a domineering will to form of a tyrannous artist already finished in himself and confronting a falsely fixed externality, seen merely as an opposition to be overcome. On the contrary, the artist often speaks of the upsurge of an indeterminate power (whether in terms of the Muse or inspiration, dream or intoxication, voice or vision) that unsettles, even dissolves the more normal, "steady" self. The artist tries to take imaginative possession of the inward split, tries to create in this split. He cultivates diremption to cure himself of diremption, alienates the self to restore the self, exteriorizes in image the inner labyrinth of desire so that desire may come to celebrate and know itself.

Nor need the otherness of being be merely indifferent matter, a servile plasticity on which is forced a preconstituted grid. In his interplay with otherness, the artist is as deeply receptive as originative. The point is to release externality from the weight of a ponderous thereness, so that the being of things loses some of its rank, meaningless density. By passing through a breaking and a remaking, the self may begin to come to itself, like a wave of becoming that flattens itself in order to rejuvenate itself. For imaginative formation may require both the ecstasy of abandonment to what is other and the self-possession of mastery. For, as Kant and others have indicated, imagination may be midway between sensuousness on the verge of formlessness and intellectual concepts as tending to abstract universality. It is not midway merely as a means of mediating between these, but rather as revealing the original emergence of articulation that holds together and sets apart the self-possession of form and the stream of sensuousness. Thus, it is not merely a derivative mediating power; it is a creative intermediate out of which self-reflection and receptivity to otherness may subsequently be derived and viewed as distinct. This is precisely its significance, that, as a creative intermediate, it holds these two together in itself as an original unity.

Thus, in articulating a sensuous image of wholeness, great art may also try to articulate, as it were, man's metaphysical *rapport* with being other to himself. I use the term *rapport* here because it implies a bond of communication, an open affinity between human beings and things. Such a sense of affinity is sometimes given to us when our experience brims over with meaning. Art may reveal human experience as thus full, as thus overfull. The rapport given here may reveal the artist's joy in his secret intimacy with creation. The artist is not a Cartesian solipsist severed from the world, for his rapport brings him into conjunction with creation. He opens up the concrete order as something more than a neutered reality. The work of art releases consciousness from animosity to existence, for we and the world are not opposed poles, armed against each other in dualistic oppugnancy. The world is not an indifferent "it," and though it may seem more than us, its excess is not negative. Rather, its being other to us is pervaded by a power of prodigal abundance. In his own creative joy, the artist may celebrate its largesse.

Great art may serve as one example of the kind of wholeness at stake here. More generally, the point is that, though it may occur only rarely, the exemplification of essential human powers nevertheless *does* occur, as in ancient Athens and Renaissance Italy, to name but two frequently cited instances of singularly revealing wholeness. The occurrence of a human all-roundedness that does not sacrifice human variousness is sufficient witness to the fact that wholeness is not merely an empty ideal. Granted also, any wholeness is a condition born out of tension and so is something won from existence despite the contrary forces of dissolution also fermenting in human existence. Thus, we sometimes come across a certain ruffle in the mirror of art; we are not given back a pure self-transparency. Something fugitive is intimated, even in the very presence of sensuous wholeness. The terror and awe of the infinite mentioned previously do not drop away into nothingness when we seek to attain wholeness. The opening of difference in desire means that there is always a kind of cleft in wholeness. Opposites may touch and the wound be healed, but it is sealed with an inerasable scar. The limp of Jacob is a sign that even human wholeness is not the whole; nor is it attained through willpower alone.

Inevitably, given the dynamism of desire, wholeness tends to be a brief balance poised with all man's frailness on time's wave. For a span, however, we find the dynamism of desire's energy balanced by the discipline of articulate form. In time the balance gives way, either to a new restlessness of desire's energy or to the atrophy of form into a dead rubric. With the upsurge of desire we are opened up to difference and otherness; with the mediation of desire through self-knowledge, this surging energy is checked from an indiscriminate, untempered expression of itself and may be gathered into an articulate unity; but the dynamism of intentional infinitude remains and these articulate forms may again be smothered, perhaps surpassed by a new upsurge of the same mother energy that originally gave birth and shape to them. So the process has to be renewed repeatedly. Yet it is not merely an endless series of stepping-stones to a goal which desire will never, can never reach. Within the ever-renewing process there are crystalized real resting places of wholeness—if you will, concretizations of a kind of Sabbath for man's questing spirit.[20]

The view I am arguing here, then, tries to find a sense of wholeness that is a middle between sheer incompleteness and absolute closure.[21] As is clear, perhaps, we may agree with Hegel that wholeness need be no mere empty "ought" or the "bad infinity." Hegel is sometimes read here as, instead, advocating absolute closure. His case is ambiguous, and elsewhere I have tried to read his views more openly, particularly in connection with art.[22] Nevertheless, we can sympathize with those who came after Hegel—that is, most contemporary thinkers—who protest absolute closure. Many of these post-Hegelians, however, seem to make a virtue of sheer incompleteness. The middle view put forward here suggests that exemplifications of human wholeness do occur, but that we need not read these in a closed manner. That is, wholeness can be manifested or realized pluralistically. There is not just one whole, like the absorbing god. Therefore, present exemplifications of wholeness do not foreclose possible future realizations of wholeness. Perfection in the present is thus compatible with genuine openness to the future and further instances of perfection. Again, the example of art is instructive. Great art in the past or the present does not make redundant future renewals of the same quest for wholeness. Nor is past or present wholeness merely a stepping-stone to the future. Nor again will future wholeness refute or negate the exemplifications we find in the past or present. All may stand on their own; yet none need be entirely closed in on itself. Each may be seen as an island of fulfillment giving us a harbor of enjoyment in the ever-renewed odyssey of desire.

The artwork itself might be said to exhibit a rich middle between sheer incompleteness and absolute closure, reflecting the very tension in desire. We might put the point thus. Art is not simple, submissive imitation; nor is it sheer creativity ex nihilo. It may provide us with an original image of wholeness. As original, it may give us a world that is whole unto itself, a microcosm. As image, it may open up to the larger whole, the world other than human, the macrocosm. Passive imitation or representation reduces human activity to an unoriginality below its real power. Creation from nothing would make human power indistinguishable from God's power. In the middle, between these extremes, art is a unity of imitation and creation. As imitation, it reveals our ability to liken ourselves to all things other than ourselves. As creation, it gives expression to our own originative power. Thus it testifies to both our originative being and our participation in being other than ourselves. It is witness to a kind of open wholeness, a world rich in inexhaustible meaning, yet never entirely closed in on itself.[23]

The artwork, as has often been pointed out, is an end in itself, not merely a means to something further. But there is something releasing, rather than enclosing, in this end, which is revealed perhaps by the fact that we inevitably speak here of *appreciation*. To appreciate something is to not be niggardly in thinking well of the thing. It is not to hold back one's praise, but rather to affirm that this thing before one is good for itself. Our appreciation of it is our witness to its worth and the expression of our pleasure in its being. Appreciation is a kind of blessing of being—indeed, a certain thankfulness for being. We take joy in the thing for itself, with no motive beyond the marking of our deep delight. Art as an end, we might say, aspires to an unreserved joy, for it aspires to moments not needing to be completed by something else. It aspires to moments that are whole within themselves, moments that are enough in themselves and not just mere transition points to something else, moments of freedom that lift us out of the rule of necessity that often dictates our more finite desires. The artwork may make present such wholeness, may be itself the sensuous presence of wholeness.

In terms of our previous discussion of equivocal and univocal desire, we might say that wholeness is dependent on bringing to a halt two different flights of desire: the flight to absolute closure in the self-negating wholeness of the absorbing god and the flight away from wholeness altogether into infinite fragmentation on external things. Human desire as intentional infinitude is not reducible to either univocal or equivocal desire, because it may traverse a manifold of paths to the same destination of concrete wholeness. Whereas univocal and equivocal desire issue in rigid unity and unbalanced multiplicity, respectively, desire understood as intentional infinitude permits us to see their corresponding positives. It helps us to proceed beyond a dualism of oneness and manyness; for out of their dialectical tension, the self tries to attain to a gathered unity with itself.[24] The self tries to stabilize itself and subsume its scattered manifoldness, but without becoming entirely folded in on itself. The wholeness it seeks need not be a completion that immobilizes desire, but may be a form of activity wherein the energy of origination lives on.

Thus, even in its manifoldness, the demand of integrity is insistent in desire. This summons to integrity is not extrinsically imposed from without on an already sedimented self. Rather, every crystalization of the human self calls for an integrity coming from its synthesis into a full development. Humans cry out to be whole in their every act, for it is there that the hunger for absoluteness breaks forth. The search for wholeness recurrently grapples with the depths of self, but may never grasp them exhaustively. These depths continually well up, but to heed them is not necessarily to deplete them. For wholeness need not be compared, as in Shelley's image, to a coal that briefly flashes, consuming itself on its own fire.[25] It is more like a blaze that, in being kindled, becomes intense by being banked. Nor need it shun struggle and suffering for a facile self-satisfaction. It may embrace the pain of negativity whereby we find ourselves at odds with ourselves and in opposition to the world. However, since our intentional infinitude is grounded in a prior affinity with being, wholeness may take the edge of emnity off our relations to existence. The point is not to come to a complete halt and then discard as dead stepping-stones our previous passage. It is to try to appropriate the meaning of our passage and in the process embody an integral existence, one that manifests the caliber or qualitative character of selfhood, one that tries to draw together and, at the best, harmonize manyness. The power of original selfhood seeks articulate unity with itself through the mediation of its determinate forms, attempting to integrate them within the embrace of its intentional infinitude.

Wholeness, then, may be seen as a drama acted out in the tension between integrity and manyness. We may fall away from integrity into fragmentation, of course, or stop short at an arrested unity by recoiling from manyness. But we can also refuse the dissolution of this inner tension in either of these extremes. We can follow through the deeper dynamism that is inherent in this tension. In letting our infinite restlessness come forth more fully, in appropriating this through dialectical self-mediation, we may come back to ourselves, be restored to ourselves. Beyond fixation in finalized determinacy or sleep in an absorbing god, wholeness may make us wakeful to ourselves and vigilant to the real. This entails no sinking into nebulous inwardness. On the contrary, it calls for a concretization, or incarnation, of the sense of wholeness in the expression of life itself or in rich images, as we saw previously with great art. Just as the desiring self cannot be dualized into a ghost and a machine, so too its efforts to embody wholeness may even transfigure its sense of concrete being, lifting it above any mere meaningless thereness.

THE OPEN CIRCLE OF DESIRE

We will conclude this chapter, and indeed round off part 1 of this essay, with a perhaps not insignificant recapitulation. Recapitulation is appropriate to this particular chapter, given the recollective self-mediation of desire examined in it. But recapitulation is appropriate in a further sense, for the attentive reader will have noticed that in part 1 viewed as a whole, we have traversed a kind of "circle" of desire. It is a circle not of closure, but, I hope, of deepening interpretation, as we now come round again with our beginning transformed into fuller articulateness. For we have moved from an initial sense of lack in desire to a sense of overdetermined inexhaustibility, from a sense of inert bodily thereness to an embodiment of wholeness that transfigures thereness.

If we retrace our steps, then, commencing with chapter 1, we see the emergence of a complex sense of identity and difference in the self, or, to be more precise, of the power of differentiation internal to its identity that makes it possible for the self to be both many-sided and whole. We did not start with some pure self-consciousness, but with an initial amorphousness—indeed, inertness—from which, with the experience of lack, desire springs, progressively developing a fuller sense of self. We then saw the internal articulation of the body into a multiplicity of specific appetites. Further, we encountered the inclination of finite desire to return to inert self-identity through the obliteration of difference, an inclination always thwarted by the thrust of desire's infinitude. Moreover, we found this last to coexist in tension with the free will for wholeness. Then we considered a negative reaction to internal difference and desire's infinitude—namely, flight outside the self toward the nugatory wholeness of the absorbing god, a flight contradicted by the self's immanent freedom.

Our task was then to develop a positive ground to give internal orientation to desire's infinitude. To this end we explored a concept of original selfhood, as centered in itself, yet in primordial affinity with being other than itself. It is not necessary to review the stages of this exploration except to say that it bore fruit in a ballasted, open conception of desire's transcendence, which we called intentional infinitude. It is this that allows us to stand between the rigidity of univocal desire and the vacancy of equivocating desire, beyond the distracted infinity of centerless sequential passage from particular to particular thing. It is this, too, that finally allowed us to move from dispersed manifoldness toward some sense of concrete wholeness.

This, then, in outline, is the course of our reflection. The "circuit" it travels is, as it were, from immersion in the body, out of the body, back to the body. Departing initially from the inert body that (as contracted into itself with too thinglike a particularity) manifests nothing, desire eventually restores us to the body as an original appearance, as an embodiment of qualitative power. Desire returns itself to heightened concreteness by transfiguring the body's lassitude into concrete ideality. Desire's dialectical self-mediation might be said to be this transformation process whereby dead determinacy is metamorphosed into a determinate incarnation, infinitely suggestive of the indeterminate power of being. Here, therefore, there is no static totalization, only the infinite demand of active self-appropriation; and this, though it gain its measure of immanent equipoise, must be sustained, perpetuated, and fulfilled further.

For desire involves this: selfhood responding to itself and to the original exigencies of its being. The false height between man and the absorbing god yields to the depth within man himself. Man is this riddle of the world, recalcitrant, passing strange. For this riddle is a question to itself; this riddle recourses to itself; this riddle must answer for itself. We find, however, that though we may desire, even embody at times, concrete wholeness, we are still not *the* whole, and that, though our desire be infinitely restless, we are still not *the* infinite. The deepest thrust of our spirit, in coming to itself, makes its way toward becoming open to genuine otherness. Thus we find here a certain decentering of desire toward otherness, even in moments of wholeness; we find the breaking open of any closed circle of merely monadic self-relation. The "ex-centricity" of desire's intentional infinitude becomes evident in its transcendence of self-relation toward real otherness. To talk of an open "circle" of desire is perhaps appropriate in this part of our reflection, given the dialectical self-mediation at work there. But, as we have seen, the outcome is not absolute closure. On the contrary, we can now take our bearings to explore how the openness of desire yields its metaxological intermediation with otherness.

PART II
ACTUAL FINITUDE

Chapter Four
Desire, Transcendence, and Static Eternity

TRANSCENDENCE, TIME, AND THE PROBLEM OF DUALISM

We are marked off as other to finite external things in their fixed particularity, since the original power of our being makes us dialectical selves capable of immanent self-differentiation. Our sense of our own difference is inseparable from the fullness of our opening out to being other than ourselves. We must now explore that otherness, not in terms of the difference between the self and external things, but in terms of what transcends the self in its finiteness. This exploration will take up the rest of the book, but my main purpose in this chapter is to look at an important interpretation of desire in relation to transcendence. We might summarize this interpretation under the rubric of static eternity. This interpretation is not adequate, I will argue; but it has an inner plausibility that we need to plot, in order to relate more appropriately to a fuller sense of transcendence. Static eternity, like the previously explored concepts of an absorbing god and equivocal desire, is a recurrent, essential philosophical possibility. These are all revealing failures, which we cannot afford to neglect on the way to a more satisfactory view.

We also cannot neglect static eternity because it is deeply related to the philosophical quest for origins. The notion of static eternity is pervasive in the tradition of metaphysical thought that tries to articulate the nature of original being—being in its primary, most original sense, relative to which the derivative forms of being found in the so-called sublunary world are to be understood, indeed evaluated for their ontological worth. Historically, this notion of static eternity has often been identified with a version of Platonism. And, although I think that Platonism is more complex than many of its contemporary antagonists allow, we may grant a certain drift toward conceiving the eternal in terms of an absolutely immutable transcendence.[1] Absoluteness, in fact, tends to be identified with immutability. In this essay the historical question is subordinate to the philosophical issue, but the following, perhaps more historical considerations may prove helpful.

Much contemporary thought, in the shoes of Nietzsche, if you will, tends to be vehemently anti-Platonic. The traditional view is conceived something like this. Time, because always becoming, amounts almost to a defective condition of being, an unreal succession of shadows, all without abiding substance. The philosopher, however, seeks an abiding reality beyond time, a realm not cursed by change, eternal being that is free of time's tyranny. Eternity is home, time is homelessness, and man struggles to return, striving through the gates of time. In the wake of Nietzsche, however, contemporary thinkers find themselves at odds with this traditional view. Such thinkers might be said to be obsessed with time, not because they seek an eternal home elsewhere, but because they are struck by what seems to be man's unrelievedly time-bound condition. There seems to be no extratemporal alleviation of our finite condition. And, it is said, least of all should we be what Nietzsche calls "afterworldsmen," people who cast an "evil eye" on this earth in their yearning to be in another world elsewhere.[2] Our being is radically, essentially temporal. The consequence tends to be an eclipse of traditional notions of eternity such that it becomes questionable whether it even makes sense to talk about the traditional opposition of time and eternity. Thinkers after Heidegger, in pursuit of Derrida's deconstruction of Western metaphysics, seek some release from posing the problem of time in terms of such oppositions.

In our previous discussion of desire and wholeness, we sought a middle ground between completely indefinite openness and absolutely fixed closure. So also with regard to the present issue (and the full argument will unfold over this and the next four chapters), I will argue for a position between the contemporary tendency to dissolution into the indefinite becoming of the sheerly temporal and the traditional tendency to take flight in the immutably determined being of static eternity. We may agree with contemporary criticisms of Platonism, if Platonism is taken as an ancient ontological version of modern epistemological dualism, in which the metaphysical oppositions of time and eternity, becoming and being, the changing and the immutable, are to the fore, rather than the epistemological oppositions of *res cogitans* and *res extensa*, subject and object, knower and known, as in the modern self-oriented project. I would agree that these one-sided oppositions often tend to feed off each other, but, unlike some contemporary thinkers who seek to escape from the terms of these opposites, I believe that these traditional opposites are attempts to formulate real, basic difficulties.

We may agree that such formulations distort the difficulty and lead to a constricted conception of the binary terms in which they pose the problem. Though we will be critical of static eternity, there is no question of being critical of the originary experience whence this conception arises or of the fundamental, essential perplexity that lies at its root. We need to recover these root perplexities even in the inadequate response itself, as well as in the critical act whereby we question the adequacy of this response. The notion of static eternity is rooted in the complex ambiguity of desire and in the enigma that transcendence presents to man. The point, then, is not simply to acquiesce in what is often a post-Nietzschean tendency to caricature Platonism. It is to penetrate to some of the deeper intentions at work even in a caricatured Platonism, intentions sometimes covered up in the polemical debunking of ancient metaphysics by contemporary thinkers. The dualistic opposition of time and eternity may not be sufficient, but we cannot banish the questions of either time or eternity. We seek a sense of the eternal as emergent through the richness of being that time itself presents.[3]

Man's original self-mediation is not to be denied. The difficulty is how we continue to affirm this, while allowing for genuine transcendence. Traditionally, transcendence has tended to be affirmed at the price of attenuating the human being's original self-mediation. Alternatively— and this is more characteristic of modern thought—self-mediation is affirmed, but at the expense of transcendence conceived in its otherness to the self. It is by no means easy to preserve both sides. We must certainly be wary of all dualisms that engender an unstable oscillation between one polar opposite and the other. Indeed, we must cease to be captive to this dualistic mentality. The modern revolt against Platonic dualism, coupled with its dissatisfaction with Cartesian dualism, can be seen as a genuine movement against dualism per se, whether ontologically or epistemologically conceived.

Thus, any excessively dualistic approach to the question must be criticized, for such an approach makes impossible any intermediation of the above extremes. But dualistic opposition, although inadequate, is not to be discarded entirely, for it has the merit of trying to preserve the sense of otherness and difference, albeit in a form that ultimately proves impossible to uphold. We must grant what is genuine in this effort to preserve difference, therefore, while trying to articulate a position beyond dualistic opposition that comes closer to realizing the preservation of true difference. Otherness is to be seen as a genuinely positive category, not as parasitical on the oscillating negation of one polar term by another such term. What this means in the present case is that we must transcend, as it were, the metaphysical rivalry presented to us by the antithesis of Platonism and Nietzscheanism. In terms of this rivalry, it is said that ancient, Platonic eternity serves to negate, or certainly diminish, the importance of time, while modern, Nietzschean temporality serves to subordinate, if not entirely repudiate, the significance of the eternal. But, as Heidegger indicates, this modern negation is itself parasitical on the ancient eternity it refuses. We need something more than the parasitical relations engendered by all dualistic opposition; for what limited power such dualistic oppositions possess, they have by virtue of being parasitical on the complexity of concrete being itself. They are illuminating to the extent that they draw life from this source, but become misleading in implying that such borrowed life is self-sufficient and absolute.

In the light of these remarks, we will pursue our discussion in three stages. First, I will plot the inner plausibility of the resort to static eternity, given a certain understanding of desire and transcendence. Second, I will outline the chief difficulties with this resort. Third, I will embark on a nondualistic approach to being and becoming that carries desire forward to a fuller sense of transcendence. We will look at this last point in the second half of this chapter, where we will consider becoming as itself a process of positive othering, which issues in the human self as free becoming, which, in turn, brings home to us more fully the basic affinity of man and becoming, desire and otherness. In subsequent chapters we will specify this basic affinity more fully, in terms of the metaxological relation.

DESIRE AND EQUIVOCAL BECOMING

Human desire enjoys no absolute, self-sufficient closure, for the tendency to such closure is always subverted by its inescapable openness to otherness. Yet this openness is not univocal, and if we examine how its ambiguity might unfold, we may discover inadequate forms of this openness and correspondingly distorted perspectives on otherness.

When desire faces otherness honestly, the other as other brings home to us our lack of self-sufficiency and absolute autonomy. A recurrent response to this is a sense of shame and guilt at the instability and lack of foundation within. We cannot be our own ground. But we may well be tempted to take flight from this disconcerting reality toward an ideal that is radically other. The ideal sought now is not an ideal self (of the kind examined in chapter 2), for this also partakes in desire's dynamism, but the ideal as a realm eternally fixed. Since there is no fixing of the self, and since the openness of its very being is temporal, we cannot find absolute stability here. Instead, we seek an ideal of a settled otherness, the other as an unchanging ideal. That is, we make otherness into a fixed idea, in a manner reminiscent of the Platonic eidos. By offering us otherness in the form of a fixed ideal, a static eternity seems to mitigate the instability that desire experiences in its own openness.

It is not just man's internal instability that feeds this flight. The character of the world—its externality to man and recalcitrance to desire—serves the same end. This world is one of becoming, in which nothing can be congealed into immobility, and all is dynamized and unsettled. Becoming loosens all rigidity. Concrete existence is shot through with contrariety, blending inconstancy and durability, converging on unity here, diverging from it there. Nothing can be stayed as absolutely the same, yet from this flux, provisionally secure identities are repeatedly rescued. The world we experience is not absolutely determinate, in the sense of being finally formed, with all possible determinations already exhaustively articulated. Not only is desire marked by openness, but the external world reveals an otherness that is itself an open process of possibility. Becoming discloses a universe of promise, a world in bud. It is both determinate and indeterminate and sometimes provokes the reaction of Macbeth in relation to the ambiguous destiny of time itself: nothing is but what is not. Becoming both is what it is, and yet is not fully what it is, because it exists only in process to its own realization. As such, it might seem to issue from an initial instability and develop toward some steadfast permanence. It might seem to point us away from its inherent unsteadiness to a fuller form of being. It might appear to be like a wave, carrying human desire away from dissolution toward what is not existent as a mere "here and now." Not just desire, but external otherness itself, might seem to be the pointer beyond becoming, the temporal arrow targeted on static eternity.[4]

What can emerge here is an unduly fractious posture toward becoming. The ambiguous twofoldness of becoming (that it is and is not) can

be regarded as a kind of ontological duplicity. In never allowing existence to stand still, in constantly annulling all stable identities, becoming
looks like an equivocation process, since for equivocation nothing is ever
absolutely the same.[5] Looked at this way, becoming seems deceptive and
illusory and incapable of furnishing desire with an unambiguous ground
of stability. The world seems to groan with ontological insecurity and
to drive us to shun its shiftiness. Here we find a flight from external
becoming reminiscent of the flight of desire from internal becoming toward an absorbing god (see chapter 1). To safeguard itself from erratic
transience, desire seeks a ground of stability. But it is afraid to appeal
to becoming, for in becoming it sees nothing but the vulnerability that
it seeks to elude, but now duplicated externally. Instead, it looks for a
ground absolutely free of the restless motion of becoming. It replaces
the indeterminacy, equivocalness, and dynamism of becoming with a
transcendent being that is absolutely determinate, univocal, and static.

Let me stress that this response is not some fantasy constructed in
the void. It arises from the genuinely ambiguous nature of experience
and is carried by a logic of its own. One crucial factor here is the common experience of time as a power opposing the self, or even stronger,
as a power opposing the self's desire for wholeness. As an opposing
power, time seems to scatter our desire for wholeness abroad on the
uncontrolled, perhaps uncontrollable, otherness of external becoming.
Against this opposing power, against this self-scattering, against the irreversible flow of time itself, it is understandable why we (who cannot
renege on the exigence for wholeness, for it is intrinsic to our very
being) might search for a realm entirely different from time, an otherness entirely other to immanent becoming. The entire motivation for
appealing to static eternity is to fulfill the quest for wholeness while
preserving our openness to otherness. But when time is seen only as an
opposing power, our own temporal condition is easily equated with one
of guilt and fallenness.[6] For then it appears that we have fallen from a
state of original unity or univocal identity into a state of dispersed multiplicity such that both desire and external becoming seem inherently
equivocal.[7] The only escape that occurs to us is to return to the univocal
unity of unchanging eternity, to abandon the actual chaos of time and
surrender ourselves to the ideal cosmos of eternity. To break through
the ephemeral and the inessential and the transient, it appears that we
must master and suppress the unsettling ambiguities of time.

The upshot is that we come to despise the motion of our own desire and scorn the ambiguity of becoming as utterly equivocal; we seek to escape contradiction, within and without, in a transcendent unity that repels multiplicity from itself. The self tries to outrun difference and diversity into a transcendent realm that is absolutely different from the phenomenal world because it is always absolutely the same, static eternity again. Here we are reminded of Parmenides' Being that brooks no contradiction, that is one with itself, homogeneous with itself, suffering no diminution or change. Nor should we be surprised that in chastizing those who make compromises with the phenomenal world of genesis, Parmenides upbraids them as "hordes who wander double-headed."[8] They wander double-headed (*dikranoi*) precisely because their thinking is divided by difference and so fails to stand beyond the duplicity of becoming as equivocal. The way out offered by Parmenides is an absolute self-identity that excludes from itself all difference.[9] Thus we are asked to negate becoming and to assuage the suffering of our passage through phenomenal difference in a beyond that is the apotheosis of static sameness. Here, things come to pass and pass away; there, being is not wounded by this curse of change. Here, becoming is travail, decay, and death; and even coming to be is only an unreal prelude in time's war with itself wherein things turn into their opposites, thereby destroying themselves. Time, the opposing power, opposes even itself. But, beyond this barren strife, static eternity annuls equivocal becoming through the calming power of changeless, univocal identity.

We see a tendency in this direction in the immobility of the Platonic eidos itself: for here is a determinate self-identity always the same, itself and nothing but itself, a univocal unity of being wherein the equivocal multiplicity of becoming is overcome.[10] The real world becomes a dependent, derivative image, one on which we cannot entirely rely, and away from which we must be directed. In itself it is next to nothing. This derogatory comportment to the ambiguity of becoming drives apart the real and the ideal into an antagonistic, exclusive rift. Each tends to be seen as what the other is *not*, this "not" being a negative divide that sunders them into opposition. The result is that equivocal becoming seems to be merely a realm of appearances, where this "merely" serves to signify something insubstantial, something hovering over the brink of nothingness, something that, to all intents and purposes, is hardly distinguishable from nothingness. Time is trapped in a dualism with eternity, and it seems that it can escape from this trap, not by fulfilling itself, but by negating itself.

STATIC ETERNITY AND ITS DEFECTS

It is understandable that desire might want to outrun the instability of becoming, but in the end this strategy is self-frustrating. Let us look at four main ways in which this is evident: in terms of ascent, descent, origin, and ground.

The ascent to static eternity here seems to be an upward movement of negation that substitutes unity for multiplicity, still homogeneity for restless heterogeneity, univocal identity for equivocal difference.[11] Moreover, this ascent by negation to what is more than becoming goes hand in hand with a similar defective approach to what may be more *within* becoming. Here we must acknowledge some aspects of the Nietzschean criticism of Platonism: namely that the latter's love of eternity is not always safeguarded against what we might call a metaphysical distaste for time, which means that nihilism is a never absent threat. Desire's openness to otherness here and now is subordinated to an otherness elsewhere, an otherness that is always eternally elsewhere. But a complete substantiality in the "other" world is hardly a sufficient exchange for the absence of immobile substantiality here. Human desire is openness to and need of the actual. But in trying to outstrip this need and overcome lack in itself, the self here tries to surmount external becoming, thereby reducing it to lack, to a sense of being that is lacking. As we shall see later, a more positive view of becoming is necessary, one that is not antithetical to our eros for the actual, an eros that must itself be viewed in a less negative light.

Even in the ascent currently under consideration, something positive is revealed in the movement of desire in and through becoming, not simply beyond it. Static eternity is a kind of frozen transcendence, indeed, a kind of catatonic god.[12] Even if we do describe our passage upward to this catatonic god in terms of divestment, this passage is not made possible by any inherent power of static eternity to draw what is becoming up to itself. As absolutely fixed and stable, such transcendent being cannot be active; it is hard to see how it might even lure human desire. Rather, what facilitates any ascension seems to be the power of being inherent in desire and becoming in their transcending of what is fixed in the world of immanence. In other words, desire and becoming seem to do all the work on the way up, while the catatonic god does nothing. Should this ascent by negation be completely successful, we would end up not with transcendent being but with nothing.

The second difficulty mentioned, that concerning descent, develops further the privative nature of this ascent. For the result of this ascent is a kind of overkill with respect to stability. It leaves us with a sense of homogeneous being in which we can perceive nothing. It is hard to see how such a sense of being could be communicated articulately; for to communicate is necessarily to break out of immobile identity. Because of the negative ascent, we cannot descend again, it seems: either we dissolve in homogeneous being, or, failing that, we merely fall back down into the heterogeneity of becoming. There seems to be no middle way by which an immobile eternity could be communicated to what is in motion, both in terms of existence itself and in terms of our discourse about it. Consequently, descent from the immutable to the mutable can only be a fall or diminution. Because descent, like ascent, partakes of movement, it too assumes a ..egative connotation, in which appearance and diversity become degenerations of static being. The paradigm of life we seem to be offered is a coagulated eternity. The tumultuous carnival of time is switched for a stilled, immortal mortuary. The generative power in becoming can come to seem like only a degeneration of ungenerating eternity.

The difficulty becomes even more complex when we consider the question of origin. An origin must in some sense be a creative source, something capable of originating. But what is absolutely determinate cannot originate: to be a creative source is to be more than a determined thing. Thus, if we claim static eternity to be the origin of the immanent world, the consequence is peculiar: we discover an original that, because it only abides within itself in self-sameness, does not and cannot originate. Not only can the self not descend again; neither, in the first place, could a static eternity, not even to the extent of falling or degenerating. For such an origin there is no way down, for from its own side it cannot initiate a real relation to becoming. By making the transcendent into absolutely determinate being, we contract its power and endow it with the uncreative being of a particularized thing. Even if we could make sense of an ascent from becoming, we could not account for a descent that might originate becoming in the first place. And this is true regardless of whether we understand this descent in positive or negative terms. Indeed, it proves unintelligible even to assert that becoming is a degeneration, since there can be no origination at all, positive or negative, if the eternal is absolutely immobile. Should we claim, therefore, that transcendent being which is absolutely determinate in a univocal way is the origin of the world of becoming, we make the latter itself unintelligible.

In addition, the indeterminate side of becoming shows us a certain diversifying infinitude in worldly existence. But what is determinate, bounded, inactively self-identical cannot be infinite in this way. Any such unity bars difference internal to itself, cannot positively generate plurality outside itself, and, instead of being the origin of being, seems to be its sclerosis.[13] Yet, when we look at becoming, we find a more extravagant, more expansive, less limited existence, one that erupts into excess and superfluity, a profuse wild abundance that does not spare itself, but prodigally and ceaselessly expends itself. Rather than static eternity beyond becoming, which, like a miser in pinched self-identity, does nothing, it is becoming itself that sets forth the show of reckless original power, its indeterminacy giving us an image of what an origin, in the positive sense of a creative source, might really be.

Finally, there is the difficulty in relation to ground. Since the ascent by which we reach static eternity is privative, the phenomenal world and its supposed ground tend to become a *dyad* set in opposition. This ground is not merely beyond becoming, but is antithetical to it, and thus, paradoxically, it creates a barrier to the grounding of becoming. In the very act of supposedly rescuing the phenomenal world from its vicissitudes, static eternity seems to infect it with a new insecurity. Hence, this ground seems to perpetuate phenomenal groundlessness. The point is more strikingly evident, perhaps, when we look at the antithesis of becoming and static eternity as a dualistic opposition of an equivocal image and a univocal original. The first (equivocal becoming) does not ground itself, but is groundless both apart from and in relation to the second (univocal eternity). The character of the gap between them, however, is such that the first (becoming as image) is thrown back on its own murk and nullity by the second (eternity as original). Supposed to be the ground here, static eternity makes present instability into something eternal, unchangeable, and unregenerate. By stabilizing becoming, static eternity paradoxically seems to make becoming eternally unstable.

There is a further important point that we need to make. Not only does phenomenal insecurity reappear, but it does so in a more extreme, articulate fashion. For it reemerges from the context of a radical dyadic contrast. Thus it sometimes happens that the longing for eternity elsewhere can prove so intense that, instead of static eternity giving desire some ground in the here and now, the present absence of the eternal can make desire more deeply distracted, and we are led to experience the process of becoming (whether in desire itself or in the external world) with a new, intensely heightened sense of groundlessness. With regard to providing ontological security, then, static eternity appears to take back with one hand what it purports to give to becoming with the other. And so in a peculiar and paradoxical way, this univocal transcendence would appear to be an equivocating eternity. For ultimately, it duplicates the equivocalness that desire in its negating movement sees in the ambiguous otherness of becoming. But most especially, static eternity fails to orient us to any ground that might be manifest *within* becoming, a ground that, while it might be beyond us in certain respects, would still be in our midst. We must reconsider the question along these lines, freed perhaps a little more fully from the temptation to negation.

But first let me summarize briefly. Any dualism of time and eternity as the mutable and the immutable that makes eternity the only source of intelligibility, ends up by making time itself unintelligible. To try to make intelligible the equivocations of time through an eternity that is absolutely intelligible in a univocal, determinate way and yet to chain the difference between time and eternity to an excluding opposition is not only to render time absurd; it is also to make eternity absurd. Again, the difficulty is not simply due to our failure to live up to the ideal of the immutable. Should we measure up to it, we would be visited with disappearance and dissolution (the very antithesis of the immutable) and hence be privileged with neither mutability nor immutability. This defect seems to be inherent in static eternity, in its inability to ground any positive relation between itself and becoming and its failure (as a supposed ground and origin) to measure up to the rich generative being immanent in becoming. Even granting a defect on our part (for static eternity can be correlated with desire as lack), there is a deeper failing, in that the concept of static eternity as the original ground of being cannot yield an appropriately creative transcendence. We must conclude that, in relation to ascent and descent, this static eternity risks being a nugatory transcendence, while in regard to origin and ground, it seems to make itself redundant. In no case does it provide the basis for a *positive two-way mediation* between becoming and its original ground. Hence, we are compelled to repair again to the world of becoming with the gain that, should we require an affirmative transcendence, it cannot forsake time but must be as rich as, nay richer than, the originative power of being with which becoming itself is internally big.[14]

BECOMING AS PROCESS OF POSITIVE OTHERING

In the remainder of this chapter I want, first, to develop briefly the point that becoming need not be viewed as lacking. Second, I want to make clear that the self need not be set in dualistic opposition to external becoming in its otherness. The first point relates to the need for a creative transcendence and might be expressed in terms of becoming as positive othering, rather than mere equivocal process. The second point sees the self as emergent from becoming, emergent as a complex form of being capable of metaxologically mediating with becoming in its otherness. In subsequent chapters we will develop this metaxological mediation to the point where we can venture some reflections on the ground of being in a manner less prey to the limits of static eternity.

Let us look at the first point regarding a more positive orientation to becoming in its otherness. For this world is no nothing; as Caliban in Shakespeare's *Tempest* knew, it is full of sounds and sights that delight often and do not hurt. It may not always be Miranda's "brave new world." Ascetics and mystics may call it a shadow; yet it possesses its own peculiar, robust substance. Dust and ashes though it be and sometimes bitter to taste, it burgeons and blossoms and blooms into life that expends, spends, and renews itself. Death may wean us from this reliable yet unreliable place, but be this weaning gentle or harsh, it discloses the power of being that in the first place promotes our flowering, and eventually even our demise. The world is insistently ambiguous: it grants life, favoring us with the freedom to break out of uniform continuity and strike out on strange paths; it takes hold of life again and, striding to its harvest like the grim reaper, cuts all things mortal with its sickle. It is the agent of life and the carrier of death, and what it gives it takes away and gives back again, in a moving drama of entrances and exits.

In short, instead of trying to pass, as if with Parmenides, from the equivocations of change to static univocal eternity, we must try to glean some truth from the equivocal, with thinkers like Heraclitus and Hegel.[15] The truth of the equivocal may be rescued in a more dialectical understanding of being, which, in its notions of identity and difference, comes closer to the richness of ambiguous becoming. Such a dialectical understanding might seem to require a volume to itself; but by now we are sufficiently familiar with the dialectical approach that we can restrict ourselves to the following remarks.

Rather than turning away from becoming as equivocal to eternity as univocal, a dialectical approach asks us to sift for what is positive in the ambiguous otherness of the world. This world of becoming dynamically discloses the original power of being and does so in a twofold way. It is not a mere image, but, if you will, an original image:[16] image in portraying the power of being, which, as source of origination, it never completely exhausts; original in effecting this portrayal in a genuinely active way. As an original image, it is a kind of intermediate: not an utter nullity, not a degeneration of being, but a middle transition, via the mediation of originative power, between nothing and determinate being. Forms of determinate being are concretized in this middle and through its power. The character of the middle here frames a world in which the creative power of being converges with possible dissolution; but it recurrently surmounts this possibility and is poured forth in determinate forms of existence.

Or, to put it another way, it cannot suffice to dualistically oppose becoming and being and then confine the active power of origination to only one side of the dualism. The process of becoming itself reveals the power of internal differentiation. It undermines from within any false stabilization of being that claims to finalize and enclose the originative dynamism it discloses. Things that seem to be closed wholes are revealed as provisional formations of this dynamism of being, and inevitably their claims to absolute self-sufficiency are prized open under the pressure of that dynamism's ceaseless power. Boundaries that seem frozen then become fluid.

At the same time, this differentiating dynamism is not a mere shifting continuum in which all delimited things melt into a homogeneous flux. Even granting the possibilities of dissolution, it is not that we find nothing defined and relatively enduring. Though becoming transcends form and particularity, the original power that it manifests also embodies itself in things that are defined by form and particularity. Nevertheless, substance in the sense of a static underlying thing is not what is properly primordial. Enduring things are derived from the more original power of being, which is never static, even when specified in determinate form. We cannot congeal what a thing is into something solidly immobile and then make this the determinate substratum that underlies change.[17] What "underlies" change is the power that generates it, relative to which determinate substance is a subsequent *result,* not the prior principle. Substance is not what is primordially permanent in becoming, as standing outside its so-called fluctuation; it is what becoming makes relatively permanent as a delimited product of its original power. Likewise, the form of a thing is the self-shaping of its own process of becoming; its embodiment is a particularized determination of the original power of its being.

External becoming, then, is neither uniform nor formless; rather, it intimates a dynamic source of original power that surges outward in manifold form. It is not like a blind, unattended rudder, a loose boom in a storm; nor yet is it a simple, determined linear process. It invokes an order that is articulated, yet open, an intermediate world between the sheerly indefinite and the rigidly determined. The determinate forms of being it originates are themselves the product of the determining power of being and, as such, are vibrant with its original energy. We might compare such an order to what we find in an imaginative creation like a poem or musical work. We have already had occasion to draw on art in relation to human wholeness, but here the metaphor is helpful in pointing to the possibility of dynamic form, moving pattern present in being in its otherness to man. As in the case of musical form, we do not have to choose between pattern and movement. My point is not to emulate Schopenhauer and proclaim the metaphysical supremacy of music as a direct copy of the will itself.[18] Schopenhauer's view does draw, however, on certain fruitful, suggestive analogies between what music as the creation of an artist intimates and what external becoming might mean as the outward expression of a primordial dynamic power. As derived from the original power of being, all pattern becomes set in motion, all form becomes the articulation of the active energy of being.

Here, too, we find a balance between formed wholeness and the surpassing—indeed dissolution—of all finitely formed wholes. The energy of being, concretized in the process of becoming, stabilizes itself in determinate things; but the articulated unity that such bounded wholes present is only a poised provisionalness, whose impermanence is disclosed by the further flow of becoming. So we find a dialectical coexistence of contraries in becoming itself, which at once both unwinds and unfolds itself, yet supersedes and undoes itself. Like an extravagant wave of life coursing toward a crest, it builds up to break itself, breaks to renew itself, and renews itself to break again. Contracting into bounded wholes and overflowing all boundaries, becoming exhibits radiant original power even in the particular entities it concretizes. In Heraclitean language, its radiance emerges from the friction of contraries and its harmony, the harmony of concord and divergence. Its emergent form distributes recurrence, process, and deviation—the circle, the line, and the interruption.

Instead of equivocal otherness, we can see in becoming's ambiguous twofoldness what, above, we termed the power of positive othering. By this I mean to point out that becoming cannot be reduced to a sheer continuum explicable in terms of quantitative homogeneity. Without making any pretension to embrace its astonishing diversity, we can say that the process of becoming comes to embody qualitative difference in this sense. It passes beyond inert identity, moving from homogeneity to heterogeneity by giving rise to identities that do not exclude internal difference. Difference erupts out of identity. Indeed, differentiation is the coming forth of identity and as such constitutes real identity. For without internal difference, the thing as identifiable would disappear into the resulting absence of distinction, and we would have the limiting case of the purely homogeneous—what in former ages was sometimes called *materia prima*. If difference is extrinsic to identity, and if, to preserve the integrity of a thing, we try to fix difference to something outside the thing in its immanent integrity, then, in fact, we destroy the real difference of things, and everything becomes the same. For when an identity is not immanently differentiated, it cannot be distinguished from what is other to it, and its distinctive reality collapses.

When we speak of becoming as a positive othering, the self-differentiation it discloses is a process of alteration which is literally just that: the power to make other (*alter*).[19] At its most developed, becoming is a process of singling out—that is, it is a differentiation process that is the source of irreducible singularity, real individuality. Where static being (with its homogeneity of uniform identity) houses different things in a kind of museum of mummies, a hushed hall of waxworks, becoming as positive othering creates a noisy festival of singing difference, a carnival of incarnation. We might also add, to continue the musical metaphor, that the work here performed is paradoxical: with no fixed score, it is always completing itself, but also ever improvising new variations on a theme. It is at once a whole, yet always in a draft stage toward harmony. It is intermediate between absolute indefiniteness and completely determinate closure. Human wholeness may mirror it (see chapter 3), as the microcosm does the macrocosm. Becoming as othering is a drafting, erasing, revising of individuals, yet also a resting in singularity. It rummages and gropes and reaches into its reservoir of possibilities, sifting opportunity and seizing upon structure wherein it may individuate and differentiate the power of being and arouse it from somnolent homogeneity.

THE SELF AS FREE BECOMING

Becoming as positive othering might perhaps be seen as an ontological identification of difference, in this sense: that through its forming power

it names the anonymous homogeneity of being (sheer flux), thereby issuing in things as original identities, while also binding up their difference. But the succession of things it produces is not a smooth seamless
series of entities. A more profound kind of discontinuity is introduced
into the succession of things with the human self. Though a product
of the world of becoming and a thing among the series of things, the
self is a product that may transcend the series of finite things. Becoming
as endless othering issues in an infinite succession of things, but this
first, external infinitude gives rise to the human self as a second, inward
infinity, something that previously we spoke of as an intentional infinitude (see chapter 3). The human self is not a simple product of the
process of origination, but a product that is a new, free original process.

With humans we find a more radical emergence of singularity and
a deeper sense of becoming's openness to otherness—deeper, because
human openness to otherness is capable of being appropriated in inwardness. We are not just the actualization of a preestablished possibility,
but a more original openness, beings capable of generating new possibility. With the human being, the creative power of the possible appears in the actual, for here we confront the emergence of free
becoming, purposeful becoming. We are a form of being open to the
really different, because we are ourselves free difference. For here we
have determinate being that is self-determining and to that extent open
to as yet undetermined becoming. With humanity is tossed up a queer,
uncanny difference; for here we have a creature who can create, a
strange indeterminate determination, a continuation turned into an astonishing anomaly.

But once again a certain doubleness must be acknowledged. This
doubleness must be seen, not as a dualistic opposition, but rather as a
coincidence of opposites. Human doubleness consists in the fact that we
are both dependent on external becoming, yet independent of it. We
are both of these because our difference consists in the fact that we are
an emergent freedom. Our being set apart from external becoming is
inseparable from our being bound to becoming in a kind of ontological
kinship. From the standpoint of this kinship, the ambiguity of external
becoming is matched by the inner ambiguity of human desire. But in
both (external becoming and our free becoming), something positive is
disclosed. Perhaps here we might glean some meaning from the myth
of the Fall.[20] In our sense of free difference we become aware of ourselves as naked, distinct, and unique. We are thrust out from the in-
nocent paradise of slumbering sameness and cast into the ambiguous

world of otherness. We are there entrusted to be the bearers of ambiguity itself, endowed with the risk of being carriers of this explosive mix of life and death, good and evil, power of affirmation coupled with the ability to despoil and negate. Yet, out of this ambiguity an outcome can be won. We can augment external becoming by raising it to a new self-presence, by being ourselves a creative form of self-becoming. The cycle of coming to be and passing away manifests a recurrence that tends to be formal in respect of particular things (the same *kind* of thing is repeated). But with humanity we find identity in a richly individualized way. We are no strangers to recurrence, but in our return to ourselves, we may seek to form an individual concretely over time, an individuality that is not to be repeated.

The human self is an original identity that in its difference recurs to itself over time. It is an open identity that, through its difference, is an original image of the original power of being that is disclosed in the world of becoming. For becoming, like the polymorphous Proteus, appears and disappears in a profusion of configurations. Yet there is one existent at least that, by being protean in itself, can take hold of ambiguous becoming in a new interiorized fashion. This is the self.[21] The self may give back an articulated image of this protean unity and multiplicity by becoming this manifoldness in its own self-relating singleness. In this we find, so to say, the mirror in which becoming can behold and inspect itself and raise the event of appearance and disappearance to a new level of articulation.[22]

THE POSITIVE PLURALIZATION OF IDENTITY AND DIFFERENCE

We need not develop this point in further detail, since much of our discussion in part 1 related to it, albeit without fully placing the self in the context of external becoming. All we need note here is that our concern with external becoming and otherness converges with conclusions already reached. We must also recognize that philosophical discourse about such matters can easily slide into nebulousness. In the next two chapters I intend to balance this discussion with a more detailed analysis of our knowledge of otherness and the different degrees of concreteness. Yet our own experience of time, whether in the unfolding of desire or the aging of our bodies or the maturing development of selfness, testifies to the unavoidability of the present theme. Let me close this chapter by trying to bring out its overall importance in our discussion. This will help us situate ourselves, and we will see better how it advances our efforts to relate desire and otherness.

Above, we were critical of static eternity, but the point of this criticism was not to debunk the question of the eternal per se. Rather, it was argued, first, that we must free ourselves from an excessively dualistic way of conceiving the issue, and second, that we should free ourselves from partial perspectives on becoming (as equivocating process, duplicitous change) and desire (as reactive to its vulnerability before otherness). Each of these perspectives has its own partial plausibility, but together they can lead to the dualistic impasse of static eternity. We then tried to develop briefly a positive sense of becoming to match a more fruitful sense of our openness to otherness. The outcome pointed to the possibility of a two-way interplay between desire and the otherness of becoming. This two-way interplay, this metaxological intermediation, gives rise to a less misleading context in which to raise the question of the ground of being, which, of course, is the profound philosophic perplexity to which the concept of static eternity tries to respond.

We see, however, that any recourse to eternity cannot be justified in terms of the evasion of time. Our element is this world, time, and the philosopher must fight with his precariousness in the flow of time, and fight it as an opposing power, not just take flight from it. Any approach to the eternal must come from within time itself, be generated from the proper expenditure of one's wealth here, not by a hoarding of it for elsewhere. The talent is betrayed when it is buried, even despite the most exalted intentions to dig it up later for use hereafter. This resurrection comes too late. Man's struggle is rooted here. Unlike the catatonic god, one cannot be a kind of metaphysical absentee landlord who coolly collects, from a safe distance outside the world, the fruits gathered from the sweat of time. It is the movement up and down that is the thing, the ebb and flow, the eternal renewal of the energy of life, renewal without end, which we may greet with joy.

I underscore how different this is from the fractious posture toward becoming that is manifest in desire's flight to static eternity. There we have an insecurity within, born of the sometimes terrifying openness of human desire, issuing in a rigidity that seeks to externalize itself by a sclerosis of being outside desire—indeed, above desire. Insecure desire here seeks to destroy an ambiguity it cannot tolerate. The position we must now espouse must be a different opening to the ambiguity of being, one that, by contrast, consents to the chance, the hazard, the indeterminacy of becoming. Nietzsche talks about the innocence of becoming (*Unschuld des Werdens*), but I do not think we need to be so lyrically sanguine. As Platonists well know, time *is* often the opposing power. This does not mean that our only alternative to the Nietzschean innocence of becoming must be to make into our holy of holies the gnomic utterance of Heraclitus concerning war as the father of all things. Human desire *suffers* from its own difference, as it does from the difference of external things. There is a deep, undeniable pathos in our periodic subjection to the density of things, as well as in the surprising power vested in our being, which may startle us with its unmined possibility. But the point is not to control the equivocal with the univocal, or to obliterate the suffering of difference in order to attain some end of fallow identity. It is to dwell watchfully with the ambiguity of being and to wrest from difference suffered some genuinely originative wholeness of being. We do not decipher the world by standing stiffly outside it, nor by lording over it in domineering fashion, but by venturing into the thick of things and vigilantly moving through them.

For time is not a lazy current on whose surface we are dreamily carried, as if on Lethe. It orders and stabilizes things, but it also sunders and scatters and devours. And the self, even when trying to gather its own internal differentiation into a unified outcome, has always still to face into the dense multiplicity of dispersed externality. The dispersions of time confront us with a necessity that is stubborn and rude. In our freedom we can sometimes be more tenacious and obdurate than this dispersion, securing some equilibrium of being, thereby countering the scattering that time will eventually effect. We may manage this gathering for only a brief span, but this may be enough. For this brief span, the warrior metaphysic of Heraclitean becoming is suspended. The other side of Heraclitus comes into its own when he tells us that what separates also unites with itself, since there can be no harmony without sharps and flats, no living being without male and female, without like and unlike, no unifying or seeking union without contrariety. After all, for us ease is not eternal sloth; ease is peace after struggle—that is, suffering faced, concentrated, and drubbed.

If becoming is pregnant with promise, humans might be seen as both midwives and offspring, or perhaps even strange offspring that midwife themselves. Without a doubt, time frequently washes up much that seems flotsam, wastage, mere wreckage. Existence is startlingly prodigal. But we deliver nothing, if we turn away from it simply because its limited stability gives no absolute surety. Suppose time is like the fitful sleep of a child. We are the child's shout in the dark. Sometimes, too, the child wakes up and even plays.[23] Our affinity with being may then become evident, for, unlike all other creatures, which seem *driven* to become, we seem capable of freely directing the development of our self-becoming. As such we may rise to affirm, indeed love, becoming. Our originative power, disclosed in the eros for transcendence, is unintelligible in isolation from the upsurge toward articulate life that appears with becoming. As a process of positive othering, becoming generates beyond itself, especially through humans as finite beings, whose infinite restlessness sets them to originate beyond themselves.

We conclude, then, with this affinity between the human self and the world of becoming, which grounds the possibility of a two-way—that is, metaxological—mediation between them. Indeed this affinity might be seen as the original bond of man with being, a bond more primordial than the dualistic attitudes explored above. For it is not just a derivative unity pieced together from absolutely separable poles of a dualistic opposition. Even the self's difference is emergent from its more primordial participation in being. Perhaps, then, this affinity might be called man's community with being. Dualism is a distorted form of this community, and indeed both presupposes it and is parasitical on it for its own limited plausibility.[24]

All things selve, the poet Hopkins believed. But we selve through an interiorizing movement to self-presence. My purpose in this chapter has been to try to preserve this self-appropriation within the context of a positive middle that both sustains the difference of the human self and becoming, desire and otherness, while allowing the forging of their articulate affinity. What we find are two sources of open dialectical self-mediation. Becoming is self-mediating, in the sense of mediating through the differentiating process of positive othering the emergence of the human being as singularly a self. The human being too is self-mediating, in a manner explored in previous chapters and now seen in the more inclusive context of openness to otherness. On the side of both the self and the other, we must grant a positive sense of identity and difference. But this redoubling of identity and difference is very important. For this ineradicable pluralization cannot be understood in terms of dialectical self-mediation alone. The form of mediation between two terms, each of which is dialectically self-mediating, cannot be itself dialectical self-mediation, but requires the fuller form of metaxological intermediation. To this we now turn.

Chapter Five
Desire, Knowing, and Otherness

We must now develop in fuller detail the notion of a two-way mediation between desire and otherness. I propose to do this by focusing on the desire to know. This focus is determined by a number of considerations. First, the centrality of reflection on knowledge in philosophy hardly needs to be restated. Focusing on knowledge will allow a certain clarity with respect to the possible relations between self and otherness as explicitly defined by different traditional positions like idealism and realism. Second, our primary stress throughout on human desire, as the thread linking the episodes of our itinerary, does not exclude explicitly cognitive concerns. Indeed, our philosophical desire to understand desire is itself an instance of desire and knowing not being antithetical at all. Third, we may agree with Plato in the *Symposium* that desire, while obviously not confined to cognition, does flower into knowing, as the articulated self-conscious form of human eros. The desire to know spontaneously breaks forth in our being as the exigence to make sense of the density of being that may initially seem foreign and indifferent to us. This desire reveals itself as an imperative of our being that we can never entirely suppress. This is related to the process of awakening self-presence and opening to otherness that we have already discerned in desire. Finally, our focus on the desire to know not only captures this awakening to self-conscious articulation; it also serves, as it were, to render knowing itself dynamic. For the desire to know pertains to a complex active process, not a static product, a certain relating or becoming related of desire and actuality, in which the human self becomes both awakened to itself and vigilant to real otherness.

The discussion that follows is in three stages. First, I will consider the concepts of immediacy and mediation in relation to otherness and will argue for a crucial distinction between self-mediation and what I will term *intermediation*. This distinction is very important if we want to avoid any improper closure of knowing and to safeguard desire's continuing openness to otherness. In relation to this, I next will discuss Hegel's tendency to treat all mediation as self-mediation and some of the ambiguous results this has had in regard to dialectic. This leads to the final section, in which I will try to clarify the dialectical and metaxological approaches to otherness, arguing that the metaxological view more adequately preserves the two-way mediation of desire and concrete being and the irreducibility of the other.

IMMEDIACY, SELF-MEDIATION, AND INTERMEDIATION

We will first consider three key notions relevant to knowledge of otherness—namely, the notions of immediacy, self-mediation, and intermediation. Let us first take immediacy, for this is often deemed essential in any knowledge of otherness. For in immediate knowing, it is sometimes claimed, the mind becomes receptive in a simple passive way to reality other than the mind, and it does so without interfering with this other reality, with a consciousness purged of preconceptions and superimposed categories. Of course, there are different versions of this immediate knowing. For instance, the empiricist's stress on pure givenness to the senses and on primitive impressions provides us with a sensuous version of immediate knowing; whereas the Platonic emphasis on intellectual intuition, or *noēsis*, provides us with a more idealistic, supersensuous version. Either way, what is important and relevant here is that the passivity of the knower seems to safeguard the otherness of the known, which is not altered by the knowing relation and stands apart from the known in its irreducible difference.

This matter could easily be developed in many different directions,[1] but the main point would come to this. While we need not object to the genuine intention motivating a philosophical appeal to immediacy— namely, the wish to preserve the dimension of irreducible otherness and to insist that a sense of genuine difference be defended—such a defense of difference does not possess sufficient subtlety. I will return later to what is important in this intention, but here what matters is that the failure of immediacy to fulfill this intention arises from the tendency to think of otherness in terms of simple external difference. The inevitable outcome is a purely external dualism of the self and the other.

For immediate knowing tends to diminish, if not eliminate, the complex, internal self-differentiation of the knower in a way that makes it difficult to distinguish knowing consciousness from an undifferentiated aware-ness. Further, immediate knowing tends to fix the confronting other too rigidly. Thus, models of the mind as a tabula rasa, like Locke's blank page devoid of characters, seem to epitomize sheer openness to what is other to the mind. But because this openness is indifferent in itself, it diminishes the complexity of the active process that is required if the human self is to gain any perspective approximating genuine openness to the other as other. The only way such an indifferent openness might be effected is through a dominating other that would externally impress itself on our awareness. But for just this reason the self and the other would in no way be intimately implicated with each other, and their cognitive conjunction would be merely adventitious and extrinsic.

The deficiency of immediate knowing lies not only in fixating the other too rigidly, but also in an incomplete self-knowledge. For there is no immediate self-knowledge that excludes all mediation. Such a knowledge would be absolutely inarticulate and thus incompatible with all knowing as a form of articulated relation. Here we might be tempted to think of Narcissus as an image of immediate self-knowing. But the real point of the story is not that Narcissus knew himself when he fell in love with his own reflection. Because Narcissus lacked any genuine sense of the difference between self and other, his inability to recognize otherness is inseparable from the fact that he lacked any sense of self. Self and other merged immediately, but the result, of course, was the loss of both. There is a certain sense in which such narcissistic knowing does not differ essentially from the too strongly dualistic insistence on the difference between self and other that we find, for instance, in naive realism. Both stress immediacy, the first from the side of the self, the second from the side of the other. But because each has an insufficiently complex sense of the self and an impoverished sense of the other, nei-ther is capable of doing justice to the properly articulated balance be-tween the self and the other.

The narcissist is dominated by an unmediated, undeveloped sense of sameness, whereas the naive realist, in so far as he is strongly dualistic, has an unmediated, undeveloped sense of difference. Both cling to im-mediacy and exhibit its defect from different directions. The narcissist says "The world is an image of me, univocally the same as me." The naive realist advances the counterclaim "I am an image of the world, univocally the same as it." To the extent that narcissism and naive realism try to explain themselves in more reflective terms, they tend to give rise to inadequate forms of subjectivism and objectivism, respectively. For they lead to different reductions of the complex relation of knower and known. Thus an exclusive subjectivism (the reflective counterpart of immediate narcissism) leads to a dominance of self and fails to do justice to the recalcitrant difference of what is other. Alternatively, an exclusive objectivism (reflecting naive realism's sense of minimally mediated difference) furthers a forgetfulness of the self and literally loses its mind while claiming to give itself over to external things. It petrifies a difference into an opposition. Both these positions forfeit something essential. If we forsake the self, we also rid ourselves of the world, for we surrender any internal principle of discrimination. If we take flight from the world, we relinquish articulate selfhood, for then we collapse into formlessness without some degree of external definition.

Neither of these extremes can be reflectively maintained, for while claiming to be based on immediacy, they are in fact supported by something they expressly deny, namely, mediation. To the extent that knowing is an act of relating, it unavoidably implies mediation, whether understood from the side of the self or from that of the other. The point about knowledge of otherness, then, is not to get *behind* mediated self-knowledge to some inarticulate immediacy. If we delve into self-knowing, as we have done at some length in part 1, we do not discover an undifferentiated immediacy, but an immanent ground of differentiation, what we spoke of before in terms of original selfness and its participation in the articulating power of being. Knowledge of otherness demands that we remedy the incomplete self-knowledge of immediacy.

In this there is the possibility of both an advance and a risk. Here instead of insisting on primitive immediacy, we must concentrate on the mediated aspects of knowledge. We must grant the knower's active power, the knower's internal self-differentiation and efforts to differentiate the initially unappropriated tumult of existence in its otherness. Here our focus is on the second notion of self-mediation mentioned above. With this, we rescue the knower from an unduly passive receptivity and counter the opposing dominance of a merely confronting externality. Concrete being is not indifferently there. With self-mediation, we discover that nothing is articulately present to the knower unless the latter openly receives what is given—that is, unless the knower indirectly gives it to him or her self. The risk of this recourse to self-mediation, however, is that we are tempted to complete the incomplete self-knowledge of immediacy by turning the knower in upon himself in closed self-relation, in complete, seamless self-reflection. When this occurs, as it tends to in some post-Kantian forms of idealism, it is the self (as the active power) that is taken to prevail over the other (as nothing for the knower unless the latter opens him or her self). Then the self tends to assert its dominance while the other is assigned a subordinate role in its self-activity, and self-mediation per se tends to become ruler of the total realm of mediation, of which it also becomes in the end the sole subject.

This approach is pervasive in post-Kantian philosophy, due in significant measure to Kant's stress on the active, synthetic powers of the knowing subject. It would be wasted effort to try to summarize here any of its historical manifestations.[2] I will look briefly, in the next section, at how it is manifested in one aspect of Hegel's thought. Suffice it to say that what is important here is not to repudiate self-mediation or the intention of its advocates—namely, to preserve an appropriately rich sense of self-identity. The difficulty is that this preservation may sometimes come to lack proper discrimination. That is, the difficulty is not with self-mediation, but with closed self-mediation. The trouble with closed self-mediation is not unrelated to that with sheer immediacy: when self-mediation points to the need to complete the incomplete self-knowledge of immediacy, it too is sometimes determined by the implicit assumptions of immediacy. These assumptions tend to be dualistic. Where immediacy is tied to an external dualism, mitigated by the dominance of the other and by the submission of the passive self, self-mediation (at least when it succumbs to the temptation of closure) becomes yoked to the same dualism; only in this case we have a *reversed* order of independence and subservience, which seems to allow for the subsumption of all external difference within the knower's own active self-development. Neither of these dualisms is adequate, either to self-knowledge or to knowledge of otherness. The stress on immediacy tends to abridge self-knowledge and so inevitably mars knowledge of otherness. Closed self-mediation tends to a reductionist outcome with respect to knowledge of the other, an outcome that eventually truncates even proper self-knowing.

An improper stress on immediacy and self-mediation can sometimes, in fact, sound a retreat from real otherness. Thus, one way to escape the other is to short-circuit all reflective, mediated awareness by immersing ourselves again in the flow of immediate being. By obliterating all reflection, we collapse the gap inevitably opened by self-awareness. Alternatively, we might try to cut ourselves off from the other by elevating self-reflection into a closed system of abstractions. The first strategy excludes reflection from concreteness and tends to produce supposedly "realist" philosophies that glorify irrational immediacy. The second severs concreteness from reflection, leading to purportedly "idealistic" philosophies that dazzle the disembodied mind with unreal logical essences. The first gives us a concreteness, but at the cost of blind experience; the second gives us abstract thought that is emptied of concreteness.[3] But submersion in immediacy and severance from concreteness in abstracted self-mediation yield but a similar indifference to otherness; that is, neither gives us a sufficiently differentiated, discriminating understanding, one that both unites and distinguishes concrete being and thinking.

If *within* themselves the self and the other were rigidly self-identical, and if their respective univocal identities made them absolutely different, then *between* them no relation would be possible beyond absolute equivocation. However, all knowing, as a relating or becoming related of self and other, testifies to the reality of such a "between." Thus the relation of knowing is living witness to the insufficiency of the categories of univocity and equivocity for understanding the connectedness, yet difference, of self and other. Knowing testifies to a complex between. It must be granted that all knowing involves some form of mediation. But it does not follow that all mediation is exhausted by one single form thereof, namely, self-mediation. The issue of otherness does not come down to an exclusive choice between immediacy and self-mediation, or between the extraversion of the knower favored by the realist and the self-reflection of the mind elevated by the idealist. The real issue is whether mediation itself is a more complex affair than active self-mediation; whether all mediations can be defined by contrast with immediacy; whether, in fact, we find a plurality of possible forms within the concept of mediation itself. In this light, the form of mediation that is fully attentive to the other need not be identical either with immediacy or self-mediation. Yet each of these must be given its due. We need to grant the receptivity and openness to otherness that is at the heart of appeals to immediacy. We need to grant the requirement of self-activity found in self-mediation, without making this absolutely self-sufficient. We must now consider a further form of mediation—intermediation— and try to bring together these different requirements.

What do we mean here by intermediation? The emphasis is on the *inter,* the space of the in-between. Intermediation is not a relation in which the knower through his self-activity overreaches the other, thereby stamping his own shape on the knowing process as a whole and exclusively determining its outcome. Nor is intermediation a question of the other imprinting its configuration on the knower, constraining him externally and reducing the self to the minimal response of mute inarticulateness. These two alternatives are each premised on a single, dominating sense of identity and difference, the first ascribing it to the self, the second to the other. Intermediation, by contrast, is premised on a plural notion of identity and difference. Let us here recall and underline the crucial conclusion reached at the end of the last chapter. Let us recall that when we there considered external becoming in its otherness to desire, we dealt with something that was itself internally complex, that revealed itself through the intrinsic power of its own coming to be, and that this process of coming to be yielded a succession of identities, not least of which was the human self as a singular individual. Intermediation deals with otherness in this complex sense. Hence, it cannot be defined as an interaction between passivity and activity, but rather deals with the convergence on a middle space of a plurality of complex identities, each actively differentiated within itself.

In this middle space we have a plurality of centers of active being. Immediacy rightly grasps the convergence of the other on this middle space, but by congealing this other and pacifying the self, it goes against the grain of its own intent to affirm otherness. Self-mediation correctly recognizes the activity of the self but, in pacifying the other, inflates the self in an exaggerated way. Immediacy and closed self-mediation fail to allow both sides of the intermediation to flower out of themselves and so to meet in a middle that neither defines completely by itself and in which neither is completely determinative of the other. So also, intermediation is not the same as the symmetrical, mutual determination beloved especially by idealistic thinkers. Such mutual determination does not reflect a certain irreducible openness that we find in intermediation. It fits better with a dialectic of immediacy and self-mediation, passivity and activity, where the determining power of self and other are pitted against or, alternatively, call forth each other. Though there is a deep mutuality in intermediation between self and other, there is also a recognition of what might be termed a reciprocal asymmetry between them. By this I mean that, mediation notwithstanding, there remains an essential recalcitrance, not only to the self, but also to the other, which intermediation acknowledges and lets be. The asymmetry is reciprocal because each side recognizes the irreducibility of the other to itself.

We will return to this recalcitrance later. For now we will further compare self-mediation and intermediation. Between these two, there is both a similarity and a difference. Neither can be said to be inarticulate, yet their respective differentiated natures are not quite the same. In self-mediation, differentiation tends to take place within the appropriating activity of *one* self which, as it were, exits from its initial inarticulateness and subsequently returns articulately to itself with the gain of some self-consciousness and self-possession. In intermediation, however, differentiation is shaped by a *plurality* of participants—a genuine plurality, whose members cannot remain genuinely attentive to the other and yet allot the other a merely subsidiary status within their own self-mediation. Moreover, the sense of difference entailed by such a plurality is not just the covert self-differentiation of a single encompassing unity like the absorbing god. Suppose, for instance, we were to try to understand a plurality of distinct individuals, each of whom exhibits some measure of what we called original selfhood? What form of mediation would be appropriate between such individuals, sufficient to do justice to the intrinsic richness of their selfhood, to preserve their genuine difference, to prevent the degeneration of this difference into dualistic opposition?[4] Self-mediation cannot be sufficient, and this despite the fact—indeed, because of the fact—that each of these individuals might in itself be inherently self-mediating. Any adequate mediation between a plurality of individuals, each marked by the power of dialectical self-mediation, cannot be exhausted by dialectical self-mediation. For, with a plurality of such individuals, neither the externality of their rich singularity nor the association of their diverse manyness can be subsumed by any single absorbing unity.

Since intermediation tries to acknowledge the other in its irreducible difference, it cannot be defined by any notion of identity relative to which plurality plays a subordinate role. Intermediation does establish a bond between self and other; but this bond does not emerge from some metaphysical nostalgia for the obliteration of difference. It should be sufficiently clear by now that any such nostalgia is inevitably self-defeating, despite the fact that human desire has myriad ruses by means of which it seeks to give expression to such a yearning. Our desire for a bond with otherness is fundamental, of course, but this kind of nostalgia grows out of a perspective on difference that regards it as ultimately a privation of identity. To remedy this privation, self-mediation is always exposed to the temptation to seek a culminating, monistic totality. The sense of difference acknowledged by intermediation is not a dispersed multiplicity to be annulled by such a totality, however. Intermediation is grounded in the interplay of a positive plurality, and this interplay has the effect of constituting such a plurality as a certain *community of being*. Each identity is greeted in its difference; nor is their meeting encased in some further incorporating identity.

I do not want to suggest that self-mediation and intermediation are to be set in absolute opposition. There is, it must be granted, a genuine incompatibility between intermediation and any *closed* self-mediation, but this is not the case with self-mediation that preserves an appropriate openness. The character of this openness has already been sufficiently established in our discussion of part 1, particularly in connection with human wholeness as intermediate between sheer indefinite incompleteness and dogmatically fixed closure. The openness and intermediate nature of human wholeness is coherent with—indeed intersects—the middle space between self and other revealed in intermediation. We might say that in the mediation of all knowledge, the desire to know always produces a pluralized intentionality. Partaking of the dynamism of desire, the intention of knowing articulates itself in terms of a double directionality. The middle space of all mediation bears this twofold intention, which expresses itself, on the one hand, in the exigence for self-knowledge, and on the other hand, in genuine openness to otherness. Knowledge of the self and knowledge of the other are both defined at the fork of this twofold intention, and each in its different way always contains something of this forking within itself.[5] It is a question of which side of this tension is in the ascendant. In the case of knowing the other, there is a certain readiness for the manifestation of difference. This readiness is a mediated achievement, hence beyond simple immediacy. But it is sustained only in struggle with an inevitable drift of desire back to the self and desire's sometimes too importunate self-insistence. Self-mediation is essential to intermediation, for without the former, the latter would collapse into inarticulate immediacy. The desire to know, when directed toward otherness, is thwarted if, at the same time, it fails to conserve self-consciousness, the concomitant of self-mediation. This requirement is intrinsic to *any* knowing, since it involves nothing other than the knower's articulateness concerning the fulfillment or frustration of his epistemic intention. Without it, knowledge of otherness would be a loss of self-consciousness in the other.

But if self-mediation is necessary for articulateness, intermediation does not dissolve the double intention of desire into the single design of closed self-mediation. There is always a strain or tension between, as it were, self-exit and self-return. Intermediation must avoid both the loss of self in the other and the subsumption of the other in the self. A prerequisite for success here is that the self struggle with itself to become appropriately open to what is other, neither refusing to recognize real otherness, nor insisting on being overbearing with respect to it. Something can be the prerequisite of a relation without defining that relation domineeringly or being identical with the relation as a whole. In this sense self-mediation is a prerequisite of intermediation. Within the double directionality of intermediation, self-consciousness is preserved without being closed in upon itself. Intermediation is not immediate knowing; nor is it self-mediation, because it *knows that it knows another*. The knower is articulately self-conscious of its relation to what is beyond self. Intermediation unfolds within the context of a positive plurality and solicits something beyond self-reflection. But it does not thereby abandon the demand for self-knowledge; rather, it charges it with a more embracing openness within the fuller community of being.

HEGEL, IDENTITY, AND SELF-MEDIATION

It will be helpful here to make some brief remarks about Hegel's conception of the relation of the knower and the known, as developed in the *Phenomenology of Spirit*. Above, I mentioned the pervasive stress on self-mediation with respect to self-activity in post-Kantian philosophy, particularly in idealistic thought. My remarks here will serve as further clarification of this issue. The case of Hegel is particularly illuminating, since one of the chief controversial questions surrounding him concerns the relation of dialectical thinking and otherness. Hegel is an extraordinarily complex thinker, and his complexity is not always devoid of ambiguity. He claims that his dialectical thought preserves difference, and this intention is not at issue here. What is at issue is the kind of difference that his dialectic preserves and whether dialectical difference exhausts the concept of otherness. This is another way of asking if all forms of mediation turn out, in the end, to be self-mediation. I have been arguing that there is a form of mediation more complex than self-mediation, whereas Hegel tends to see mediation in terms of self-mediation. Hegel, like many idealists, has a very penetrating understanding of the original dynamism of knowing. Though knowledge of otherness presents difficulties for idealism, I believe, my purpose here is not simply to reject idealism in favor of a more naive realism or empiricism. We need to preserve the dynamic dialectic of self-knowledge that often forms the core of idealism. But we also need a more discriminating sense of otherness and a more sophisticated realism that is faithful to the full complexity of concrete being.

The goal of Hegel's *Phenomenology of Spirit* is insight into what knowing is.[6] This goal, Hegel argues, is not reached in immediate consciousness, for whatever we take as immediate turns out, on reflection, to be also mediated.[7] Thus the merely immediate cannot maintain itself on its own terms; in forgetting the contribution of mediation, it makes claims about itself that are the opposite of what it really intends.[8] What Hegel is doing here roughly corresponds to what we spoke of above as completing the incomplete self-knowledge of immediacy. Hegel sees mediation as providing our access to truth, and unlike some other thinkers, he does not greet it with "horrified rejection."[9] Within the vast panorama of the *Phenomenology*, Hegel examines an extensive series of relations between the knower and the known. The specific details of this series is not what is chiefly at issue here, but rather the fact that throughout the series something remains constant—namely, the *form* of mediation. This form is what interests us, since it specifies a definite relationship between identity and difference.

How does Hegel describe this mediation? "Mediation *(Vermittlung),*" he says, "is nothing but self-identity *(Sichselbstgleichheit)* working itself out through an active self-directed process; or, in other words, it is reflection into self, the aspect in which the ego *(Ich)* is for itself, objective to itself."[10] Elsewhere he says that "the living substance, further, is that being that is truly *Subject,* or, what is the same thing, is truly realized and actual solely in the process of positing itself *(Sichselbstsetzens)* or in mediating with its own self its transitions from one state or position to the opposite. As Subject it is the pure, *simple negativity,* and just on that account it is the sundering of the simple; or it is the process of duplicating *(Verdopplung)* and setting factors in opposition which [process] in turn is the negation of this indifferent diversity and of the opposition of factors it entails." Very significantly, he then goes on to say: "The true *(das Wahre)* is merely this process of *reinstating* self-identity, or reflecting into its own self in and from its other, and is not an *original* and primal unity as such, not an *immediate* unity as such. It is the process of its own becoming, the circle which presupposes its end as its purpose, and has its end for its beginning."[11]

In these highly significant quotations from Hegel we see the centrality of mediation, here understood as self-mediation. We also see how through self-mediation he endeavors to complete (captured pictorially in the image of the circle) the incomplete self-knowledge of immediacy.

Notice again how self-mediation is not radically different from immediacy; both are dialectically continuous—indeed, identical—in that self-mediation is the explication, the developed articulation, of what is already implicit, albeit as yet undeveloped, in immediacy. The end (attained in full self-mediation) is only the beginning again (immediacy), but now set forth in fully developed form. In self-mediation, the end rejoins the beginning, and the circle is closed.

I underline the importance for Hegel of the continuity of immediacy and self-mediation, for this continuity determines a resulting conception of difference or otherness that has far-reaching repercussions, particularly with respect to the issue of whether self-mediation is to remain radically open or become closed in on itself. For Hegel, immediate consciousness is shot through with a difference between the subject and the object, in that immediate consciousness takes its true object to be a reality other than itself. Now Hegel tends to understand this difference as a dualism, as a yet-to-be-mediated opposition. He then attempts to bridge this dualism by adverting to the self-consciousness that is presupposed by consciousness of an other. For self-consciousness, Hegel holds, is such that the object of the subject is the subject himself objectified. That is, self-consciousness can span the two sides of self and other, thereby interiorizing their difference and establishing their dialectical identity. A crucial consequence of this for Hegel is that the difference of the other becomes the *internal* self-distinction of experience; what consciousness takes to be a dissimilarity between ego and object is really their inner distinction.[12] The upshot is that the negative of difference that consciousness at first takes to be outside itself proves to be really due to consciousness itself and its activity.[13] In a word, self-mediation seems to encompass the self and the other, and all differences are caught up in its self-contained circle.

What is at stake here in this very abbreviated presentation of Hegel? Hegel's positive insight is that articulateness and differentiation presuppose self-consciousness; on the positive side too is his insistence on some sense of the other. Yet he tends to let the prerequisite of self-mediation dominate the whole—indeed, in certain respects, be the whole—in a manner that belies a certain notion of the other. From the outset, otherness tends to be defined negatively: it is the dualistic other of immediate consciousness, in relation to which Hegel proceeds through a dialectic of immediacy and self-mediation. In this dialectic the other essential to consciousness is progressively incorporated within the identity of self-consciousness. Since, from the outset, otherness is tainted with the negative possibilities of dualism, Hegel does not seem to entertain a radically affirmative sense of otherness. Consequently the end he seeks is to subordinate otherness to a subsuming unity. He does not seem to develop an intermediation that goes beyond immediacy, self-mediation, and their dialectic.

Here, in relation to Hegel's thought, let us try to restate the distinction between intermediation and self-mediation. In the first, we are dealing with a plurality of identities, each of which is different and one of which is the knower as internally differentiated. In the second, there tends to be but the single identity of the knower, with the negative duality of the other subordinated to the self's interiorized difference. Since Hegel's mediation articulates the process of self-identity by progressively making the other internal to self-consciousness, an equation is forged between recognition of the other and self-recognition. But ultimately what is being recognized tends to be the self, albeit in many different guises. By contrast, the pluralized identity and difference of intermediation cannot be defined by the singular identity and difference of self-mediation. For there is a difference in intermediation which is not the internal difference of its participants, but arises in the middle ground where these participants are both individuated and bound together. What is other in intermediation is not the mediating self objectified. Hegel has a tendency to blur distinctions among a number of senses of difference, speaking of them all as ultimately self-differentiation. The result is an underplaying of a more pluralized sense of identity and difference, which would prevent the collapse of intermediation into self-mediation.

It is because of this, perhaps, that there arises the suspicion of Hegel's antagonists that his Absolute is finally an absorbing god, an absolute totality wherein sameness has an undue dominance over otherness. I do not want to underestimate Hegel's insistence that he aims to preserve difference—as, for instance, in his criticism of Spinoza's Substance or Schelling's Indifferenzpunkt. Yet he undoubtedly seeks an integrating unity of opposites that mitigates and subordinates otherness.[14] He is extremely elusive, but it is difficult to completely shake the suspicion that he does not clearly enough distance himself from an absorbing god. Not surprisingly, Hegel's own disclaimers notwithstanding, some of his adversaries have felt that his Absolute is reminiscent of Spinoza's Substance, but now, after Kant's transcendental turn, made into Subject.

Thus, once again we come across an encompassing unity that interiorizes the immanent self-differentiation of self-mediation and completely defines itself in the process.

If, however, there is more than one self-mediating center of being, then the mediation between the members of such a plurality cannot be self-mediation once again and still do full justice to the inherent intricacy of these members and their interplay. As long as we think of the other exclusively in terms of immediacy and self-mediation, its difference can very easily become just an adverse antithetical reality. We are then tempted to seek to overcome its seeming opposition. As a result and at worst, we are disjoined on a dualism. At best, we may seek, like Hegel, to unify opposites. But although this effort is certainly positive, the question is, is it positive enough? Is it positive enough to do justice to irreducible difference?

A self-mediating process that unifies opposites does not completely exhaust intermediation, for the latter can be said to seek not just a unity of opposites, but rather, and more properly, the community of plurality. It may be, of course, that profound thinkers like Hegel, though sometimes tempted by language like that of the *coincidentia oppositorum* (as, for instance, in Hegel's famous definition of the Absolute in terms of the identity of identity and difference), really intended something more like the community of plurality, and that a generous hermeneutic will be able to grant the significant proximity of the dialectical and metaxological approaches to the mediation of otherness. And it is certainly true that one is never absolutely sure that one has done justice to the richness of thinkers like Hegel.[15] Be that as it may, the idealist, like the immediate realist he contends with, is tempted to assign to difference a sense of opposition and then to claim to reconcile this opposition in some more ultimate unity. This approach has an obvious cogency if difference is the same as opposition, but this is not always the case. For a community of plurality may mediate difference, but it need not subordinate otherness. The intermediation it may accomplish can reach out to, can really reach the other, yet in all this, it need not overreach the other.

For the goal of human desire need not be to attain identity with self alone, but rather to attain an individual place within the space of the rich plurality that makes up the community of being. There, the other is not the self's own otherness, nor is it there simply to be owned. Neither disowned nor possessed, it may pose the challenge of an unencompassed alienness. There is a certain paradox here in that we are asked to be at home with the alien. Thus the form that intermediation gives experience is not that of an enclosure within which self and other are distinguished merely internally. A real external recalcitrance continues to exist, and not because this has *yet* to be included and enclosed. From within the experience of intermediation we acknowledge what is not encompassed, what rather bounds and embraces experience. Within self-experience there is one negative, but in desire's openness to otherness we meet another negative, which brings home to experience a different limit. When we face it, the vanity of any will to encompass the other is brought to light.

Let us conclude this all too brief consideration of Hegel with one final remark. Hegel's response to difference might be seen in terms of the distinction (which he took from his predecessors, especially Kant) between understanding *(Verstand)* and Reason *(Vernunft)*. Understanding tends toward external analysis, and Hegel criticizes this for *dividing* being and thinking, dissecting them within and holding them insuperably apart. In response, he cites both the negative and the positive power of dialectical reason. Dialectical reason is negative in dissolving the fixed opposition between being and thinking set up by analytical understanding; it is positive in affirming a deeper unity between these opposites. In the latter respect dialectical thought becomes speculative reason, wherein we find the synthetic function of Vernunft through which is constituted the unity of divided multiplicity.[16] The difficulty here is this. Analytical understanding subordinates unity to difference, which, in turn, easily becomes dualism, dispersion, and dissolution. To counterbalance this, Hegel is sometimes tempted to subordinate difference to unity. Yet he risks taking his cue from the analytical understanding's concept of difference. Because this concept can lead to dualism, opposition, and exclusion between knower and known, it might be regarded as a degenerate form of difference. Hegel correctly seeks to transcend this form of difference, but in the process runs the risk of identifying difference as such with dualistic opposition, something to be subsumed into a further unity. The question here, then, is whether there is a positive form of difference that could match Hegel's positive unity, one that is not secondary because it is equally primordial and rich.

If there is such a positive difference, we may agree with Hegel that it is not to be gained by reaching back *behind* the unity of reason and the distinctions of analytical understanding toward some primitive sensuous immediacy. Yet, in contrast to Hegel, the desire to know seems to go *beyond* the interplay of sensuous immediacy and understanding and their sublation into dialectical reason. If, first, we speak of sensuous immediacy as the univocal relation between thinking and being; if, second, we speak of the dividing, analytical understanding as the equivocal relation of being and thinking; and if, third, we think of Hegelian reason as their dialectical relation; then desire's openness to otherness demands that we add a fourth possibility, what we have called the metaxological relation. For this acknowledges the truth of dialectic relative to identity but explicates more subtly the nuances of difference.

THE DIALECTICAL AND THE METAXOLOGICAL RELATIONS

I now want to bring these reflections together in terms of the contrast between the dialectical and the metaxological. I need not remind the reader that there is no question of excluding the dialectical or diminishing its importance. The problem is to avoid incorrect closure. A more fundamental mediation between desire and otherness is to be sought beyond dialectical self-mediation. While averting closure, nevertheless, we need not deny the importance of concrete wholeness. In its dialectical self-mediation, human desire can strive to subsume within itself the dissolving difference of equivocity and the coagulated identity of univocity. As original selves, we can be dynamic ends within ourselves and yet be perpetually attentive to the other. The metaxological names the significance of this attentiveness in a way that goes beyond self-mediation. But such a standpoint does not entail a lack of wholeness. It tries to name the mediation between a plurality of wholes.

First consider very generally how dialectic takes shape. Dialectic responds to difficulties that arise when the identity of univocity splits apart and we are confronted with the dispersed dyad of equivocity. Hence it is a response to a lack, a deficiency—namely, the absence of articulate wholeness and centered difference. This defect or lack cannot be overcome simply by sticking to the terms that defined it initially—namely, univocal identity and equivocal difference. Such identity must be developed and such difference appropriated. The process of desire witnesses this development and appropriation. The appropriation involves both openness and comprehension, and this reveals what a dialectical relation entails: it is a relationship of inclusion in which opposites are transcended and encompassed in a more comprehensive unity. This is impossible without an acknowledgment of opposition and contradiction, of course; yet such an acknowledgment takes us beyond unmediated difference and inarticulate unity. Dialectic, then, arises in response to a lack of articulate identity, proceeds to master this lack via its ascendancy over dispersed difference, and aims at a unity that includes what it transcends.

What presents itself to desire at this point is the possibility of *an* end but not *the* end, a possible whole but not *the* whole. Put in less abstract terms, we can know ourselves as ends in ourselves without mistaking ourselves for the unsurpassable end of all; we can think of ourselves as possible wholes without confusing ourselves with *the* whole; we may discover an absolute dimension to our beings without regarding ourselves as *the* absolute. Granted, this is tricky and ambiguous. But let me mention two significant courses that would seem to be available to us. On the one hand, we might mistakenly think that we are at the end and perhaps, to sustain the feeling of openness, seek to perpetually relive the dialectical interplay between the univocal and the equivocal.[17] On the other, we may realize that only now is it possible to begin in a truly positive sense, for only now is concrete wholeness, in some measure, operative in and already constitutive of our being. In the first case, we put the emphasis one-sidedly on unity and identity so that difference, opposition, and dualism are alleged to be completely behind us, in the sense of being subordinated and subsumed. In the second case, however, although a secondary, negative sense of difference may be behind us, before us, as yet unappropriated and perhaps never to be appropriated, is the possibility of positive difference: positive difference that matches the positive beginning disclosed in the now operative presence of wholeness.

In the first case, dialectic risks closing in on the One differentiating itself and courts something not unlike an absorbing god. In the second, dialectic opens to the other in a different sense; it ceases to be self-mediation pure and simple, because the plurality before it is composed of members, each of which is internally complex. And though the dialectical knower must move outside himself, the middle into which he enters is peopled by others not available as function of subsumption; self and other are both self-othering. If there is an appropriation here, it involves openness, comprehension, and further openness, and not, as in the first case, openness, comprehension, and subsumption. Equivocity adds a dyad to simple unity, but dialectic adds a further third: it adverts to the internal complexity of one of the terms of the dyad (in this case the knower), which allows it to seek to appropriate the other. Dialectic fully open to the other, however, must add a fourth to this third: for if both terms of the dyad are marked by the power of internal differentiation, not merely one of them, then the middle of their interplay cannot be subsumed by dialectical self-mediation, a third. It demands the fourth of intermediation, the metaxological middle. And this fourth, although neither simple unity nor divided difference, cannot be exhausted by the idea of dialectical inclusion.

Let me put the matter in terms of a number of philosophical metaphors drawn from the history of philosophy. Dialectic, as it were, releases the dense sphere of Parmenidean being from its immobility and homogeneity, impregnating it with the self-relating power of internal differentiation. Yet it restrains any Heraclitean flux from whirling away into loose multiplicity and dispersing itself in ungathered difference. It achieves a Hegelian unity of oneness and manyness. But this is only one side of the complexity of being, one that points us toward positive unity and away from inert identity and confused difference. Another side of the complexity of being points us toward positive difference. Here dialectic *(dialegein)* must be understood in a manner consonant with its etymological meaning of "to talk," "to converse," "to communicate." No one will deny that to be conversant with what is involves talk, and that this talk obviously exhibits univocity, equivocity, and dialectic. But talk at its richest fights against the tyranny of any of these. Talk, dialectic in this sense, is a metaxology, again in the etymological sense of a logos of the metaxu: a discourse of and in the middle, standing in, regarding, but not effacing, difference.

As Aristotle reminds us, there is not just one, and only one, dialect of being. And any dialect, any language, always leaves a gap between communicants, an interval not only wherein it must leave off in silence, but one that itself points to the ground of communication. Otherwise such talk would degenerate into interminable chatter. In this second respect, we find a transmutation of the dialectical into the metaxological; and in a manner analogous to the way in which the Platonic dialogue, consenting to the identity of its participants, is always mindful of the drama of their difference, never closing this off, even when it in some measure comprehends it. The metaphor of the Platonic dialogue is especially instructive with respect to the metaxological. For Plato understood eros as both a drive to self-fulfillment and an arrow to the beyond. Plato also understood human eros in metaphysical terms, and the *Symposium* situates the proper activation of eros within what is explicitly called the metaxu. The Platonic dialogue itself, in its intermediated balance of self and other, might be seen as articulating the field of the metaxu, wherein the dynamic eros of human knowing is energized, without in any way closing off its fundamental receptivity to otherness.[18]

Thus the sense of difference required by the metaxological relation is not dualistic opposition, but positive plurality. This, of course, is conditional upon difference of identity. But if different identities are already rich centers of originative existence (like participants in a Platonic dialogue), they are not, relative to themselves, catatonically alone; nor, relative to others, need they be estranged. On the contrary, original identity gains its fullest expansion in its concourse and kinship with an other original existence. Were its members not akin in being original in themselves, a plurality would be nothing but an adventitious collection. The metaxological relation, by contrast, constitutes a community of being that is formed in the interstices and interplays between a plurality of originals. This community cannot be included within any one final whole, because its composition is framed by the difference and identity of more than one whole. It is not defined by a dialectical self-mediation between one original and its images, but by the space between different dialectical originals, a space that is not dialectical in the first sense alone. The balanced equilibrium here between identity and difference neither declines into the univocal or the equivocal, nor does it spiral into the dialectical, if this is taken to imply a circumscription of otherness.

What are the consequences of this view in relation to knowledge of otherness? A fuller consideration of the consequences will be our concern in the next chapter, but we may conclude this chapter with these remarks. The desire to know, in its openness to otherness, finds its full activation in the community of originals just mentioned. But such a community reveals a certain primordial affinity between the self and the other. So the question of otherness does not involve connecting extrinsically a self-contained subject and a subsistent object. It is rather a case of understanding the significance of a difference and a bond that are already there. Otherness is not known by a monadic self that, out of its self-sufficient solitude, bridges an external dualism between itself and the rest of being. Desire reveals its directedness to being, for its self-development occurs always within the community of being composed by the plurality of originals. Desire is an openness to being, because originally it is in metaxological affinity with the other. In this respect, human desire is always beyond itself, both driven by its own internal dynamism and drawn out of itself by its relation to otherness. What we saw earlier as the double nature of desire (as both seeking to fulfill itself and reaching out to being beyond itself) may now be seen as grounded in the irreducible plurality of the metaxological. Desire is an implicit kinship with the other. From the start, the call of the other sounds within the self-development of desire. Desire is defined in community with otherness. Our express recognition of the other brings this community to consciousness.

This also means that the other cannot be defined as simply what is posited by the self and for the self, as often happens in idealistic thought. We may relate positively to the other, for it is there for us. But we may do this, not because the other is simply there for us, but rather, because it is for us to assent to our difference from, yet our bond with, it. The thereness of the other is neither an immediate thereness nor yet a singularly self-mediated thereness, but rather a metaxological thereness. No doubt, our sense of this thereness may remain undeveloped. But, whether we acknowledge it or not, this thereness grounds the community of self and other, manifesting their participation, as a plurality of originals, in the primordial power of being. Our knowing of otherness thus involves a certain restoration of concreteness: the original thereness of being that was present all along but perhaps not acknowledged or affirmed in any articulated way. The concept of the metaxological is an effort to name this thereness of being. Thus, though our knowledge of the other may involve a sophisticated, developed articulation, there is also a return to something quite elemental. This might seem to be something like a second immediacy, though strictly speaking there is no pure immediacy. But knowing the other calls rather for a release, not from mediation per se, but from distorting mediations, mediations that clog the spaces between us and the other. In fact, such clogging "mediations" should not be called mediations at all, for any genuine mediation must make possible real communication across the spaces of difference. But let us now look further at this thereness and at the metaphysical sense of concreteness that it reveals.

Chapter Six
Desire, Concreteness, and Being

DESIRE AND THE IDENTIFICATION OF OTHERNESS

It may be helpful here to recall the overall purpose of our argument in part 2. First, we should remember that in the self's quest for immanent wholeness (the focus of part 1), desire inescapably faced toward otherness, and as we saw in chapter 4, it did so not in any casual way, but with the intention of discerning some sense of the absolute or the unconditioned with respect to transcendence. In chapter 4 we considered desire's relation to otherness and unconditional transcendence in terms of static eternity and the difficulties connected therewith. We considered why we need to understand external becoming in a less negative, less dualistic light, in terms of a two-way mediation between desire and otherness. In the last chapter, we developed this two-way mediation more fully. Now we must develop this intermediation even further, with respect to the sense of concreteness that has emerged. This will then enable us to approach the question of the unconditional more adequately than we could in chapter 4. In this chapter I will develop the sense of being, or metaxological thereness, spoken of at the end of the last chapter.

I will outline a movement of the desire to know through a series of progressively richer identifications of otherness. Here the desire to know will be understood, in accordance with the concept of intermediation previously developed, as manifesting an ideal power capable of the identification of difference. When I speak of the identification of difference, I imply no subordination of the difference of the other to the identity of the self. To identify the other—that is, to name the irreducible difference of the other—may require one to identify with the other in some measure. This is perhaps implied by the community of being revealed by metaxological intermediation. But to identify with the other is not the same as to be identical with the other. The difference remains as a difference.[1] To identify the difference of the other, to name being as beyond incorporation in closed self-mediation, involves recognition, not subordination, of the other.

One way in which we are commonly misled here is by treating the desire to know as we treat the desire for food—as issuing in some kind of ingestion and consumption of the other. The desire to know reveals the concrete ideality of the human being (see chapter 2). This ideality allows one to know the other, and this knowing includes both the intentional identification of the other's difference, and at the same time a letting be of the other in its otherness. The desire to know may attain an original identification of difference, thereby mediating an emergence into articulateness of our affinity with the other. As such, it displays the original power to open itself to what is different in such a way that it comes to affirm that the other is and to achieve some identification of its being. Hence the desire to know is a principle of both real receptivity and articulating activity. It is an active openness that is beyond the extremes of passive voyeurism and self-absorbed self-activity. It thus allows for a release of the self toward the density of being in its rich otherness. It may even enter into a more ultimate submission to what is beyond the self, insofar as its release toward the other is not its consumption of the other, but its love of it.

This progressive identification of otherness, this release toward concreteness, may be explicated by means of the categories of the univocal, the equivocal, the dialectical, and the metaxological. Such categories are not to be seen here as merely subjective concepts, however. Rather, they serve to reveal the internal complexity of the self and the other, both in their respective realities and their mediated interplay. That is, relative to these four possibilities, we may speak of both a mode of identification on the part of the self and a degree of concreteness on the part of the other. Desire reaches out to being other than itself, but in so doing, it becomes increasingly articulated within itself, even as it comes to a more penetrating appreciation of the internal complexity of the other. Its relation to the other takes the form of a different mode of identification, corresponding to these four possibilities, just as, correlatively, the emergent complexity of the concrete may itself be interpreted in terms of these possibilities.

Before looking at the four, let me add that I am sensitive to the fact that my account may be too brief to do justice to all the necessary intricacies. However, I must confine my discussion within the limits dictated by the overall intentions of this essay. I am also sensitive to the possibility that I may seem to be superimposing a schema on the matter ab extra. I do not believe that this is so, though undoubtedly simplifications may creep in. I am trying to sketch a complex emergence, not trying to impose a categorial blueprint on being. My wish is to try to name philosophically what is there, not to pass off conceptual abstractions for concrete being. In fact, as we shall see, there is no absolute categorial schema that can encapsulate the otherness of being and the radical limit that human desire ultimately faces. By now, of course, the reader will be well aware that the above four possibilities constitute something of the essential categorial core of this essay. I will try to indicate that the four modes of identification and degrees of concreteness are not abstractions spun out of nothing, but are consonant with a typology of many of the principal traditional philosophical positions, and hence genuinely helpful in probing the issues in question.

UNIVOCAL PARTICULARITY AND EQUIVOCAL PREDICATION

Suppose, then, we ask what is there as the being of a thing. On a first, least complex level, we might immediately simply identify the thing by locating it in its bare particularity, as nominalists tend to do. We might call this simple denomination the univocal identification of particularity. For it is barely distinguishable from a mute gesture and is thus minimally articulate. We point to the thing, that thing, meaning to designate by our pointing nothing more than a circumscribed entity, as in certain doctrines of so-called ostensive definition. The "thatness" of the thing just is; it is marked by an inert, rigid self-sameness and so is itself minimally articulated. Thus the thatness of the particular thing is here considered to be univocal, to have one sense only, as when Butler speaks of a thing as simply being itself and not anything other. Something of this approach is undoubtedly at work in the effort to fix our reference to things. Yet this fixing can also cause a false freezing of our identification, so that we lose sight of the dynamism of relating that is involved in identification. It can also cause a falsifying congealing of any dynamic power that the thing itself may exhibit.[2]

Still, especially when seen in a broader perspective, a significant advance has occurred here, regardless of the minimal articulateness that marks this stage. For when any "vocality" or articulateness comes to light, though it be simply univocal, we are incipiently in a highly complex world of communicability—indeed, in the world itself as a community of being. The thing in its univocal thatness is not nothing. It is. Thus it stands outside sheer nothingness. When we speak of a thing simply in terms of the fact that it is, when we identify it as ex-isting, we have some first intimation of it as standing out *(exsistere)* in being, beyond absolute nothingness. So too, this univocal unity of a thing is a fuller articulation of the power of being than would be a bare undifferentiated continuum of amorphous matter, what the ancients hypothetically called prime matter *(protē hulē)*. In the world there is an eruption of initial differentiation ("That!"), which is mirrored in the eruption of our identification ("There!"). Think here of the child's "There!" which explodes the primitive undifferentiation of James's "booming and buzzing confusion." There can be a kind of joyous yes in that "There!" uttered in rapport to the sense of a cosmos emerging from out of the initial foreignness of otherness.

On a further, more complex level, we recognize that there is more than one material particular. There may seem to be an infinite plurality of such seemingly atomic unities. The sense of such manyness inevitably pluralizes our initial univocal identification into the assertion of a possibly unlimited sequence of "thats": that, that, that, . . . *ad infinitum*. I will return to such an infinite succession in the next chapter. Here we will restrict ourselves to one thing intensively, rather than deal with an infinity of things extensively. The particular thing itself calls for and sustains a more probing attention. On deeper acquaintance, the particular thing, far from exhausting itself in being a bare univocal that, may manifest a possibly unlimited sequence of properties or attributes. To identify such a thing and the possibilities of its concreteness requires that we enumerate the sequence of its *differentiae*, which it presents to our attention from a multiplicity of different perspectives. The thing in its otherness might be said to be potentially infinite in this sense: that it might require an infinite sequence of attributes to match the manifold of aspects it might present to a multiplicity of perspectives; for it can be seen as a, as b, as c, . . . ad infinitum.

I am not saying that in practice we make this potentially infinite analysis in a single act of perceiving a particular. But we might try to make it, even though in actual fact we abbreviate the probe of our attention and often satisfy ourselves with an identification that circumscribes, hence limits, the manifold properties of a thing. At this second level, we do not leave the univocal behind entirely; and each property is often thought of as itself univocal, like the immediately particularized thing. We find this tendency in the empiricist philosopher who inhabits a world similar to that of the nominalist; for the thing is first seen as a discrete unit, and its properties are also first viewed as discrete sense-data.[3] But this raises the crucial question. Can a potentially unlimited sequence of properties, each of which is particularized and univocal, allow of anything more than an extrinsic connection? Can this do justice to the otherness of the thing in its fullest thereness? If the properties of a thing are radically discrete, their connection will be adventitious, and it will be impossible to see them as emerging out of the intrinsic unity of the thing itself. If they are genuine properties—that is, proper, appropriate attributes—then they must be bound more intimately to the thing itself and, through it, to each other. Think here of the way in which classical empiricism first seems to soundly stabilize the particular thing for our sensory perception and of how it then seems to offer a clear-cut differentiation of the discrete sensory data of the thing. Yet, as we know from the history of classical empiricism, it ends up with deeper perplexities about such data and, in the extreme, dissolves entirely the stabilized being of the particular thing, as Berkeley does with respect to the material thing, and Hume with respect to the self understood as an inward particular.

This risk of decomposing the particular is related to the potentially unlimited sequence of properties mentioned above. How do we prevent, at the level of the univocal, this sequence from being open-ended in a sheerly indefinite way? We do not seem to be able to reach a term that exhausts a thing's manifold aspects, and so we risk losing the immediate definiteness and unity of the first degree of concreteness. An indefinitely unlimited sequence of properties seems to disperse the univocal unity of the thing. So we are forced to ask whether this interminable univocal predication can any longer suffice. Can it do justice to either the thereness of being or even the complex unity of a thing?

Below I will indicate why being cannot be a predicate in the above sense. As regards the unity of a thing, we might venture that any univocal predicate, if dwelt with long enough, might generate its own infinite variety of aspects. Thus the original atom of univocal unity might be dissolved into an infinite kaleidoscope, in which there might be an infinity of infinite kaleidoscopes, and so on, like a mocking hall of mirrors without end or exit. In this manner the univocal unity of the thing seems to dissolve into an immediately rich, but totally unmediated, multiplicity of properties, or differentiae. To try to lay hold of this dissolute manifoldness, the second mode of identification tends to become equivocal. In this mode, the thing itself becomes equivocal, for it appears to be a potentially unlimited series of attributes without intrinsic connection. Thus, we assert univocally about it now this, now that, only to find that the different assertions together often lead to contradictory or opposing characteristics. Unfortunately, I cannot follow the analysis further here. But, for a classical example of what tends to happen in this situation, I refer the reader to Hegel's analysis of perception in the *Phenomenology of Spirit*. This is an anatomy of bewilderment regarding the mind's desire to synthesize the unity and the plurality of a thing that remains at a level dominated by what we are calling the univocal and the equivocal.[4]

DIALECTICAL COMPREHENSION AND FORM

We must now proceed to a third level of consideration. For in defining the concreteness of a thing we need not be confined to either univocal identification of particularity (the first level) or equivocal enumeration of attributes (the second level). Instead of dissolving into an indefinite multiplicity of properties, each indifferently equal in status, the thing may suggest that it is marked by some essential properties. Its unity seems to be more than bare thatness, its differentiation marked by more than indifferent attribution. That is, its identity and manifoldness indicate a more essential, less accidental wholeness. The thing may be internally differentiated into the essential and the accidental. Correlatively, the knower must discriminate between what is to be included and what excluded from a definition of what makes the thing to be what it is, as, say, in Aristotle's notion of *to ti ēn einai*.[5]

Here the thing may appear as informed by an identity that appropriates the seemingly unconnected manyness of its manifest properties. What is this identity or unity? The empiricist tends to see it as derivative—that is, as a subsequent unity that we build up from a concatenation or cluster of essential properties. This empiricist unity is thus a posterior unity of aggregation. But though such a collage-like conjunction of properties is more richly concrete than univocal particularity and more integrated than equivocal distinction, there is a prior form of wholeness that is even more fundamental, a wholeness inherent in the thing itself and not just the result of our aggregating activity. For properties may be said to manifest the inherent self-differentiation of the thing itself, thereby also defining its difference from other things. They may present the thing as a self-mediating phenomenon, not only in terms of the derived unity of aggregated attributes, but also in terms of the prior unity of immanent essence.[6]

Here the thing is not seen just as a unit of bare particularity; it is also seen to be essentially articulated. Its essence is to be articulated within itself, to be gathered together in the form of a whole that is prior to its parts. This prior whole is not the sum of its attributes, but is rather the formal intelligibility that relates the parts in an integrated pattern. Indeed, it is what makes aggregation itself possible. So too, to the extent that this wholeness is immanent in a particular attribute, it makes that property an essential property. On this, the third, degree of concreteness, the unity of the thing is self-mediating and self-differentiating, expressing its characteristic essence in what is proper to it, holding itself together as a whole in its differentiating appearances. The whole makes the parts intelligible, just as the parts make the whole articulated. We might say that the whole is in the parts in a manner reminiscent of the way the whole person may sometimes appear in the eyes. The eyes are said to be the windows of the soul. Things, too, have, as it were, like sleeping selves, their sightless eyes.

For the thing presents itself and distributes its qualitative wholeness immanently throughout its parts. It does this because its self-mediation is dynamic. The qualitative form of a thing is not something static, but something that emerges from the self-shaping of its own power of activity. Form is dynamic. Now dynamic form in this sense defines what we are calling the third degree of concreteness. For this third degree is actively more inclusive than bare particularity and merely extrinsic, external attribution. Of course, we might be tempted here to rigidify form and make it inflexibly determinate, a danger that is present perhaps in the Platonic notion of eidos. Or we may try to particularize form and reduce it to the first degree of concreteness, as empiricism and nominalism tend to do. But this unity of dynamic form is more rich, not less, than the bare unity of particularity. Similarly, its immanent difference is not reducible to the second degree of concreteness. The difference here is one of self-differentiation, such that form is actively held together by the unity of forming power that is its source. In a word, dynamic form is a more or less determinate immanent structure that the original power of a process of coming to be assumes and crystallizes in a definite, particular embodiment.[7]

At this third level we begin to see how our understanding of a thing can place us in a dynamic world of genesis, which brings to mind the view (introduced in chapter 4) of the world of external becoming as a process of positive othering. At this third level, too, the knower must open more fully to the complex concreteness of the thing, and like the otherness of the concrete, must also become self-mediating and self-differentiating. The knower must become a dynamic unity that can immanently appropriate an otherwise unconnected manyness. The knower requires dialectical mediation, beyond univocal identity and equivocal difference. Hence we might speak of the third mode of identification of concreteness as the dialectical comprehension of form.

What is implied by this? It implies that the knower (like Aristotle's *nous poiētikos* perhaps, which is said to be capable of becoming all things),[8] must be seen as a concrete ideality marked by an indeterminate openness to otherness and so capable of assuming in the ideal order the same dynamic form that in the real order is inherent in the thing itself. Knowing as such an ideal power of openness can penetrate, as Hegel tells us,[9] to the initially hidden essence of the thing. In dialectical comprehension the indeterminate power of knowing ideally appropriates and interiorizes dynamic form. Thus, on the one hand, it tries to give an account of the unity of the thing without falling into an exclusive either/or between the thing's identity and difference. On the other hand, dialectical comprehension tries to pierce the thing's supposed equivocalness and grasp both the unified manifoldness and the self-differentiating unity that the thing makes present in its otherness.

This ideal power of the mind to be an unreserved openness to otherness is one of the chief philosophical enigmas. And, of course, this protean indeterminacy may assume many different guises. Much of our previous discussion of original selfhood related to this enigmatic indeterminacy, at once an active power and a receptive openness. Here we must confine ourselves to what is perhaps the chief difficulty at this third degree of concreteness. It is the temptation to think that we have now exhausted all the possibilities of being. The very wealth available here may make us vulnerable to a peculiar impoverishment. For the mediated convergence of knower and known that takes place at the third degree of concreteness and the power of the knower to ideally interiorize the form of the known might suggest that formal wholeness constitutes a completed totality beyond which there is nothing else at all.

Then we invite a double contraction that is untrue both to the concrete thing and to the deeper reaches of man's openness. With respect to the thing, the danger is that existence is circumscribed by essence and essence is thought to be more metaphysically ultimate than existence, while existence itself becomes narrowed to the less rich concreteness of the first and second degrees. With respect to the knower, the danger is that the idea is taken to dominate the being of the thing, and knowing becomes a logical dance of bloodless essences, an unreal whirligig of categorial shadows. Essence is separated from existence, the ideal from the real, and we allow a "purified" version of ideal essence to entice us away from the bewildering complexity of real being. Then, in a dialectic that is ontologically deracinated, abstract form calls out to abstract form; severed from the sap of being, such shadows intermingle, with only the void as a supporting medium. For, if we inappropriately separate "pure" essence and identify its domain with the full totality of being, then we may end up inverting being into nothing and forfeiting the full concreteness to which we came so close. These are dangers to which idealistic philosophies are particularly prone, dangers that have been noted throughout the tradition of philosophy, right down to contemporary thought.[10]

THE METAXOLOGICAL AFFIRMATION OF BEING

The question to be asked here is whether the original power of being revealed in dynamic form is exhausted by the process of transition from form to form. It is possible to conceive of this process of transition in terms of either the interplay of the knower and the known or the immanent procession of forms that make up the phases of development of a thing or the sequence of logical categories that make up a dialectical process of thought.[11] But does form, however conceived, direct us to a more primordial dynamism? It is in response to this question that the fourth degree of concreteness comes into play, for here we encounter a sense of being in all its plenitude beyond form.

We must return here to the thing as self-mediating and consider precisely why its form of wholeness is dynamic. The suggestion here is that such a dynamic wholeness is itself the issue of a more primordial source of activity, the original power of being. The intelligibility of what is is grounded in that in virtue of which it has its being. Form may be an ingredient in the intelligibility of a thing, but does it by itself ground the intelligibility of its full being? The form of a thing is sometimes said to be its essence or nature. But here we must think of nature as the result of a process of origination, as in the Greek notion of phusis or as implied in the word *natura* itself (nature as *natus*, something born).[12] As such a process of birthing, nature may be said to be grounded in the original power of being. Similarly, essence might be said to give form to the determinate coming forth into existence of the power of being.

Recall the *ex-* of *exsistere:* "to stand forth," "to come forth," "to spring forth." While the *-sistere* (the "standing there") of a thing might denote its formed wholeness, the *ex-* implies its relation to an origin, indeed the grounding of formal wholeness in an originating, forming source more primordial than form itself. So we might say that the power of being forms itself in self-shaping activity, manifests itself in a potentially unlimited sequence of appearances, sediments itself in particular things. But if form is a prior unity relative to particularity and its succession of properties, this power of being is more primordial still. It is what is ultimately prior, for it is the origin of all the other degrees of concreteness. Though we have called it the fourth degree, it is really the first. Its thereness is more than those of the other three, for it is what makes possible their concrete being. Without it, particularity would not emerge from the homogeneous continuum, internal difference and its distribution in manifest attributes would continue to slumber in inert particularity, and form would be nothing but an unactualized possibility. More radically still, without the original power of being, these others would not *be* at all; there would not be anything at all; there would be nothing.

If there are grades of communicability in the prior degrees of concreteness, ranging from the contracted to the more expansive, here we touch an acme of communicability. Concreteness here overflows like a plenty. There is a dimension of opaqueness and indeterminacy here, but in a sense exactly opposite to that contained in notions like absolute nothingness. The latter might be said to be opaque and indeterminate because it is an absolute lack, whereas here the power of being is indeterminate in an affirmative, not a privative, sense. It reveals a surplus, an overabundance. It is not indeterminate because it lacks determination, but because it is overdetermined. It is more than, not less than, limited particularity and finite structure.

Hence this fourth degree of concreteness is not a residue reached by abstraction from the plenitude of being, such that being becomes just the most impoverished universal or the emptiest abstraction. (In thinking of being in such terms, Hegel and Nietzsche prove to be unlikely bedfellows.) The more realized the individual thing becomes, the more concrete its universality becomes. This universality is not merely formal, but springs from its participation in the originative power of being. The individual is thus not merely a contracted particular, but a participant in this creative universality. It is not appropriate to say that being is "mere" being, since in the sense intended here, being is the real plenitude that sustains the other degrees of concreteness. Thus (relative to the first two degrees) being is not a predicate, though without it, predication would be impossible. Nor, relative to the third degree, is being just a universal form or logical category in the idealist's sense. To the extent that it recognizes the peculiar universality of being, that being is not an "ordinary" universal or a general concept, the transcendental understanding of being that we find in the Aristotelian-Thomist tradition may be said to come closer than empiricism or idealism to naming this original supporting plenitude of being.[13]

Just as the original power of being supports all the degrees of concreteness, so all modes of identification, as crystallizing the desire to know otherness, are penetrated by a dynamic orientation toward being. The fourth mode of identification might be called the metaxological affirmation of being. In it the desire to know reaches a culminating fulfillment in its least clogged openness to otherness. For this metaxological affirmation assents to the ontological affinity between the knower's being (as original selfhood) and the being of the other (as grounded in the original power of being). We might say that here the "I am" of the self comes to recognition of its metaphysical bond with the "it is" of real otherness, thereby issuing in the double affirmation of "we are." (Later I will speak of this "we are" in terms of agapeic otherness.) This affirmation must itself be redoubled—that is, repeatedly renewed—if it is to remain living spirit and not just become dead letter. But here we encounter the most fundamental sense of thereness. Though this emerges last in the order of explicit recognition, it is first in the ontological order. To reach this metaxological affirmation, we must be released from any effort to either contract being or finalize the desire to know at any of the three prior levels. This does not involve denying these prior levels; it is just that if these become separated from the full fourfold, they may easily become abstractions from the concrete. But in the larger setting, we see that the lower levels presage, but only imperfectly fulfill, what the higher level comes to realize. The metaxological identification brings us to a certain limit, crowning the desire to know with an express affirmation of otherness in its full concreteness.

Suppose we try to speak of this affirmation in terms of the assertion "being is."[14] We need not utter an empty tautology or regress to a mute gesture toward bare particular thatness. The affirmation is reminiscent of the Greeks, tired from their trek out of the heart of Asia, shouting

"Thalassa, Thalassa!" on reaching the open sea. Affirming "that some-thing is" or that "being is" on the fourth level is a little like this shout: the limiting shore that we reach, instead of constraining one, widens before one. The affirmation telescopes within itself, as it were, the pro-cess of arriving, even though in terms of sequential speech, it might take an infinity to unravel what is coiled and compacted there. It is a packed affirmation, rolling up within itself the threads of its trek. And because it epitomizes a certain plenitude of being, it may serve as a directive to the same plenitude of being opening before us in the space of otherness. Far from speaking an empty tautology, to say that "being is" may be to speak a ripe, ontological yes. It may be double affirmation in that being appears twice over; being appears over and over; it appears as more, as excess, as surplus, as overflowing; being appears infinitely. When we say that being is, we may affirm *its* affirmation—namely, that it is not nothing, that it is the original power to overcome negation and elaborate its energy plurally. Least of all is being reduced to homogeneity. Rather, its deepest heterogeneity emerges in the communicability of its original power, which prodigally disseminates itself into a plurality of beings.[15]

The reader may here be tempted to ask whether, in talking of seem-ingly glorious generalizations such as "being is," we may not have lost sight of the concrete thing in its thereness. I admit the danger of ab-straction in this matter, but our sights are still aimed at concrete oth-erness. For I have spoken of the affirmation "being is" only because, in every particular affirmation that takes the form "that something is," there is implicit the more radical outreach to being as a whole that can be seen to open before us in the affirmation "being is." The "it is" marking even a minimal naming of a particular thing can thus be seen to participate in a more englobing sense of being. In its full complexity this sense of being requires a metaxological naming, if it is to do justice not only to *what* the self and the other are in themselves, but also to the fact *that* they are at all. Each is irreducibly different in being, but both are radically bound together in the community of being. This funda-mental sense of being is indicated in the "is" that springs up in language, this commonest, most inescapable, yet most enigmatic of words. We tend to be blind to this, its very prevalence concealing its enigma. We take for granted the being that is there as granted, "given" in this fullest sense; its crowding strangeness seems to stun us, and we bypass what should engross our gaze. But the very elemental presence of being ought to subvert every form of simplemindedness and challenge us to the highest sophistication and the deepest openness. The commonness of the "is" indicates its significance; its commonality is the communicability spoken of above. We have our metaxological being in this commonality; we participate in, draw on, exhibit its communicating energy.

So also, because of the need to understand the community of being in a dynamic way, we must avoid reducing being just to objectivity. We must avoid a misleading objectification of the originative power of being. In this respect the metaxological is like a field of energy in which articulated relations are defined, but which is always dynamically vibrating in a certain way. In this field, centers of energy may be stabilized, but they must not be overly objectified; these centers might be seen as "knots" of the primordial energy, but their energy is just to be in interplay. Being at the fourth degree of concreteness brings before us this shimmering, infinite energy. Even the particular thing is not reducible to an object, if by this designation we mean to deprive it of its own participation in the dynamism of being. This is not to deny that the particular thing may be seen as an individual whole. It is to affirm this, but also to add that such a whole, as participating in, and hence suggestive of, the infinite power of being, might also be called an image of something infinite. It is not just we who radically open out to being. The thing in its wholeness opens out to its participation in the infinity of being—infinite because its originative power is not exhausted by particular finite things. The finite thing is like a window that may enframe a definite space, but when we look into it, we behold the interplay of energy that eventuates there; and so we find ourselves looking out through it, and the seemingly enclosing picture, no longer a closed whole, widens out to the infinite horizon.

THE FOURFOLD SENSE OF BEING AND TRADITIONAL PHILOSOPHICAL VIEWS

I will speak of this sense of the infinite in the next chapter, but let me conclude this chapter, first, with a brief summary of the four levels considered and then, with a brief indication of how they might relate to certain traditional philosophical positions.[16] Proceeding in reverse, from the fourth to the first degree of concreteness, we see that the thing's most primordial concreteness is its existence as an original participant in the power of being. Thence follows its derived unity of dynamic form, here meaning the self-shaping in a particular embodiment of its ontological power. This form is then seen to express itself in a multiplicity of properties, which finally define the character of the particular. The concrete thing, we might say, is an original whole, but also an image of the infinity of being. Proceeding now from the fourth mode of identification to the first, we see that the underlying intentionality of desire is oriented to the affirmation of being as it is. The metaxological naming of being does most justice to this intention, but the other three identifications—namely, the dialectical comprehension of form, the enumeration of attributes, and the perception of particularity—all contribute to our overall desire to know otherness. Relative to the metaxological affirmation, our identifications of essential form, manyness of attributes, and singular particularity are transformed into interrelated phases of a more discriminating, yet unitary, response to what we might call the polyphany of being.

How do these four degrees of concreteness and modes of identification fit with some traditional philosophical positions? The following remarks must suffice. On the first level, we tend to find the naive realist and the nominalist, who immediately identify the other as an object, a bare external particular. On the second level, we often find the empiricist, who tries to describe the immediately evident properties of this bare particular, but who, because of the ambiguities and equivocalness of such description, is often forced (like Hume, who provides us with the reductio ad absurdum of empiricism) into the position of the skeptic, who cannot say for sure whether the other, as "object," is "in here" or "out there." On the third level, we tend to find the type of idealist who asserts that what is true about the object is not its bare externality but its internalized appropriation by the self's knowing activity. On the fourth level, we find what we might call the complex realist or, in our terms, the metaxological realist.

This last agrees with the naive realist that we really do reach to the other. But, unlike the naive realist, he sees that this knowing is more complexly mediated, and that the other is more concretely rich. Like the skeptical empiricist, he grants the difficulty of setting up a hard and fast distinction between inwardness and otherness. But he ascribes a positive significance to this, as showing the poverty of the first degree of concreteness if taken in isolation. He sees the failure of the first two levels, when abstracted from the fuller sense of being, as negatively mediating a richer notion of the respective identities of the self and the other and as making possible a conception of their difference in other than dualistic terms. This rejection of sheer oppositional dualism is shared by the metaxological realist and the idealist. But, just as he asserts a richer otherness than the naive realist, so also the metaxological realist conceives a relating to difference that is more complex than the internalized appropriation by the actively mediating self that the idealist recommends. Thus he does not subordinate the other in its difference to any immanent identity of the idealistic knowing self. So too he is open to the transcendent in a way that is different from that of the idealist.

A similar perspective emerges if we consider directly the four notions of the univocal, the equivocal, the dialectical, and the metaxological. In passing from the most rudimentary of these four to the most complex, the desire to know strains to be an identification of otherness as it is, and does so by a deeper and deeper interpretation of being as it shows itself, as it appears. First, the naive realist states that what he knows *is* truly knowledge of the thing and correctly clings to the is. But in his hands, the "is" becomes univocal. It has neither openness nor hidden reserves, and, as a consequence, the naive realist forgets the mediating self and its "is-ing" and also has difficulty in accounting for the internal complexity of appearance. Second, when the empiricist develops this line of thought and becomes the skeptic, he asserts that we know nothing absolutely of what is, since nothing we claim as knowledge is ever absolutely certain, but always tends to be equivocal. Everything thus tends to be mere appearance, a phenomenalistic labyrinth out of which we cannot step and into which any stable selfhood or irreducible otherness seems to disappear. Third, the idealist tends to accept the skeptic's claim about external appearance, but by contrast, he may grant the realist's claim that there is one fundamental reality but not, however, as the realist sees this, namely as externality. For the idealist, this one fundamental reality tends to be the actively mediating self that is now the dialectical Ariadne's thread that leads us through the labyrinth of equivocal, external appearance. So also for the idealist, the true goal of knowing is often not external appearance as what is, but rather the knower as the one who actively orders external appearance. What is and "is-ness" thus tend to be defined in terms of dialectical self-mediation and self-identity.

Finally, the metaxological realist, like the naive realist, grants that we know what is in its otherness. But what is other does not exclude appearance; rather, it is more rich, more open, more mysterious than as conceived by the naive realist. Thus, like the skeptic, he admits that external appearance is not univocal and shares a sense of the limits of our knowing. He shares with the empiricist a desire for fidelity to experience. But, unlike the skeptic and like the idealist, he is not daunted by the ambiguity of experience; rather, he sets himself to interpret its positive import. Nevertheless, the metaxological realist, somewhat differently from the idealist, is reluctant to attribute this import predominantly to the self. Since appearance and what is other do not bifurcate absolutely, we may gain access to the actual on two fronts, both from the side of selfhood and from the side of otherness. Thus the metaxological realist tries to avoid the two extremes of identity and difference. Against the dispersed multiplicity of naive realism, he takes his stand on the affinity of the self and the other, of knowing and being. Against the totalized monism found in some forms of idealism, he sees that there is to be no closure to this affinity. For he sees the "is" that articulates this affinity as not just univocally identical or equivocally different or dialectically self-identical. He sees the "is" as metaxologically pluralized.

Chapter Seven
Desire, Otherness, and Infinitude

DESIRE, INFINITUDE, AND THE BETWEEN

The desire to know is capable of unreserved openness to otherness. It is openness to what is given. But what is given, we now see, cannot be restricted to the contracted concreteness of the particular thing. Thus the four degrees of concreteness previously discussed are modes of appearance of the thing, progressively more complex presentations of its otherness; correlatively, the four modes of identification are increasingly ample acknowledgments of its inherent richness. As the immanent self-articulation of the thing becomes more concretely communicable, so the matching openness of a human being moves from the immediate, through the dialectically self-mediated, to the metaxologically inter-mediated. Appearance is the convergence of these two sides, and the given is at its deepest at the fourth level. If we understand the given in this complex sense, the individual thing might be seen as a participant in the energy of being, itself suggestive of an original power not completely exhausted by determinate particulars. That is, in the finite thing something more than the finite is intimated, something in excess of finitude. In this sense the individual thing in its dynamic otherness might be said to provide us with a certain image of infinity. It transcends itself, its concreteness going beyond contracted particularity to an infinite sequence of properties, and beyond this again, through dynamic form, toward the plenitude of the original power of being.

In this chapter I want to say something concerning the sense of the infinite in this regard. First, I will briefly relate the problem of infinitude to man's intermediate being, his condition of being "between." Second, I will develop three senses of infinitude relevant to this. Third, I will

145

discuss an exemplification of the third sense of infinitude by considering the sublime as an aesthetic infinite. The reader will recall our previous discussion of art as a way of illuminating the possibility of human wholeness. We will continue that discussion here, but this time from the side of an otherness whence a sense of a radical infinitude emerges. In the final section of this chapter I will discuss what we may call *agapeic otherness*. Here we have the possibility of radically rich otherness within the community of being constituted by a plurality of originals. With regard to agapeic otherness we confront a call for the transformation of desire, despite its importunate self-insistence, into an unconditional moral openness to the other, a transformation that does actually occur when human desire assumes the form of goodwill.

I have pointed out some of the difficulties in chapter 1, in connection with the infinite restlessness of human desire. The idea of infinity tends to dizzy the intellect, for, by definition, the infinite is beyond limit; yet thinking tries to define itself in delimited ideas. How, then, can we think a determinate thought of the indeterminate? How can one define what overflows every defining boundary? To think the infinite would seem to be to exhaust the inexhaustible, to fix what eludes all fixity—a contradiction, it seems, that staggers the mind with vertigo. I will discuss the kind of philosophical discourse appropriate to this issue at the beginning of the next chapter. Here, let me remind the reader of our earlier discussion of metaphysical metaphors.

The difficulties with infinity are evident in a number of different historical responses. In ancient and medieval cosmology, the whole tended to be seen as finite, albeit enveloped by the divine.[1] Though radically finite, the world was capable of being an image or symbol of the divine. Things had both center and circumference; hence the self might situate its finite being in relation to the infinite Being. But in modern cosmology there appears to be no privileged center and no circumference. The center is everywhere and nowhere, for the whole is not finite. Infinity opens up into the vast immensities of outer space and also into the unfathomed recesses of inner consciousness.[2] Infinity seems to destabilize the older order wherein humans made homes for themselves within the whole. Indeed, if the whole is infinite, it is not clear how we can have any whole at all. With this new metaphysical homelessness, human finitude appears even more nakedly manifest.

Here we might note two significant responses. Think first of the unsettling, disturbing cosmic feelings induced, most notably in Pascal, by the idea of an infinite universe. Think of his trepidation and anxiety before the empty infinity of space. With the advent of modern, mechanistic science, the eternal silence of cosmic space ceased to jubilate with the majestic music of God, the music of the spheres of ancient Pythagorean cosmology. Empty space came to seem like an infinite void, in which the individual shrinks to nothingness and insignificance. A dizzying vertigo of lostness strikes, and we seem to fall without resistance into an abyss of vacancy. But there is another experience, at the opposite extreme. Instead of Pascal's chastening, cold meaninglessness, we might think here of Bruno (at the beginning of modernity) exulting at what he saw as the fullness exhibited everywhere. We here encounter an infinity of richness, rather than an infinity of indigence. Whereas Pascal felt anguish at the idea of an infinite universe, Bruno was intoxicated with infinity and the prospects of endless energy he believed it promised, even in humanity itself.[3] Closer to our own time, Nietzsche celebrated the "innocence of becoming" and the release of our infinite promise, now unshackled, he believed, from the fetters of old religious idols.

Clearly, then, infinity is an ambiguous, even dangerous, concept. There are perhaps two extremes to be avoided. On the one hand, there is the taboo in the religious tradition that prohibits us from attributing infinity to anything but God, with the result that the human being appears as impotent and paralyzed, smothered by an overwhelming divine majesty. In tension with this is the infinite restlessness of human desire. We do manifest something inexhaustible, something not to be smothered, if only our endlessly recurring disquiet before the unremitting enigma of the universe. Our adventuring, inquiring spirit may be unrestricted, at least potentially. Indeed this our power to be radically open to the whole may be our glory and highest dignity.

On the other hand, there is the modern aggrandizement of the self. Against the transcendent infinite of traditional, other-worldly religion, the modern self has often sought the infinite within this world and, indeed, has tended to interiorize the infinite within itself. Nature itself has sometimes been seen as but limitless space for our self-expression, an empty stage on which human desire struts and frets and believes that it conquers. Where paralysis and impotence may follow from a rigid traditionalism, an unrestrained will to power may be the issue in this unanchored modernism. Despite the fact that modern cosmology denies any privileged center, it is an extremely common strategy in modernity for the self to try to insist on itself as the center of all things. But very often this is clearly an act of cosmic bravado (a counterfeit of Bruno's exultation) or else just metaphysical whistling in the dark (as we shrink from Pascal's anguish). What I am suggesting here is that the between we have been developing in our consideration of desire and its openness to otherness asks us to avoid these two extremes. Against the extreme traditionalist, it asks us to grant the modern sense of inward infinity, acknowledging its right to be released from metaphysical impotence, while insisting on the need to give human desire a more primordial ontological anchoring. Against the extreme modernist, it asks us to grant the participation of our power in the more primordial power of being, such that the opening that unfolds through our infinite restlessness becomes a vigilance that must be attentive to the infinity also emergent in otherness itself.

Another important consideration here has to do with the contemporary question of limits. The metaxological view, though its continuity with the tradition of metaphysics should not be underplayed, also shares the concern of contemporary philosophy with the affirmation of finitude. The metaxological thereness of the other resists any simple appropriation and so is not subject, I believe, to the charge brought against the so-called metaphysics of presence to the effect that it seeks to reduce being to univocal identity. Again, my point is that our finitude cannot be such as to deny our infinite restlessness. A genuine limit can be defined only by allowing the full thrust of that restlessness. Here the sense of infinity, emergent in otherness, proves important.

Of course, in the minds of many contemporaries, the idea of infinity is associated with the purportedly Hegelian absorption of the finite into the infinite.[4] Hence some contemporary thinkers, inspired by Kant rather than Hegel—for instance, Heidegger and his followers—take their stand on human finitude explicitly against the purportedly Hegelian absorption into the infinite. Much existentialist thought, beginning with Kierkegaard, can be seen in a similar light. If, here, we begin again to speak of infinity, is this just a resuscitation of the supposedly Hegelian absorption of finitude? I do not think so, for a number of reasons.

First, Hegel himself is too many-sided and complex to be simply summed up in the language of absorption. Second, no genuine affirmation of human finitude must be such as, wrongly, to *reduce* man. This is not what is at stake in the question of limits at all. Third, there must be no diminution of radical otherness in its inexhaustibility; that is, we must give full weight to the emergence of the sense of infinity in the being there of otherness. This means that what is at issue here is not a supposedly Hegelian dialectic between the finite and the infinite, ending with a dialectical Aufhebung of the finite into the infinite. It is a question of the limit defined by the nature of the metaxological inter-mediation that is possible between different, potential infinitudes—namely, the self and the other. The issue of limits is not a matter of retreating behind the self's intentional infinitude or of diminishing the inexhaustibility of otherness. Rather, both these are to be seen as symbols of a more radical infinitude. Paradoxically, it is in the face of this sense of infinitude that our finitude is most insistently manifest. Finitude here may be an anchoring in being that is irreducibly positive, not just an ontological lack or defect such as underlies desire's flight to an absorbing god or static eternity. Let me now pursue this further.

THREE FORMS OF INFINITUDE

It will be helpful here to distinguish three relevant senses of infinity; let us call them infinite succession, intentional infinitude (a term we have used already), and actual infinitude. Infinite succession relates to the kind of potential open-endedness that we discover in the world of external becoming. For external becoming might be seen as the dynamic process of coming to be and passing away that concretizes particular entities, yet is not spent by the plurality of already realized particulars. It is open to the possibility of bringing into being and endlessly continuing the line of such entities. Thus, the infinite succession of external becoming may be seen as a series that is never completed. Moreover, because we cannot predict any determinate termination to this procession of particulars, we find here a certain indefiniteness. Becoming in-definitely repeats and ceaselessly generates a potentially indefinite sequence of particulars. It is not that this infinite succession is totally indefinite, for the things it produces tend to be crystalized into things of the same kind. Time does not just give rise to an indefinite number of, say, cats and dogs, indifferently; rather this indefinite number is differentiated into a definite plurality of different kinds.[5]

The linear image is significant here. Thus, we speak of generation as continuing a line and of different generations as continuations of the same family line. So we might say that natural kinds contain a reference to generation, for the natural is what is born (*natus*), while a kind is what is kindred or akin, what has kinship with its own relatives, its own kind—that is, with those bound together through their issue from a common origin.[6] Such an interconnectedness of natural kinds might be seen as one disclosure of the metaxological affinity of being, the presence of unselfconscious community in natural things.[7] Be that as it may, the main point is the openness of external becoming as an infinite succession. This openness is not a mere possibility, but one that is realized over and over again. Becoming perpetuates the same kinds of particulars in an as yet undetermined sequence of generations. We can neither impose a prior limit nor predict a determinate termination to this infinite procession. Because of the indefiniteness in the progression of particulars, a possible variability may be introduced, even into the notion of "the same kind." We cannot assert in advance that all the determinate kinds or forms of existence have been exhausted. We might say that this notion of infinite succession tends to be tied to the categories of univocity and equivocity in this sense. Our immediate inclination is to perceive the external world as a dispersed multiplicity of univocal particulars. In time, inevitably, this fixed definiteness is loosened up by our recognition of becoming and its open-endedness. Things in their determinate particularity, carried beyond themselves by the generating power of becoming, pass away and ultimately disappear into the indefinite succession of other particulars.

The second form of infinitude, intentional infinitude, helps to rescue the infinite succession of becoming from being solely a scattering or equivocal process. Intentional infinitude specifically refers to the power of open dialectical self-mediation displayed in the articulation of human desire. The self can rescue its own multiplicity from being scattered into a succession of unrelated fragments. It can span a process of becoming and recollectively bring its significant moments together in some unity or concrete wholeness. We have treated of this extensively in part 1, and it suffices here to briefly note the difference between intentional infinitude and infinite succession.[8] In an infinite succession, the connection of particulars would be merely an extrinsic juxtaposition but for the fact that the process of becoming, as repeating the same kinds of things, provides for some measure of formal self-mediation and thus some unity for multiplicity over a line of generation. Intentional infinitude provides for multiplicity a similar self-mediation and unity, but in an explicitly self-present, consciously recollected form. Unlike an infinite succession, which is linear with respect to particulars, intentional infinitude may be said to be circular, not only in self-consciously knowing the forms of particulars, but, most important, respecting the human being's effecting of its own self-knowledge.

Just as universal form is sometimes thought to extend itself over an indefinite sequence of instances, so human desire as intentional infinitude can be said to ideally range over external multiplicity and indeed, to scan our own self-exteriorization in a plurality of embodied acts. We are not bounded by the particular thing. In our excursion into the stunning diversity of the external world, we may mediate with its initial indifference, increasingly bringing hitherto hidden unities to utterance, and at the same time bringing ourselves to some self-comprehension.[9] Intentional infinitude refers to human desire as the intention of the infinite, an intention that is itself infinitely restless. As in infinite succession, there is an open-endedness here; but, in contrast to infinite succession, it is not merely indefinite. It refers us to the indeterminate power disclosed in original selfhood, which enables us to mediate between unity and multiplicity in our search for wholeness. But though we are pointed to wholeness here, this same indeterminate power does not permit any unsurpassable closure. In this respect our intentional infinitude testifies to the possibility of a recollected openness to being in its inexhaustible otherness.

This brings us to the third form of infinity. For, in the intermediated convergence toward metaxological community of the original self (as intentional infinitude) and external becoming (as infinite succession), we are opened up to the sense of something more. What I am suggesting here is that this intermediation intimates a sense of infinitude that is beyond intentional infinitude and infinite succession and is not reducible to these two forms. Since a radical sense of the inexhaustibility of being is disclosed here, we will use the term *actual infinitude*. The metaxological affirmation that being is gives us a glimpse of this infinitude, as we have already seen. We are not dealing with an empty tautology, but with a sense of being as unlimited, for outside being, there is nothing. "Being is" might be seen, in fact, as affirming the very opposite of nothing, as affirming an absolute plenitude: not an empty identity, but an "identity" that doubles itself, appearing twice over. Thus it may signify a fecund, originative "unity" that generates a many and gives rise to an abundant scattering of being in a bountiful diaspora.

I grant that here we come close to paradoxical language, since it seems that we must couple completeness and openness, wholeness and infinity. Yet original selfhood and external becoming themselves provide us with images of the power of being as both full in itself and yet inexhaustible, hence as open-ended even in fullness itself. Part of the difficulty here may be in thinking of all forms of infinitude in terms of linear endlessness. Such endlessness tends to trail off into indefinite possibility that is never actualized. But even external becoming as infinite succession cannot be circumscribed by such an essentially privative infinity. No thing is so absolutely static as to lack the reserve of something further. And the openness of things is not just the mere possibility of an unending accumulation of additional quantitative factors. It has to do with the qualitative presence concretized in the being there of the thing. Things are images of the original power of being and radiate beyond themselves. Similarly, external becoming, macrocosmically considered, might be said to be qualitatively open, since through it appears the ontological power of its original ground. It might also be seen as an original image of the dynamic power that gives and grounds its being.

There is a further point. If we grant this disclosure of a sense of something more, it is not the case that this more is merely derivative from original selfhood (as intentional infinitude) and external becoming (as infinite succession). A kind of reversal is at work in this regard. These two forms point to a more that is more absolutely original, relative to which they are to be seen as images, as ontologically derivative, despite the originative powers of being that they exhibit in their own right. That is, these two point to their own ontological ground, but this ground must be seen as originating by way of excess, not by way of defect. Hence, this original ground is to be seen as an overabundance. Here we see the rationale of the paradoxical coupling of wholeness and openness, completeness and infinity. The actual infinitude is an overwholeness, as it were. It is not empty indefinite possibility; it is more than finite determinacy; it is overdetermined—that is, indeterminate in a positive, not a negative way. This overabundance is sensed in those moments in which we feel that the power of being, even though it prodigally spends itself in unreserved diffusion, is in all this never spent, but rather shows forth a further infinite reserve. Becoming is grounded in the appearance of this infinite reserve, such that every seeming stasis is but slumbering energy that with time will wake. This reserve, never exhausted by determinate objectifications or diminished by particular things, is related to what Hopkins, speaking of the grandeur of creation despite its sometimes soiled surface, calls "the dearest freshness deep down things."[10]

This sense of excess, positive indeterminacy, inexhaustible reserve, is very important in preventing any philosophical hubris that might claim to encapsulate the actual infinite in a system of concepts. I will develop this point in greater detail later in this chapter and in part 3. It should be stressed here that we are not dealing with a dialectical comprehension of its form—it cannot be reduced to form—but with a metaxological acknowledgment of its presence. But this "presence," though it gives rise to a sense of plenitude, is not to be incorporated in any so-called metaphysics of presence. The excess, the reserve, the indeterminacy of this plenitude, are beyond, transcendent to any such simple univocal presence. Indeed, if we approach the actual infinite in terms of the thingness of bare univocal particularity, we may very easily invert this positive indeterminacy into the sheerly negative indeterminacy of a kind of black emptiness, or nothing.

Granted, in some traditions, being full and being empty, absolute being and nothingness, presence in plenitude and absence in all recalcitrance, God and the void, approach each other very closely.[11] I am not against the profound intention of this kind of language. Quite the reverse. Thus, in the present instance, the actual infinite is no determinate thing; yet it is overdetermined, more than any finite determination. As reserved, the actual infinite is inevitably dark to us; but as originating ground, it propagates its own peculiar light. It might even be called a kind of black light. Any familiar ease that we have with the things of the world must be disquieted here. For if we are under the domination of their limited form of being and if we then try to turn directly upon this light, inevitably, the eye will see nothing. But the black light, though no thing, is not nothing. It is what invades the crusty borders of things with visibility. Should we forget this and simply fall upon things, things themselves lose their shine and sink into a different, dull darkness. We mistakenly think that we can place ourselves at a remove from this light. But all we can really do is to turn our backs. And even then the light still casts its jet shadow over our shoulder. At best we are like frail moths: squinting creatures of twilight and dusk who, though dazzled by the light, still cluster and clutter about it.[12]

The consequence of this discussion must be a radical acknowledgment of limits. Here, congruent with previous considerations, limits must be understood in a double sense. The first sense has to do with the multiplicity of finite things appearing in the process of becoming; the second with the excess of actual infinitude. The first sense does not give us an absolute limit: the self as intentional infinitude, at least in principle, may try to comprehend an indefinite number of things. The case is different with the second limit: it cannot be reduced to the first sense, since there are reserves to its positive indeterminacy that elude any completely fixed determination. In itself it remains free of any such determinacy, because it is eternally in excess of this. It is not like a line that, when we draw it, we are already beyond it. To try to fix the second limit in this way is to confuse our approach to actual infinitude with the project of trying to make definite the indefiniteness that marks infinite succession. We do not draw this limit; it draws us. It is not like a wall that can be scaled or smashed; it remains insuperably free, mocking every pretension to finitize it in a finally fixed way. There may be a metaxological affirmation of this second limit (and, as we shall see, a metaphysical metaphor), but there is no dialectical encapsulation of its essence. Its difference dances away from and beyond the third mode of identification.[13]

Again, this second limit is not just some cramping barrier. As positive indeterminacy, this limit is also an unlimit: instead of confining us, it fulfills and frees us, frees us to the enjoyment of irreducible otherness. Here, finitude appears in its positive power, for our finitude is not exhausted by the complementary polarities of resistance and resignation— resistance that would defy finitude as something merely lacking, resignation that would surrender wearily to the same lack, for resignation is often only defiance defeated and grown abject.[14] In being freed to the enjoyment of the other, our finiteness may be emancipated into its own positivity. There is no need here of a dialectical alternation between a poverty on one side (human finitude) and a plenitude (the infinite) on the other. On both sides there is an excess, a more. Transcendence is doubled, for its power is manifested in both the self and the other.

Here we are harassed out of every false closure. Every time we lock the door of immanence from the inside, another key is turned, and another door, out, is opened. This double transcendence is mirrored in the fact that in our finitude we must confront a double call: within our own being, the call for transformation, and relative to the larger world of being, the call of conversion to the other. We cannot respond to either call with one simple, finalized answer. Relative to the transforming of self, there is a more within that ever escapes, and to this we must have recourse again and again. Relative to the other, its inexhaustible thereness escapes finite encapsulation. But this escape is not a failure, but just the point itself. Our appropriate comportment here is to own that we do not appropriate or own being in its otherness. When we know this, we also know that we do not know.[15]

THE SUBLIME AND AESTHETIC INFINITUDE

Let me now offer what I think is a significant exemplification of the above sense of infinity, drawn from the realm of aesthetic reflection. I want to make some remarks on the sublime. I focus on the sublime because it provides us with a suggestive embodiment of the infinite.

Though what we are dealing with here is extremely elusive and in the view of some thinkers abstract or even empty, the sublime gives us a pointer to the concretization of the infinite in a certain sensuous manifestation. The sublime presents us with what we might call the *aesthetic infinite.*[16]

We focus on the aesthetic because of its ability to recharge our sense of the world. Often we maneuver through the world with vision that has been neutralized by mechanical perception or dulled by humdrum familiarity. But the aesthetic may sometimes restore us to a rich concreteness. The sensuous sphere that it offers us is not some indifferent externality that we can just sanitize and bundle up. On the contrary, it often creates the feeling that we are enveloped by a mystery that we must acknowledge but cannot manipulate at will. Thus, some great art reveals the world as pervaded by a certain qualitative presence. It may solicit our imaginative rapport with being in all its otherness. The world here is not dead or inert, but discloses a power that surpasses every effort at reduction. It shows being in its excess, a profuse plenty spilling over the fixed confines of all spare, determinate concepts. A work of art may present this dense abundance through the imaginative plenitude of its own original image.[17] We might think here, for instance, of Monet's late paintings at Giverny: the pond, the lilies, the water, the Japanese bridge, all partake of a shimmering energy, out of which they struggle to emerge and into whose vibrating heart they are enfolded again. We cannot absolutely fix this originary energy that forms itself and decomposes again, that comes to shape, yet eludes every stasis.

Thus the artwork embodies in a rich image something of the excitement of the process of becoming. Yet at the same time it may address the enigmatic presence of things. We sometimes have the experience that things just are, without a why that we can manage to say. Beings simply are there. But how can we name this thereness? An artwork may accomplish this sometimes. There is a kind of scientific objectivism that prides itself on its disinterested fidelity to the "facts." But the artist does not respond with any aseptic detachment to the sheer fact that things are. He may name the elemental thereness of things and do so not by some neutral labeling but in a creative act that celebrates—even praises and renders thanks for—this thereness. There is nothing bland in such a celebration of the being of things. In that sense art may aid in our recuperation of the sense that the world is not sterile.

The notion of the sublime is intimately related to this recharged sense of the sensuous and to an aesthetic attitude toward the world that has no interest in dominating things. Of course, the sublime is a very old idea, one that featured in ancient thought, most notably in that of Longinus. It is also of significance in the aesthetics of the modern age, in Burke, in Kant, and in a variety of important Romantic artists.[18] Indeed, some recent aesthetic thought is concerned with reconsidering the notion.[19] Part of its importance, I suggest, is that it provides us with a sensuous sense of powers transcending our own limited selves, more ultimate powers than all finite being. The sublime is also important if we wish to counteract the Promethean hubris of modern humanity in seeing itself as the sole overlord of nature. The sublime chastens our will to power when we seek to subordinate the otherness of being to our own mastering power. It answers to a desire for a restoration of a sense of the beyond, a sense of transcendence not reducible to our own immanent self-transcendence.

Often the sublime is depicted in terms of settings in nature that display aweful, terror-inspiring power: hurricanes, wild storms, craggy peaks of mountains, turbulent clouds, irresistible rivers rolling over high waterfalls and tumbling into an abyss. Yet this awful energy fascinates us, releases in us a strange excitement, even joy. Why so? Perhaps in part it is the energy released in us by the proximity of danger. But more deeply, I suspect, it stems from a desire to experience the closeness, the perilous closeness, of a mighty beyond. We find the need to experience the overpowering presence of something other than the human, something beyond human will, whose ambiguous majesty—for this storm or gale or flood might kill us—seems to lift the individual to a strange, seemingly superhuman exaltation. The danger is courted out of an almost religious desire to experience the transcendent in nature itself.

Some thinkers—Kant, for example—have reminded us that the experience of the sublime demands that we, the beholders, not be so threatened as to be unable to rise to some contemplative standpoint. If we are simply swamped by the sublime, the naked danger to our existence will reduce us to animals seeking merely to survive. The sublime has a higher significance. In recognizing the awful, destructive power of nature, but standing fast before it, something of a human being's higher calling may shine out, even in its precarious finitude. I will return to this below. Here we note that there is always something unmastered about the sublime, which is why it is not inappropriate to call it the aesthetic infinite: the sensuous manifestation of the surpassing power of being that cannot be reduced to merely finite proportions. Nor can this manifestation be encapsulated in clear and distinct concepts. As already implied, something about it spills over every delimited boundary within which we might try to enclose it. Consider what might be termed an empty version of the sublime: the void Arctic spaces. Here, nothing particular occludes the gaze, which opens out into the illimitable. Yet the sublime may be manifested because, in the barren openness of the sensible realm, a presence may come to be "there." A somewhat different example, mentioned by Schopenhauer,[20] is that of the American prairie, where, once again, we have an experience of the illimitable. No finite thing seems to be able to stand in the way of the aesthetic infinite. Likewise, the otherness of being may be freed from the provisional domestications often imposed on it by humans and may shine forth with a renewed elemental thereness. We are not—nor can we ever be—complete lords over this infinity. At best we can be fellows at its celebrations.

This aesthetic infinity is related to the notion of positive indeterminacy discussed previously. The beautiful and the sublime are often distinguished because of this unmeasured illimitableness. I might point out that this distinction between the beautiful and the sublime is not unrelated to the contrast between wholeness and infinitude that played such an important role earlier. Beauty seems directly related to the idea of wholeness, for it invokes ideas of harmony and measure and the joy of recognition when like calls to like. Here the self recognizes a certain sameness that it shares with the other. The sublime, by contrast, in being unmeasured, may sometimes entail disorder and disharmony. It may force disquiet on desire and insist on the acknowledgment of something radically different, something other in a way that is irreducible. But beauty and the sublime, what is akin to us and what is beyond us, need not always be separated thus. A certain open wholeness, or unclosed beauty, may itself be suggestive of the inexhaustible sublimity of being.

Here our previous discussion of becoming as infinite succession is relevant. Time flows through us and around us as this infinite succession that we cannot master. Time yields no static foundation on which, motionless, we may stand secure. It reveals the ontological frailty of finiteness. The ambiguous world is often like the Sphinx: beneath the breasts that suckle, we see the claws that twist and rip. Finite things come into being. They eventually decrease; they decay; they meet their decease. Yet they still strain beyond themselves for what they lack. They are, in multiple ways, the points of intersection between life and death. We are such intersection points made self-conscious. Though we know that becoming as infinite succession will scatter and disperse finite things, nevertheless they *are* now, partakers of a feast of being that will infinitely outlive them. Just as a form is more sharply outlined when emerging from a surrounding blur of fog, so too, when negation looms in an ultimate form, a new luminosity may light up the mysterious being of things, that they simply exist at all. We are moved to appreciate the beauty of things simply as being at all.

This beauty is not static, something that appears at a fixed time, once and for all. Nor is it manifested progressively. Often it simply towers up before us, as if erupting from a different dimension. There is an ultimacy here that we miss if we are dispersed on existence as a mere aggregate of passing particulars. Particular things may be beautiful; as beautiful, they may be radiant; but as radiant, they implicate a power that they, as particular, do not expend. What appears in their presentness may have the bite of infinite power. It may intimate an unmastered reserve, even in the embodied radiance we sometimes encounter in the beauty of things. The beauty of being is essentially fugitive. The beauty of things cannot be kept back. But this fading is not a failure, for something more may be intimated that is beyond brute facticity. Something is held there, held out for us. It fades, and we feel a profound pathos. This is something great art can signify in its celebration of things in their transience. The creative act of man can become a kind of affirmative pathology, a logos, a bespeaking of the pathos. It can become a kind of healing mutability canto.

This fugitive beauty may indicate how beauty, as a formed wholeness, can open out to the sublime as suggesting something unmastered and infinite. Beautiful things are presented to us, briefly whole and harmonious, but since they are fugitive, they cannot be held eternally still, they cannot be mastered absolutely. Thus, fugitive beauty answers our desire, yet subverts and dislocates it. It helps us to be at home here; it also exposes and unshelters us. Time as an infinite succession will not stay its course for us; it forces us to see the world in its openness and otherness. We cannot think of all beauty as a closed harmonious whole or in terms of a serene stable form. For, even when fugitive beauty evinces wholeness, it still pushes against the boundaries of any closed whole. A ruffle of resistance passes through the serenity of stable form. Even the most serene beauty is pierced by the hint of a presence that is beyond all form. Within the heart of all harmonious wholeness we receive intimations of infinity, a pressing against the edges of enclosed form. The unmeasured sublime invades the fugitive presence of finite things, and every effort by man to close the whole explodes wide open once again.

This contrast between beauty and the sublime recalls the distinction between the third and fourth degrees of concreteness. The third degree of concreteness in our discussion in chapter 6 was greeted by the dialectical comprehension of form, while the fourth degree occasioned the metaxological affirmation of being. What we have been looking at here is the aesthetic version of this sense of being and our affirmative greeting of it. Our encounter with a radical limit may release our creative power in such a way that our yes to being can be sensuous too. The manner in which the fugitive nature of finite being pushes beyond the beauty of closed form to the unmeasured sublime is an aesthetic exemplification of the intimation of the fourth degree of concreteness that we find in the third degree. Fugitive beauty points to the other side of form and essence, to an originative power whence form and essence spring. If you like, the beauty of form is beyond form, since it is grounded in and powered by the sublimity of being, as the ultimate originative source. As we saw in our previous discussion, the third degree of concreteness exhibits dynamic form, which points to the original power of being on the fourth degree. Beautiful form is pierced by what is beyond form. The sublime (as in the Latin *sublimis*) is what is beyond the limit, what is above our finiteness. It reveals, as it were, a certain vertical sense of being. The sublime is a sensuous symbol for an ultimate space that is between us and what is transcendent and that emerges through the vastness, the variousness and the inexhaustible power of being that we see generating in successive time.

Many people feel that this otherness of the sublime, this unmastered power of the aesthetic infinite, threatens to radically unshelter humanity, thereby reinforcing human finitude in a manner that causes the individual to dwindle to nothing. But we do not have to look at the sense of limit here in a solely negative manner. Being unsheltered might instead be seen as a kind of homecoming to positive finitude. In consenting to this radical otherness, we may come into our own and be restored to a sense of the perduring mystery of being. The world bursts in on us, and its staggering beauty stuns us. It is there again, not to be taken *for* granted, but rather, to be taken *as* granted. Out of this may be born a certain metaphysical gratitude for being, which in turn may flower into gratuitous origination of the kind that we find in great art and other creative human acts. Let us focus for a moment on the artwork as indicative of this positive response. For the artwork might be seen as an original image that concretely sets forth a defined, but dense, presence wherein we enter into metaxological rapport with what is other.

It is not defined exclusively by the artist's power but is rather a sensuous middle that intermediates between the artist's power and the animating power that informs and vitalizes the heterogeneous world. It points as much beyond the artist as back to him. The artwork may be a kind of double mediation: it may mediate between the self and its own original power; but it may also intermediate between the self's power and the original power of being.[21] This second power of otherness need not squash human creativity, but may rather invite it—indeed, help ground and support it.

As finite, we find ourselves as originated beings. But as originated, each of us is a creative origin; and as an origin, a created creativity. Our finite being is double: we are created, yet creative originals. Thus our original power is not simply our own private possession. There is a certain gratuity here, in that we are given to ourselves, but in a way that asks that we enrich what already is, that we give back more and not bury the talent. We are entrusted with the care of what is original in the different world. Each of us is an intermediate original, created, yet a creative power. Art affirms the first, while putting the second to work.

Thus, on the one hand, art arrests any inflation of the self into everything. The creation it calls forth prevents the self from cutting its ties with the world to be alone with its own pure image. It refuses to pander to the truncated, narcissistic selfhood that is infatuated with its own fatuous reflection. To puff up its stature, such vain "creativity" becomes unrestrained, swaggering self-assertion; it also becomes shackled to an opposition that, in keeping its eye only on the pretense of its own originality, is dead to whatever is original in the heterogeneous world. Then the other becomes simply a rival, and originality degenerates into unfruitful self-protestation. On the other hand, the artwork is not a mere imitation, something so subservient to the other that it abnegates the self's creative power. Were it so, it would not be an original openness to the world, but an empty image that falls away from it. Mere imitation sets up an opposition between the self and the world from the side of the world. Sheer self-creativity sets up a similar opposition, but inverts it from the side of the self.

By contrast, a great artwork, while remaining balanced in itself, may radiate out beyond bare particularity. Its double mediation may seize on our own doubleness and turn us to the other in the generous spirit of positive plurality. What it may concretize is the sense of what it means for us to be original participants in a universe that is itself original. It may thus capture our co-agency in the process of creation. It is not enough for us to offer a mere imitation of the world already there, nor yet a self-creation which claims that the self alone is the world. We must give a new imaginative world that jubilates in concert with the articulation of being into a community of originals. Creation shares its power, deals out its boon. It is given ungrudgingly. In accepting creation's favor, our creative act must be a gratuitous origination.

Such augmenting origination may mark a condition of positive finitude attuned to the aesthetic infinitude suggested by the sublime. But if we see the sublime as calling for the concretion of a certain transcendent ideal, it would be a mistake to identify this ideal with any sentimentalized "sweetness and light" of the kind so often satirized at the close of the Romantic period (by Dostoevski's underground man, for instance).[22] The full negativity implied by the unmastered power of the sublime—at the extreme, the scattering of finite being in death—cannot be evaded. It may be relevant here to relate the ambiguity of becoming to the daimonic. The daimonic is central to our concern with desire, of course, since Plato spoke of eros as a *daimon*—a middle poised between earth and heaven, mortals and divinities. The daimonic reveals something of the powers of infinitude *within* the self, something gripping the whole person, breaking up neutrality (see Bruno's heroic furor), and exposing the self to the emergence within of what may not be mastered finitely. It may dissolve isolated singularity, but the uncontrollable power it sometimes looses may easily veer in a destructive direction. From without, it may submerge the self in the impersonal and the anonymous, making the human being into a thing, passive in the hands of outside powers. From within, it may find expression in an urge for self-assertion and self-aggrandizement that smashes furiously at the difference of the other. The daimonic may then unloose an irrational violence that ransacks the external world and execrates the inner.[23]

Although such possibilities must not be denied, the gratuitous origination of art may be more than irrational power within or blind impersonal power without. Art may stand in the ambiguity of the daimonic but, its creative act, by contrast, may stand against the dominance of these devastating powers that wreck the promise of the middle. Everything great gambles on the ruin of human powers. Thus art is suspended in the ambiguity of the daimonic; yet, in weathering its stress, it may be matured in this suspension. But it is not a question of loss of self. Nor is it one of either skirting or surrendering to the dark side of the daimonic. Despite this dark side, the other side of the ambiguity of becoming, the fact that the being of things is actually given is also affirmed. The sense of difference between the human self and the otherness of being is not obliterated; rather, difference is released from the animosity of dualistic opposition. Similarly, any sense of difference we may have between inferior and superior powers may also be relieved of animosity. The temptation to try to usurp these superior powers is allayed. The point, however, is not to be submerged anonymously as one part within an absorbing whole. It is to realize one's distinctiveness as an original whole within the bond of the community of being that passes beyond finite encompassing. Art can remain true to the difference between us and what is beyond. To praise and preserve this nonidentity is the very pathos of art.

The sublime, then, does not require that the self become a lifeless vehicle manipulated by a power beyond. It is rather a question of openness to an ultimate that emerges in the middle. The middle is not the property of anyone. To be true to the middle is to speak within the interval between beginning and end and there to strain to the utmost possible. It is to transform the middle from an indifferent space between arbitrarily posited limits along a succession that is otherwise indefinite. It is to make the beginning and the end as much present in the interval as at the boundaries. In gratuitous origination, the limits may enter the middle, making it a completion that is also an awakening, an awakening that rounds off a movement. Moreover, the ingress of the extremes is not because we have overreached them. On the contrary, in reaching out to them, we are startled to find that they reach in, since they cannot be fixed to determinate finite points or coordinated to our will. Thus the artwork may image the aesthetic infinite by embodying the fecund power to suggest a significance that, as inexhaustible, we cannot pin down without residue to one definite prosaic meaning. It always harbors a fresh difference, one that is not consumed by determinate explications of it. It recedes into a reserve. This does not mean that it excludes struggle; rather, that it seeks to embrace discordant elements within a concrete whole that, despite exemplifying wholeness, is not closed off. The result may allude to conflict requiring repeated confrontation; yet, in presenting the struggle, enmity may be transcended.

The artwork may be a whole within itself that is radiant beyond itself, a tense coexistence of centripetal and centrifugal power, an intensive self-sufficiency that is nevertheless the packed suggestion of infinity. It may compose a singular whole that, as a unique intermediate, is yet big with infinity. It transgresses the simple unity of bare literal univocity without losing itself in merely equivocal ambiguity or closing itself up within a totalizing dialectic. It passes into the middle space between the self and the world as both original, a space in which our speech may be both unique and irreducibly pluralized, as poetic speech tends to be. We must search out words most faithful to the milieu of middle existence, cognizant that no one word alone can usurp this middle. And if there is any return to an origin, it cannot be one origin alone, but rather an origin that is articulated into a plurality of beginnings.

AGAPEIC OTHERNESS

I now want to offer another crucial exemplification of the metaxological sense of being, in which we find the same suggestion of infinity. I will offer some remarks on what we might call *agapeic otherness*. Previously we explored the metaxological in terms of the self's intermediation with nature, or external becoming as other. But metaxological intermediation is most richly disclosed when the partners in interplay are each explicitly and fully selves, self-knowingly activating the possibilities of open dialectical self-mediation. What is at stake in agapeic otherness is the character of community constituted by a particular concourse of such selves.

We must try to clarify briefly the "we are" mentioned above. This is a very important theme in contemporary thought, which is sometimes spoken of, as, for example, the problem of intersubjectivity. We find it in Martin Buber's discussion of the between defined by the "I-Thou" relationship. Gabriel Marcel treats of the ontological significance of the "we are," whereas the later Camus focuses on the same "we are" as revealing a profound solidarity at the heart of revolutionary action. Heidegger is concerned with *Mitsein*, and Sartre with the other as essentially in conflict. It is the concern of Levinas in regard to the "face to face" of the ethical relationship.[24] Much of the contemporary discussion has taken place in the shadow of Hegel's dialectic of master and slave, regarded by some thinkers, though not Hegel himself, as the essence of human relations.[25] This dialectic has bequeathed a whole host of problems to Hegel's successors, including Sartre and, notably, Marx in his transposition of this dialectic into the class struggle. Our discussion of agapeic otherness will involve an attempt to point to a human possibility that is not enclosed within the circle of the dialectic of master and slave, one that is called for by the metaxological sense of being.

Our discussion must be confined to key points. We can say here that agapeic otherness names a certain inviolable value in the being of the other, one that is especially acknowledged when desire takes the form of goodwill. There is an appropriately Kantian ring to this latter notion, in that, for Kant, goodwill may reveal something morally unconditional or absolute about the self as a person.[26] With agapeic otherness we are also concerned to argue against modern atomism, the result of isolating the self from the rest of being; such isolation is present in many areas and is not unrelated to the separated subjectivity of the Cartesian tradition. In passing beyond the instrumentalized desire that seeks to objectify the other, agapeic otherness leads to a rupturing of the functional, isolated self. Goodwill may reveal a nonobjectifying recognition of otherness, which responds to the appeal of the other with a nonpossessive solicitude.

Agapeic otherness continues the theme discussed in relation to the sublime—namely, desire's ambiguity and the unsheltering effected by human finitude. It reveals something radically positive in being unsheltered, for it demands a radical openness to otherness that sifts desire's ambiguity, allowing the possibility of both a supreme affirmation and a supreme debasement. Suppose we think of two human beings standing before each other face to face. There is always a nakedness and a vulnerability possible here, both a danger and a promise. Think of eye-to-eye contact as imaging this encounter. Eye contact always risks violating the other in the intimacy of that other's inwardness, as well as being violated in turn. There is an implicit infinity compacted in the eye of another, for the eye may reveal an abyss of inwardness. When the eyes meet, whole worlds may pass between two selves in such brief, overdetermined moments of exchange. Such exchange cannot be maintained indefinitely. It is fraught with all the dangers of violation, in which the eye becomes the baleful glare that beats the other into submission, instead of the delicate communication of welcome or salutation. Goodwill, I suggest, reveals something of the positive promise of radically unsheltered difference because, in the ambiguous vulnerability of the face-to-face encounter, it lays itself open to the possibility that its own openness may be radically rebuffed. Yet, despite the possibilities of such radical refusal, it may issue in a gratuitous yes, a self-justifying yes to otherness, in a free, unmotivated acknowledgment of the unconditional in the other as other. Only in this way can openness to the other become trust in the other and the human being's vulnerability and unsheltering become a homecoming and a healing.[27]

What is noticeable here, precisely because of the ambiguity and danger and vulnerability, is how fallen, disfigured relations assume prominence and are easily mistaken for our essential promise. This promise and the failure to realize it fully may be discovered in different forms of will emergent from the double nature of desire, as both seeking self-fulfillment and opening to otherness. Let us concentrate on the contrast between goodwill and what traditionally has been spoken of as self-will. Will can be understood as the self's love in action, mediating the transformation into deed of the original power of its being. Given the relation of will in this sense to the whole self, self-will and goodwill here are not to be taken as particular isolated acts, but rather as philosophical mnemonics for ways of life, metaphysical metaphors for extended comportments to being.

By self-will here is not meant natural animal drive or proper self-love;[28] it refers to the attempted closure of infinite desire upon the separated self. It is a falling away from consent to the self's metaxological affinity with being in its otherness. It may range from minor metaphysical tantrums all the way to Satanic refusal. Man's defenseless vulnerability may cause one to rage against one's finitude, to be furious with one's own frailty. Self-will emerges at that juncture between our precarious finitude and the limitless power of negation that we possess by virtue of our being infinite desires. It is a response to the givenness of being that insists on refashioning the given in its own image. Thus it is blind to the otherness of the given; indeed, it wills that there be no given at all in this sense and seeks to erase any irreducible otherness. Here we find a spirit of negativity that sees in the given an unacceptable limit—unacceptable, because it bespeaks our frail finitude. Since the person marked by self-will wants to reject this frailty, so also, that person tends to reject the otherness of the given. Of course, to do this absolutely is impossible. At most, the given is redefined as something indifferently there, a mere matter for our use, literally seen as worthless until self-will confers value on it.

The human being marked by self-will sees the worth of the other not in terms of the intrinsic inviolability of the other, but in terms of itself and the products of its own power. The other, thereby redefined as matter for the use of the self, becomes valuable only after self-will has imposed its own stamp on otherness. The difficulty is that this process turns out to be endless. For what is given in the present must be mastered ad infinitum, since only such mastery gives otherness any meaning; and no matter how much self-will might will it to be otherwise, the otherness of being persists in its enduring thereness. Thus the person of self-will is forced to drive into the future, manifesting the infinity of human desire as a kind of devouring willfulness. For the future, when we reach it, also endlessly becomes indifferent matter for mastery. So self-will becomes a distended desire, not unlike equivocal desire, in that nothing will satisfy it absolutely.[29] But a will that nothing at all can satisfy is indistinguishable from a blind will. Hence, though self-will seems to be the pure expression of power, what it really manifests is an unredeemed lack, not unlike Sartre's nothingness, which culminates in an understanding of man as a futile passion. But, as in the case of Ahab's consuming hatred for Moby Dick, the root of the self's angry rancor toward otherness is a helplessness before what cannot be mastered by willpower alone. The force of its rage is the hollow power of directed—or rather, misdirected—powerlessness. In a word, self-will cannot let go or let be. In one sense it wills to be unified absolutely with things; but, given the impossibility of obliterating difference or of having the other on its own terms alone, it turns against otherness. Self-will cannot say its amen to being, because it cannot endure the pathos, the suffering, of difference. Indeed, in that it hates what it cannot control, there is really a despair, both of itself and of otherness, in its defiance of finitude.

Let us now contrast this with goodwill. Goodwill is not infected by this blustering rancor to being.[30] The value of otherness is not due simply to an act of will of the self. Where desire as lack may long for the other, desire as goodwill belongs with the other. For goodwill, to be is to be good: it desires what is good because it is good; what is good is not so simply because we desire it.[31] The goodness of the other is not what we project on him, but what is his due, given the metaphysical worth of his being. Even when faced with negation, goodwill is ballasted with a deeper affirmation, with a certain metaphysical respect for an intrinsic integrity or rightness of being in the other.[32] It grows out of desire's fidelity to our metaxological affinity with being. For it is open to what is good in the given, what is of worth in otherness as such. What is good in being is not merely a function of my projecting will.

In a sense, goodwill is one of the simplest, most elemental conditions of spirit; but, given the tangled, sometimes tortured, inwardness of the human self, it is often the most difficult to attain. In a way it is not an attainment at all, in the sense of something achieved as the product of will alone. It is more a release of the will to the given in a gracious way. Because of its trusting assent, its consent to the self's affinity with being in its otherness and its appropriation of the lack in human desire are essentially different from what we find with self-will. For goodwill is not the desire to consume or incorporate the other. It takes desire beyond an infinite sequence of appetites and frees us from an acquisitive fixation on an endless succession of finite things. It carries desire beyond lack in greeting the depths of the other across the space of difference. Goodwill radiates forth in a decisive transcendence of lack. For it reveals that desire may be more than an erotic rush from lack to wholeness, that it may be an agapeic pouring forth from a wholeness already real. Goodwill is thus a free overflow of wholeness that reveals the whole self in an infinitely dense kinship with what is other.

We see too how goodwill recalls the gratuitous origination of art and other creative acts. It is freely given, and in being poured forth, it may offer something for no particular reason beyond the intrinsic good of the giving itself. Goodwill is an original image of agapeic being in that it is a living embodiment that is suggestive of the excess of being. Thus a person of goodwill may exemplify agapeic otherness in his relation to an other self, indeed in his relation to the whole of being. What is other, he respects as itself a whole. Goodwill, as a saturated, excessive desire, cannot but communicate itself. I am not saying that the person of goodwill is naively idealistic. Such a one may well have plumbed, if only imaginatively, the twisted pathways of defiled desire and may be acquainted with the seductive darkness that lures self-will. Nor is it a question of glorifying some future that may never come or smugly contenting oneself with the limitations of the present. Goodwill knows the ambiguous indeterminacy of man, but sees even in self-will the twisted cipher of a betrayed infinity, an indeterminacy whose genuine flower is the overdetermination that marks rich selfness, the overdetermination that ripens in agapeic overwholeness.

I know that in desire's ambiguity resides the possibility of a debasing dialectic. I know, too, that man is a bottomless pit needing to be loved, and that to transcend self-insistence, to love and not insatiably demand to be loved, is both rare and hard. Human desire unavoidably seeks its own wholeness, and, just as unavoidably, this search coexists in tension with its openness to otherness. This is just human doubleness. Or better, we are always a middle between these two exigencies of our being. The deformation of desire's doubleness emerges when we try to close dialectical desire into an absolutely self-sufficient self-mediation. Then the voracious desire to fill one's own lack swamps the different affirmation of goodwill, and desire's openness to agapeic otherness is short-circuited. Then we are misled into treating human desire as a drive to consume. This reveals the monistic proclivity to envisage fulfillment as entailing the obliteration of difference. The other is reduced to an instrumental thing that serves as a subordinate means to my satisfaction. The self puffs itself up like an obese absorbing god, ransacking the other and ingesting its free difference. A limited form of desire, desire to possess the particular telos (see chapter 1), is mistakenly seen as the paradigm of all desire.

This understanding of desire—it might be called the shadow cast by Hegel's dialectic of master and slave—is common in contemporary thought and is perhaps most notoriously expressed in Sartre's claim that the essence of human relationships is conflict. It is related to the tendency to see desire as essentially defined by lack and negativity and to see otherness as a dualistic opposition to be surmounted. But since, as it turns out, the difference between two selves is irreducible and cannot be overcome in such terms, the danger is that their relationship degenerates into a dialectical collusion of the sadist and the masochist, as tends to happen in Sartre. It is said that a sadist is one who is kind to a masochist; and indeed, they are made for each other. Yet their dialectical collusion reveals a double failure to recognize the original in the other. There is a mutuality and a complicity here, but they are barren. The sterile power of one may be increased in the diminished subject flesh of the other. But in this subjection, there are no subjects, for both fall from their promise. To hold another in subjection may be a victory of sorts, but, at a deeper level, it is a more desolate defeat. For, when the other is deprived of original freedom, our own freedom is despoiled, and the grasp of our possession closes about a dead thing. Triumph has flown this hollow conquest, and again we are frustrated and numb and empty. We are clogged within ourselves, and our reach to the other is blocked. And our odium for the desecrated other breeds our vile self-hatred.

With agapeic otherness and the metaxological community of being, no self can be treated merely as a curb on desire's freedom, a limit to be surmounted. There is something held in qualitative reserve in the other that cannot be held in subjection or exhausted in any sadomasochistic collusion. This reserve recedes beyond such a dialectic. For we are dealing with the second kind of limit discussed previously, a positive indeterminacy relative to which genuine finitude may be forged. This sense of finitude is not our passive lacking existence which, of course, is inevitably shaken up by desire's infinite restlessness. It is emergent rather in recognition of the inexhaustibility of otherness, the suggestion of infinity in the agapeic other. Here is no degrading of finitude, but an open space eliciting the creative power of finitude, while curbing the individual's pretension to be the sole original. The degrading of finitude occurs, rather, when desire deforms its own possibility and through the power of negation tries to diminish the other to a subordinate role in desire's own self-aggrandizement. If we withdraw recognition of the other's reserved indeterminacy, we become pinned to our own negativity, and a sterile dialectical struggle with the other ensues. Each protagonist thinks that his antagonist's submission will establish and complete his own identity. But there is never any victor here, only different victims at odds. Any brief ascendancy of one individual over another is but an uneasy lull, and retribution is invariably called forth. To obviate reprisal, the self must shore up its ruins with incessant offense, now in the form of a devious sortie, now a more blunt battery. The expansive powers of difference are blocked, and we shrink to fearful, lacking, closed combatants, touchy at the slightest hint of a threat.

With agapeic otherness, by contrast, we cease to be chained to this closed dialectical circle. No dialectical circle encompasses the possibilities of human wholeness or its radical openness. Nor can a closed dialectical circle do justice to the metaxological otherness that goes with agapeic otherness. For goodwill assents to the other's reserved indeterminacy, refusing to let the empty inflation of the power of negation pass muster for original being. Original being is beyond dialectical possession. Relative to agapeic otherness, there is always a certain affirmative asymmetry—that is, a mutuality that freely consents to a difference. This, we must insist, is essentially different from the parasitical mutuality of sadist and masochist, the one powerful, the other lacking. Agapeic otherness is not defined by a lack of something, over which power is sought. It is beyond both lack and possession. For it is not that the masochist lacks what the sadist, as power, possesses. The latter's possession is itself a lack. Possession and possessed are but two phases of the same lack, manifested now actively by the sadist, now passively by the masochist. But both sides are radically deficient. By contrast, goodwill does not consist in dialectically surmounting a lack. It consists in being metaxologically at home in a community. There the positive excess of being spills over into a middle that gives both the self and the other the space to be themselves and to be bound together even in their difference. Peace with the other here is not covertly for fear of retaliation, should we dare to negate him. Rather, we find a trust in the integrity of being and in the intrinsic rightness of the other. As we have seen, there is a vulnerability and a risking here, but of a qualitatively different sort. The space of the middle wherein self and other are embraced may bound them but, like the embrace of love, it need not pinion them.[33]

Agapeic otherness makes possible a certain fellowship of being as a living exemplification of metaxological intermediation, but where does this leave the sense of differentiated individuality? What is to be avoided here is treating individuality either as an inflexibly separated particularity or else as merely an instantiation of some indefinite generality like "humanity." The place of the individual, understood in its richest possibility as original selfness, is the community of being in which fellowship may draw out the individual's infinite promise. Indeed, in this fellowship the individual may himself be pluralized, become an original image of community, in this respect. Such a one may have to ceaselessly develop the power of openness, make itself available to all otherness, trying unremittingly to see things also through the eyes of others.

There is here possible an imaginative identification with difference, the identification with difference variously called love of neighbor, universal benevolence, or unstinting sympathy or compassion for all. Since this identification is metaxological, it does not entail any dissolution into anonymous impersonality or, alternatively, the fantasy that we are the all. It carries us beyond dialectical identity, checking any temptation to the monistic inclusion of the other. Without respect for an irreducible difference, community collapses. The choice is not between perversely obstinate particularity of a quasi-Kierkegaardian sort and the evaporation of individual distinctiveness in a larger absorbing whole, as advocated by totalitarian views. The metaxological intermediation of fellowship draws the individual beyond catatonic confines, mediates particular differences, yet may support the real distinctiveness of individuality. In a sense, fellowship may be said to originate the individual, in that it names him humanly. It is a kind of baptism, offering him a new beginning in a different world. Thus we sometimes speak of love as bringing us out of ourselves. In this sense, a community of love is not something subsequent (an aggregate derived from preexisting units), but a rich source, a radically originating middle.

When we turn to another in this light and exclaim "ipse homo," we delight in a difference. We do so not simply because we recognize ourselves in the other, but because, more deeply, the agapeic other has turned to us and we ourselves are recognized. That is, we find that we make a difference to the other, and so we delight in a double difference,

our own and the other's, and in its shared recognition. Community engenders this complex unity, because it manifests this common delight
in difference. And it preserves an openness; nay, it is simply openness.
We recognize the other; the other reciprocates; indeed, we become a
"we" precisely to the extent that we consent to a reciprocation that is
infinitely open. When we close this off, greeting becomes embarrassed,
welcome ashamed. Nor is this open infinity of reciprocation merely one
of mutual self-interest, a case of the hand washing the hand. Informed
by goodwill, it may extend limitlessly beyond such a particularized motive. Not counting the cost, it may give for nothing, in solidarity even
to the point of suffering for the other.

Clearly I am talking about human promise, but this is not a merely
empty ideal. Given the pervasive understanding of human relationships
in terms similar to those of the master and slave dialectic (after a certain
reading of Hegel) or in terms of the will to power (after Nietzsche) or
a *libido dominandi* (after various strands in contemporary psychology that
take the darkness in man as what is elemental); given the undeniable
fact that *homo homini lupus*, one is made guarded in affirming the real
elemental promise of fellowship. But the essential need not be the
seamy. Our discussion has made us clearly aware that the promise of
the essential ideal is easily wrecked. For, just as self-will may fall away
from agapeic otherness, so we can come across fallen forms of individuality and community—what we might call the atomic particular and
the factional aggregate. Since these are common views of self and otherness, corresponding roughly to modern individualism and collectivism,
some brief remarks may be in order.

A person becomes an atomic particular through a certain withdrawal
from fellowship and through a shrinking back into an infertile difference. Selfhood destroys itself if it ceases to give itself; here we meet the
spirit of negation turned against itself. The atomic particular may not
know this; indeed, often it thinks of the other as the object of negation.
It defines itself by the assertion of its difference, but the empty freedom
it arrogates to itself is inseparable from its aversion to the different self-
transcendence demanded by fellowship. The loudness of its protestation
of its own freedom conceals its recoil from the freedom of another. Before another freedom, it does not know what to do except to clamor
more loudly about its own freedom. Atomic particularity is not individuality, but catatonic subjectivity chattering to itself in order to avoid
having to speak to, and even more, listen to, someone else. Its chatter

is a mask without a face, a mask expostulating about its absolute difference, behind which hides nothing.

We can see how this empty individualism leads inevitably to a correspondingly empty collectivism. For no man is an island, not even the
atomic particular. His petrified individuality will inevitably seek a com-
pensating outlet in the larger context of otherness. Here what we called
the factional aggregate becomes the fallen form of fellowship. Particularization and aggregation have this in common, that they both feed
on a negative difference. The particular is this particular because it is
not that, *not* the other particular, ad infinitum: thus we absolutize an
indigent homogeneity. But this results in every particular being indifferently different—that is, indifferently the same; so we can put them
all in the same bag, as it were, in an aggregation that extrinsically bun-
dles them all together. In the first case, by loud clamor about its own
difference, a self crowds out the difference of any other; in the second
case, by indifferent submission to the crowd, the self dissolves all difference into uniformity and external conformism. The atomic particular
and the conformist aggregate are correlative, and each, in its respective
sphere, is an ontological bully. The aggregate is merely the atomic particular writ large. For it is but a faction, monadic in a more general way,
to which any outside difference is a menace; hence, any dissent within
its own ranks must be crushed with summary cruelty. Thus the self-will
that pervades the atomic particular also permeates the faction and in-
sinuates itself into its war with other factions. Overall, there is a dissolution of fellowship, a hardening of individuality, a disrespect for
otherness, and a failure of agapeic goodwill.

Individuality and fellowship, understood metaxologically, are beyond
the negative difference of inflexible particularity and the negation of
difference of homogeneous aggregation. A real recalcitrance does exist,
but it is not to be treated in the above averse fashion. The other's reserved indeterminacy is both an openness and a recalcitrance. Agapeic
otherness spins the self back on its own difference—that is, it makes it
face itself and any self-inflating pretension. At the same time, it draws
the self into the common middle, where merely asserted—perhaps I
should say, shouted—difference is just not adequate. Through the suffering of difference, the genuine will holds fast and is tempered. At
bottom, the atomic particular who asserts his difference is the one who
is repelled by difference, and hence his sometimes easy surrender to
being engulfed by homogeneous aggregates. Learning the language of
a different concord, a language that converts the lack of desire into

goodwill, is like trying to coax a new tongue to supplant the quacking tongue of its chatter. We are a conversation, Hölderlin held. Man is the being who is tongued with hearing.

Let me stress once more the transcendence of agapeic otherness to any closed dialectical whole. While emerging from an immanent wholeness, goodwill is a free care for the wholeness of the other. So it requires a paradoxical wholeness that is infinitely open. It is beyond not only mechanical, but also organic, models of community. It is always tempting to view wholeness, whether individual or communal, in terms of an organic whole.[34] True, the organic is an inherently richer form of being than the mechanical, for, unlike the mechanical, it exhibits an immanently developing principle of unity, even in its manifoldness. But organic unity is problematic as a paradigm of free fellowship, for it tends toward a holism in which relation to the other becomes the power of the organic whole to assimilate the part. The open wholeness of free fellowship cannot be exhausted by any logic of parts and whole. The other here is not a limited part to be assimilated by the organic whole. Free fellowship lets the other be as other. There is a freedom here that extends even beyond the self as a whole, for it allows for and vouchsafes the warranted being of the other. Moreover, to let the other be is not a matter of indifference or neutral noninterference. It is not merely not constraining. To let be may be the highest act of cooperating respect.[35]

Free fellowship may be more open than any organic whole. Yet often, human relationships are more broken than organic relationships. It is this brokenness, perhaps, that arouses nostalgia for a vanished homogeneous unity in which the burdensome hazard of freedom seems alleviated.[36] But if we flee the demand of agapeic otherness or become metaphysically hostile to difference, inevitably we end up with perverse parodies of freedom and wholeness. For instance, self-will may try to build for itself a castle of bondage in which, seemingly in absolute control, it acts out its parody of freedom: man's will to power becomes a tyranny, in which he is both despot and charge, overweening and servile, slave master of others and slave of himself.[37] But with self-will, we really carry around with us our own invisible dungeon. We become chained to ourselves as our own degenerate necessity. We make it our lot to be as are the lost, impotent to break out beyond lack and negation, blocked inwardly from retracting our retraction from being. And even when we touch another, we do not seek to be released from our bondage; rather, we scheme to draw the other into it, to be our partner in woe. We encircle the other in a double bind, but only redouble our own state of seige.

Here again we see the perverse parody of mutual wholeness involved in the dialectical collusion of sadist and masochist. For their union is discord itself. Each loses himself and drives the other to the same lapse. Both sink into a bondage that, being a closed and confining circle, is, on its own terms, inescapable. Each hates the other because he hates himself, and each hates himself because he hates the other. If you like, their union—what they have in common—is their hatred. But since this hatred eventually becomes an indifferent one, equally extending to the other and turning back on the self, it becomes a boundless hatred. And this, of course, is hell itself. If this is the promised end of otherness, Sartre is right: *L'enfer, c'est les autres*. Here Sartre and Hobbes are blood brothers. But in the war of all against all, the Leviathan who would tame all does not bear the olive branch, unfortunately, only the apotheosis of the ailment. When we hiss at this hell, we succeed only in stoking its chill fires.

Between this circle of hell and agapeic goodwill lies an absolute rupture. Agapeic goodwill discloses what is beyond contestation and antagonism, what is beyond agonistic lack. From the circle of hell, agapeic goodwill has no reason; the latter requires a *leap of trust*, the terms of which self-will cannot justify. Hell is right, but for the wrong reason: goodwill is indeed a leap, but only because self-will is a fall. To gain goodwill, self-will would have to reverse its fall and leap upward; but this, ensnared as it is, it cannot do by itself. It requires the ingression of something from above, rain to water its droughted roots. We would never return home, be restored, unless we were called home, loved.

We love what lets us be, what sets us free. The metaxological community of being is exemplified in agapeic goodwill, because the difference it affirms is not a breach within one absorbing unity but a free expansion between original unities. Self and other cannot be reduced to objectifiable things, for they are worlds within themselves. Thus their communication can be a kind of transworldly reach, supporting a middle space wherein none has to lose himself and in which isolated lack may be most fully overcome. As an enjoyment of the other, goodwill is not a desire that, in being saturated, disappears. Rather, it is intensified by enjoyment, renewed in its joy. It stretches out to the infinite. It is as if self and other, in sharing joy in each other, were sharing in and supported by something beyond them both. It is as if, in turning to the other, we are drawn to something more, whose elusiveness and inexhaustibility not even the finite, beloved other can capture. It is as if our outreach to otherness were a transwordly reach for the infinite ground. When all the chatter ceases, even when all the genuine talking is done, a deeper stillness takes over that envelops and invades.

PART III
ACTUAL INFINITUDE

Chapter Eight
Desire and the Absolute Original

In parts 1 and 2, we tried to see how desire might pass beyond dialectical self-mediation to the metaxological community of being. I now want to develop the possibilities afforded by the metaxological view to provide some further picture of that limiting otherness, especially as it is disclosed through the sublime as aesthetic infinitude and through agapeic otherness. I will draw on many of the key notions discussed previously—for instance, the contrast between desire as lacking and agapeic goodwill, the sense of overdetermined being of original selfhood, the coexistence in human desire of an exigence for immanent wholeness and an infinite openness to otherness, and the notions of the absorbing god, static eternity, and the original power of becoming—to suggest an even more original power of being. I want to speak of this last power by means of a metaphysical metaphor that we might call *the absolute original*. The absolute original is a metaphor for the ultimate good of desire, the truth of knowing, and the sublime beauty of fugitive being. The more original a reality is, the more desire is drawn to it. Here desire is quickened to the maximum, as if it were always an implicit opening to the absolute original, one that is revealed even at the most rudimentary level of desire's incapacity to remain mere lack, revealed in the restlessness that remains even after desire has expended itself on an infinity of particular things, revealed in the insufficiency of enclosing human existence in an immanent self-sufficiency, revealed in the willing consent to the radical difference coming before us in the sublime and in agapeic otherness.

THE ABSOLUTE ORIGINAL AND THE METAXOLOGICAL VIEW

Above us the sky, the eagle and the dove, birds buffeted and borne by the air; surrounding us unmastered sea in ebb and flow, whales singing in its streams and nameless things in the teeming, terrible deep; around us, fire and sun and stars and light sent through the immense spaces of cold galaxies; beneath us, the round, rolling earth, under it the worm and louse, roaming on it beast, bear, bull and man, the humus of whose being binds him to lower things like hair, mud, and dung—things the young Socrates thought beneath philosophy.[1] Of things I name an infinitesimal few, yet the world still seems a fantastic infinity.

We cannot negate this vast variousness. Why then ask about the absolute original? Is this not to travesty this diversity in its sometimes bewildering, oftentimes delightful, profusion? Our question here, however, is whether the self and the infinity of particular things exhaust the originating power of being, and if not, what there is more. Put in terms of this more, the question implies an unshakable acceptance of plurality. It is such plurality, in fact, that allows us to pose the question. The issue of the absolute original does not bear on the absolution of plurality and the dissolution of difference. Rather, it seeks some ground of plurality in the ultimate origin of real difference, a ground that supports and preserves plurality. The point is not to get behind or beyond plurality to some unity that overcomes difference as if it were a metaphysical defect. Such ontological nostalgia that would dissolve difference as dualistic opposition has already been seen to be lacking, as in such notions as the absorbing god and static eternity.[2]

Moreover, in inquiring about the absolute original, we do not seek a specific finite cause in the sense of the prior conditions that determine and effect a present event. We are not regressing along a sequence of determinate events in order to find in the earlier events the conditions that determine and make intelligible the later events. Nor are we asking about the relations among finite events in which one event serves as the determinate explanatory source of another. For instance, when we ask after the origin of this signpost on the road, we can answer in terms of the workmen who placed it there and so on, backward. This question and answer are not concerned with the fact itself, the signpost on the road, except in its intelligible relations to prior facts. By contrast, the question of the absolute origin is not about the relations among finite events, but about the finite event itself at its deepest degree of concreteness, about every event and the whole system of their relations, the fact that they are at all, what we earlier called the metaxological thereness of being. The question of a conditional origin, which stops short at facts and their relation, is on a different level from this question which seeks the absolute origin of finitude itself. The latter probes the fact at a deeper level, at which no determinate fact can suffice, for the being of any such fact must itself be questioned. Seeking the metaphysical ground of the fact itself, it is not within the order of a sequence of facts, but is at the second limit.[3]

Relating the absolute original to this second limit implies that we are not dealing with a problem about something outside ourselves that we can objectify and handle easily. We participate in the origin, and our very being is implicated in the question.[4] That is, our metaphysical place in the whole of being is at stake. The metaxological view implies that we cannot stand *sub specie aeternitatis,* if this means our disappearance into some divine anonymity. Rather, we must try to intermediate between man and what is beyond. We cannot name the origin except from the middle, in the middle, and through the middle. The difficulty is that, in the middle, we seem unable to assign anything but finite categories to what purportedly is beyond all finitude, being its origin and ground. If we name the absolute origin in terms of finite categories, we seem straightway caught in a separation of subject and object and their mutual limitation. Hence it seems impossible to name anything unconditional or absolute. The very act of naming articulates a difference between the namer and the named and thereby seems to limit what is asserted as unlimited. Furthermore, if we could name the origin and overcome the difference, it would seem that all determinations, including the self and the name, would vanish into pure undifferentiated activity. If we proceed from the limited to the unlimited, are we not defeated in our success, the very act of naming being a reassertion of the anonymity of the named?

Here, I suggest, the metaxological standpoint again proves helpful, for it involves a complex intermediation between the human self and otherness, such that it is impossible to give a direct account of, or have immediate access to, the absolute original. Our access is rather a periphrasis via the intermediate, which means that our philosophical discourse cannot be an absolutely univocal, determinate language. It must remain tentative and open, suggestive of what is elusive, rather than dogmatically assertive with regard to some reality supposedly mastered. But I am not, as should be clear, enjoining any sheerly equivocal language. The metaxological requires a more richly pluralized speech. Direct access or univocally determinate language would falsify not only the metaxological, but also the absolute original named from the intermediate. Further, this pluralized language and its periphrastic indirection need not be a lack. It may reflect a positive necessity, imaging a genuine acknowledgment of otherness. From the perspective of the present chapter, the discussion of this entire book and the unfolding of desire explored therein can be seen as such a periphrastic indirection, at last enabling us to venture some philosophical remarks concerning the origin.[5]

Here we might recall our earlier discussion concerning the need for metaphysical metaphors. The same requirement of the language of image and metaphor makes itself felt here in relation to the intermediated character of the metaxological. Metaphor, from the Greek word *metapherein*, literally means to carry between, to carry from one place to another. Thus, a metaphor may be said to imply an intermediation. But again, in that the *meta* may also mean "beyond," metaphor can also be seen as a movement that carries us beyond, as well as between. That is, it may concretize some dynamic sense of the beyond right here in the middle itself. But there is a further ambiguity in the etymology of the term that we might note, if only to curb any pretension to have mastered this beyond. In its etymology, *metaphor* may also carry the meanings of "to change," "to alter," and, indeed, "to pervert." Metaphor, if you like, carries a kind of self-interpretation of its own ambiguous nature since, being intermediate, it may involve a transfer of meaning or simulation, which at the same time runs the risk of being a dissimulation and a perversion. It is like a kind of proxy who, in getting the message across, plants some suspicion that something may have been altered in the deliverance. Thus, metaphor may be a creative act of naming that stretches language beyond "literal" univocal determinacy, yet at the same time always reserves the right to call itself into question and to dissolve any pretension to unsurpassable absoluteness regarding the name that it has uttered in the middle. This subversion of claims to mastery in the very act of articulation opens the space of irreducible difference once again.

As metaxological, a metaphor need not be the identity or sameness of two dissimilar things; it can be the open identification or nonreductive naming of the different. It may carry language to a limit, providing a bridgehead to the unknown and a breach of our alienation from it. In a sense, then, the image comes into its own when we try to think what no image can encapsulate, namely, the absolute origin. Here, too, it is severely tested: to know what is radically other, we must find some continuity with it, but without being seduced into mistaking a likeness for an absolute sameness.[6] A metaphysical metaphor must seek a breakthrough beyond the oppositions of finite categories; but, since it cannot fully avoid their opposition, it must be carried by what is positive in them in the very act of going beyond them. It must at once be a paradoxical mixture of affirmation and negation. What the absolute original calls for is not proof in the usual sense of demonstrating an intelligible connection between one finite item and another. The too fixed concepts and determinate categories involved in such proof would objectify the absolute original and in the process be a living disproof of what was supposedly proved.[7] We must move through the middle, neither fixing irrevocably nor getting fixed to the extremes or the middle.

To use a Platonic metaphor, there is a sense in which we can never entirely leave the cave behind. It is the movement up and down that is the thing. It is the movement of desire in the metaxu that affords us a glimpse of the sun. And the imaginative language required to articulate what is seen always ties us to the intermediate and to the sense of otherness emergent in its concreteness.[8] To move thus through the middle is not to be moving elsewhere. It is to try to articulate what is involved in the deepest degree of concreteness. We need language beyond the dualistic exclusiveness of finite categories, with its either/or between affirmation and negation. The middle demands a both/and. Thus, in one respect, to move through the middle may entail a kind of heuristic negation: starting from where we are and naming the absolute original by anticipation, we may strip from the anticipation what cannot be sustained. The outcome need not be an absolute *via negativa*. Since the origin may be suggested metaphysically by the originated, a heuristic negation of what it is not may point to some apophatic affirmation of what it is. Let this suffice for now on the imagistic, metaphoric aspect of the matter, since we will be touching again on this.

THE ABSOLUTE ORIGINAL AND THE GIVENNESS OF BEING

Let me try to further clarify what kind of question I am asking here, and how we might respond to its peculiarities. In rational discourse, the ultimate appeal is frequently taken to be a recourse to the facts; these are supposed to provide a basis for rational agreement, thereby settling disputes. With regard to the question of the absolute origin, however, the fact that a thing is at all is close to the ultimate enigma.[9] By the fact of being here is meant the fourth degree of concreteness. At this limit, finite reason encounters what is not finitely comprehended or explained. The fact that being *is* settles no ultimate question. Rather it raises it. The fact that being is, is given to metaphysical thinking as a beginning. This is the question that Leibniz, followed by Schelling and, in our own day, Heidegger, saw as the ultimate metaphysical issue: why being at all, rather than nothing? why not nothing? The same question might be seen as implicit in Aquinas's third way, when he questions the entire universe in its radical contingency as to why it might *be* at all.[10]

Our question here is not whether there is a being beyond becoming, a static eternity abiding in absolute determinate self-identity. That the world is at all is the wonder, that it is there, an exceedingly astonishing given. The point, then, is not to ascend to being from becoming and leave becoming behind. Being already appears in the givenness of what is. The question is what gives the given, what the giver might be like in terms of what appears as and in the given. Now the givenness of being in becoming gives us a world in process that is both determinate and open and hence suggestive of the power of being as overdetermined. The givenness of being is not an immediate thereness, not a dialectical self-mediated thereness. The givenness of being is metaxologically intermediated. Hence its thereness, while constituting a world unto itself, also points beyond itself to a power it also images.

The world, in the thereness of things, presents itself as something originated. As originated, it is not identical with its origin, even if it does image it. But it is not a mere image. As a world in becoming, it shares in the original power of being. We might then speak of the givenness of being as an original image: original, as constituting its own dynamic world; image, as pointing beyond itself to something more. It is hard to avoid the analogy of the artwork. Being as given is then seen as a creation, a poiēsis of the overdetermined power of being, its artwork. The very word *poiēsis* carries in its etymology connotations extending beyond human origination to any process of origination, any coming into being, as Plato notes in the *Symposium*.[11] As an original image, the world manifests the concreteness of a creation that reveals an infinite, radiant, and reserved power, suggested by a present sensuous embodiment. Thus the world as image and original might be seen as a mighty work in itself and a metaphoric disclosure of the power of the absolute original.

A certain open indeterminacy in the givenness of being is important here. Just as an artwork may be a paradoxical determinate indeterminacy, an original image at once both defined and formed, yet also open to a plurality of interpretations, so becoming is both determinate and indeterminate, an originative process generating determinate entities, yet also disclosing the positively overdetermined power of being that is not exhausted by finite things. The fact of being is not any absolutely finished reality. Its positive indeterminacy, in the sense *that* it is at all, opens us to an original power beyond *what* things are, where what a thing is refers to its definite structure, form, or essence. Even the meanest thing, such as a stone, a worm, or an insect, is more than structure; it evinces a certain being there that is not structurally comprehended or circumscribed. Structural understanding abstracts a determinate "what" from a "that" (in the sense of a particular thing), but the "that it is" of being (the fourth degree of concreteness) cannot be abstracted as a "what." There is no finite determinate structure, eidos, *Gestalt,* of the power of being as such, even though that power is only disclosed to us through the intermediation of certain forms of its determinate appearance. One merit of seeing the givenness of being in relation to becoming is that we are kept from being mesmerized by structure, immobile being, static form, and from canonizing these as the essence of existence. Existence manifests essences, but in a sense, being as such has no finite essence. Finite essence is not an unoriginated structure prior to existence. It is posterior and derived, an originated determination that issues from the original forming power of being.

If the givenness of being is thus overdetermined, there is a sense in which there are no absolutely univocal or literal facts. If the world is seen as the poiēsis of the power of being, its thereness is closer to a condition of poetry than of prose. This means that any metaphysical talk about the fact of being cannot itself be simply matter of fact. The world as an original image is more than the sum of finished determinate facts, and its thereness cannot be exhausted in univocal speech. I cannot dissemble the enormous difficulty regarding what constitutes genuinely intelligible philosophical discourse on this matter. For, in a way, we cannot say "what" the absolute original is. Commonly the what of something refers to its determinate, intelligible structure. But such intelligible structure is a category that is more appropriate to our efforts to understand finite, particular things. Once again we must ask whether we can say anything at all about the absolute original? For if it is more than finite structure, is it then formless, structureless, and so beyond all articulate discourse? Or should we speak of it as more the structuring than the structure, as intelligence acting rather than intelligibility produced, as overdetermined power rather than determinate product, as active differentiating rather than differentiated term? And even if we do speak of it as dynamic originating, what more can we say about this?

My response here is that, though we cannot circumscribe "what" the absolute original is, we may still say something on the basis of finite realities that are not themselves circumscribed by the limited intelligibility of finite structure. Are there exemplifications of being beyond the antithesis of categories like fixed form and formlessness, finite intelligibility and unintelligibility? Such exemplifications would be finite beings that themselves give evidence of an infinite dimension, a dimension that may be suggestive of an even more radical infinity. And have we not seen before how determinate finite being may open up to the indeterminate—for instance, in original selfhood, and in the otherness of the sublime and agapeic goodwill? Such exemplifications resist reduction to fixed particularized finitude, but image, through their finite thereness, the reserved indeterminacy of being. On such a basis let me venture an image of the absolute original, drawing on original selfhood as an intermediate original—that is, taking the self not as some Platonic soul alone with itself but in the context of its metaphysical place in the metaxological community of being.

THE ABSOLUTE ORIGINAL, THE REGULATIVE IDEAL, AND THE *ENS REALISSIMUM*

One possible approach, which takes into account human finitude and the limitations of our discourse, might be to think of the absolute original as the unconditioned in a Kantian sense—that is, as a regulative ideal.[12] Taking our bearings from becoming as an infinite succession, we postulate some ideal unity to regulate the series of things and give it some semblance of totality. The process of becoming itself seems to deny us any one unconditional thing, since nothing in its succession of beings escapes coming into being and passing away. As a consequence, we might be tempted to *project* something unconditional, either at a remote origin that we cannot actually recover or at a distant end that we can never completely reach.

One merit of this approach is its heuristic, anticipatory character, and hence its recognition that we cannot master the unconditional. Yet the anticipation is ambiguous. It points to the unconditional as a possible project, one that offers a formal unity to guide and systematize experience. Yet its merely possible, regulative character prevents us from acknowledging more fully any sense of the *actually* unconditioned. Thus our anticipation of the unconditional as a regulative ideal risks being an empty anticipation. Its indefiniteness is such that, as we try to approach the unconditional, it seems to recede into nothing, and we are left with a dissolving *progressus ad indefinitum*. There is also the difficulty that it is, after all, the human self that here supplies the movement of becoming with a projected unity. The danger, then, is that the sequence of becoming becomes indifferent *in itself*. Its unconditional dimension is externally imposed, and even then, it is only an ideal projected by us, an ideal that will never be real in otherness itself. Moreover, the unconditional as a projection of the self is an absolute that we *will* to be, not an absolute that we can grant as actually being there in otherness. As regulative of a project of willing, the unconditional *ought* to be, but what ought to be is not yet actual. Hegel's criticism of Kant must be taken seriously here, with respect to both this "ought to be" and the progressus ad indefinitum, which Hegel calls the "bad infinite."[13] The Kantian regulative ideal risks being an absolute that can never be actual and hence an absolute that is not absolute at all.

The empty indefiniteness of the regulative ideal easily causes the absolute original to evaporate into nothing, which often happens in post-Kantian thought. Another approach, related to this, seeks to avoid indefiniteness by fixing the absolute original in strongly determinate terms. Again, taking our bearings from becoming as infinite succession, we might try to seek unity in *one member* of the series of things, seek an origin in its first member. The absolute original is then said to be the ens realissimum, the first or highest member of the series of things. This approach puts complete definiteness in the place of the indefiniteness of the postulated ideal that is nowhere realized. The absolute original is reduced to the greatest determinate entity, the highest substance. This concept of the ens realissimum anticipates that the absolute original will be no different than any other determinate entity, that it will be one being among others, even if it is the highest. But this is just the difficulty. For we wrongly substantialize the absolute original and risk identifying its being with finite originated being. Thus we distort the nature of the question of the absolute original, as previously outlined. In Heidegger's terms, we treat the issue as ontic rather than ontological, as a question regarding beings rather than Being. The concept of the ens realissimum feeds on a univocal sense of being, as in the case of the naive realist who pictures God as the greatest being in a manner that attenuates the irreducible difference separating the divine from finite things. If the anticipation of the absolute original as a regulative ideal tends to be vacillating, even equivocal, the anticipation of it as an ens realissimum tends to be rash, even idolatrous. The image is put in the place of the original; the anticipation is confused with explanation.[14]

These two approaches are similar in that they are bound to becoming as infinite succession. Each has difficulty conceiving an unconditioned that is actual and hence more than a mere postulate, but whose actuality is not merely that of the highest entity in a sequence of things, since its being is not that of a thing at all. On this score, however, there is something positive in relation to the regulative ideal. In terms of a sequence of becoming, the absolute original is said to be *not yet,* in that no member of the series of things can supply us with the absolutely unconditioned. This "not yet" can be seen positively, both as the thrust of finite man beyond himself and finite things and as suggesting the reserved dimension of the unconditioned. Of course, we misinterpret this reserve if we restrict it either to the series of things or to the totality of things that would close the series. The not yet points us beyond the infinite succession of things, beyond its highest being and even its postulated totality. The absolute original can be reserved and yet not be a member of the series of things, because it is not a thing at all, but rather, the reserved overdetermined power of being that constitutes, without being consumed by, what exists in a determinately finite way.

The ens realissimum is bound to the sequence of things in its determinacy; the postulated ideal is directed to the indefiniteness of this sequence, seeking to close it by way of a projected unity that is never real. The former is tied to finite facts, the latter to the system of such facts. Neither fully appreciates the metaphysical fact of being and the significance of its givenness. Neither reaches a real ground of the fact of finitude. In that the absolute original is the real ground of the fact of finitude in its metaphysical givenness, it cannot be identified with any entity within the world or even with the world considered as a cosmic totality of entities. Nor can it be identified with a static absolute, because precisely in being static, it would be unoriginating and so could not effect the world. Should we identify the absolute original with the totality of entities, we compromise its absoluteness: the sum aggregate of conditional and originated things is not itself unconditional. Should we make the absolute original a static absolute, we sacrifice its originality: the product of activity may be relatively static and determinate, but there must be more than static determinacy to the power of origination, precisely as actively originating.

THE ABSOLUTE ORIGINAL AS WHOLE AND INFINITE

Can we proceed beyond this equivocal indefiniteness of the regulative ideal and this univocal definiteness of the ens realissimum? Can we avoid this polarity and say anything affirmative regarding the overdetermined, constitutive being of the absolute original? Here I want to draw on the image of constitutive, overdetermined being provided by original self-hood as metaxologically placed in the otherness of being. As an intermediate original, the self revealed itself as double—that is, both as a desire for immanent self-relation and as infinitely open in terms of its exodus into what is beyond. It desires to be whole; yet, as infinitely open, it may become actively originative in relation to otherness. Wholeness and infinitude in this sense can be seen as two ultimates defining man's deepest relation to himself and otherness. Perhaps we might now use these two notions, by way of heuristic negation, to give us some image of the absolute original. Wholeness may help us make sense of the absolute original as an ultimate unity in itself; the idea of infinity may help us make sense of its difference and its power of creation in relation to otherness. Thus we may preserve, first, the absoluteness of the absolute original in itself and, second, its relatedness, through its originating power, to finite being other than itself.

Likening it thus to original selfhood, the absolute original might be said to be qualitatively whole. In this, it differs from a regulative ideal that supplies a formal, and then only a possible, qualitative unity with respect to a quantitative aggregate of things. Furthermore, its self-relation must be active, not static. As an absolutely qualitative whole, its activity would be bound by nothing but itself. How are we to understand this nothing? Does it imply that the absolute original was once nothing, only becoming itself through some even more primordial origination? If this were so, the absolute original would be conditional on a process of development, becoming what it is not. This conclusion follows, I suggest, only if we conceive of self-relation from the viewpoint of desire as a lack. But since the absolute original is not here to be seen as the intention of, but rather as actually, a qualitative whole, the more appropriate likeness is selfhood as a positive power, as excess of being rather than a deficiency thereof. The better image is not lacking desire but goodwill in relation to agapeic otherness. In this light, the absolute original need not be seen as becoming itself via a progression from lack in itself to positive power. What is negative and what is positive need not mutually define each other, as tends to happen in a closed dialectic of self-mediation. The absolute original may be seen as the positive power of being that defines the negative but need not, in turn, be defined by it.

A helpful distinction here might be between what we might call an *erotic absolute* and an *agapeic absolute*. An erotic absolute is one that *needs* to become actualized in time, one that is ontologically lacking without this temporal self-realization. By contrast, an agapeic absolute is one that originates freely from a wholeness already actual, one whose absoluteness is not lacking prior to temporal manifestation. Time is not identical with the radical self-becoming of such an absolute. Any moment of time may be privileged with an epiphany; hence, later times are not more privileged than earlier ones, which, of course, is not to deny man's capacity to develop his vigilance to such epiphanies. In the language of wholeness and infinity, an erotic absolute is like a desire that is initially indefinite and inchoate, but also dynamic and infinitely restless; the unfolding of its dynamism searches out absolute wholeness in such a way that the temporal process may bring such wholeness to concrete determination. By contrast, an agapeic absolute, like desire as goodwill, is already whole in itself, indeed overwhole; yet it may be infinitely open in its overflowing of itself and so originate otherness as something irreducible and not simply another side of its own self-realization.

The problem of preserving divine absoluteness in its otherness will remain intractable, I suspect, if we stay tied to erotic desire as our primary model of dynamic being and fail to perceive the metaphysical primacy of agapeic love. Many post-Kantian versions of absoluteness (even when such notions remain implicit and even in thinkers who seem to be explicitly "atheistic") suffer from ambiguity here. The contemporary spirit of metaphysical distrust finds it hard to credit agapeic otherness or the sheer gratuity of goodwill or any love given purely for the other. It suspects a secret self-will or will to power or covert egotism or self-insistence. We could look at a number of examples here,[15] but our discussion will focus on the contrast between the absolute original and Hegel's absolute. The latter, however complex and ambiguous, in the end seems more erotic than agapeic, not surprisingly perhaps, given the inadequacy of closed dialectical self-mediation for dealing with agapeic otherness.

The absolute original as an agapeic otherness differs from Hegel's conception of affirmative infinity as the negation of the negation. The absolute original is more like positive, creative origination in that it may define the negative but need not be defined by it. In Hegel's absolute, by contrast, the positive and the negative mutually define each other in a dialectical manner. But a double negation, a negation of a negation, on its own cannot originate or create. Though it may be an ingredient in creation, a double negation (a lack negating itself, as in erotic desire) cannot produce positive content from itself unless it is grounded in a prior and more ultimate affirmation, an affirmation that in itself is more than, radically in excess of, negation (like the release to the already implicit yes to being encountered in agapeic goodwill). The absolute original tries to name a certain metaxological asymmetry between being and nothing in which the affirmation of being has absolute priority. Hegel's absolute (at the beginning of the *Logic,* say)[16] is defined by a dialectical mediation between being and nothing, in which both serve as moments to the self-becoming, self-mediation of the absolute.

Consider again the affirmation "being is." As we have already seen, this might be regarded as a compacted affirmation rather than an empty tautology, a double affirmation in which being appears twice over. Being appears as more, as overdetermined. This affirmation cannot be reduced to a double negation in Hegel's sense. Instead, we seem to have a kind of yes that indicates a radical priority of being over nonbeing, suggestive of the kind of being we are trying to think with respect to the absolute original.[17] Or consider the point in terms of Parmenides' famous injunction not to speak of nonbeing. Parmenides warns us off this speaking because, should we speak thus, we will be forced to assert what looks like a contradiction—namely, that nonbeing is. We might put a somewhat different interpretation on this, however. In saying that nonbeing is, we seem to give the honors to nonbeing, but in truth the prize goes to being. For even in speaking of nonbeing, we cannot escape affirming being. There is no escape from being, even into nothing. This necessity of acknowledging being, even in relation to nonbeing, is a measure of its metaphysical ultimacy. So it is not, as Hegel would have it, that a double negation issues in affirmation; it is rather that negation brings us round, in spite of itself, to a double affirmation of being. We return again to the asymmetry of being and nothing. Being is not generated from lack, but from generosity, as it were. The absolute original might be seen as this redoubled affirmation of being over nothing. As self-relating wholeness, it masters nonbeing; as infinitely creative power, it gratuitously originates. It is as if the absolute original not only says "yes" and loves itself, but also says "yes, yes" and creates the world. The metaphor of this generous yes is meant to suggest something of the overflowing, creative bounty of the primordial ground of being.

Thus our strategy of heuristic negation does not state that the absolute original is not this, not that, ad infinitum. Such a negation would be privative, indefinite, and ultimately reductive of both the positive being of finite things and a genuinely affirmative sense of infinitude. It would be like the via negativa of desire in its flight from the otherness of the world into static eternity. We have already criticized this, but here we may agree with Hegel's criticism of the progressus ad indefinitum, albeit without fully accepting Hegel's way of bending this progressus back on itself in circular self-mediation and so dialectically subsuming the finite into the infinite. There is always something more in terms of the metaxological sense of being. Our heuristic negation does not see the givenness of finite being as something lacking and hence as something to be dualistically negated in the manner of Platonism or dialectically negated and hence to be *aufgehoben,* or subsumed into a self-mediating infinitude in the manner of Hegelianism. We proceed from the givenness of being as positively excessive, and our heuristic negation denies that the power of either the self (as intentional infinitude) or external becoming (as infinite succession) is absolute enough. The point is to heighten rather than diminish, to enrich rather than impoverish.

This is the intention behind our attempt to think the absolute original as the togetherness of wholeness and infinitude. We want neither to falsely fix the boundary of the whole nor to let being dissolve into a bad indefiniteness. The togetherness of wholeness and infinitude means, first, an openness to the whole, since the infinite cannot be bounded; and second, against sheer indefiniteness, the possible concretion of infinitude in real wholeness, since one of the stunning givens of being is the astonishing intricacy of its articulations. If we take our bearings from original selfhood as metaxologically placed in being, we may better understand the possibility of a "unity" that is paradoxically indeterminate precisely because it is originative. We might say that the absolute original is a kind of double acting, an equilibrium of the centripetal and the centrifugal. If it were centripetal only, contraction into the void could not be avoided, and the absolute original would become a kind of black hole. But since its centripetal wholeness is balanced by its centrifugal infinitude, it cannot be shut up in itself in a catatonic impotence. Rather, it manifests its being as inexhaustible energy and expansive fecundity. Its overfullness is not given to it by another external being; rather, it is the source of what is given in finiteness. As an originating whole, the absolute original is self-originating; as creative infinity, it is the ageless origin of the finite world. And though it may help our understanding to distinguish between originating wholeness and creating infinity, within the absolute original, being and originating must not be thought of as really separable.[18]

Least of all can the absolute original be called a homogeneous unity, like the dense sphere of Parmenidean being;[19] although one would want to say that, like Parmenides' being, the absolute original contains no vacuity, inspissation, contraction, fixation, inanity, ponderosity, obtenebration, deprivation, and such like. Nor is it the Hegelian unity, which is initially implicit only to become explicit and immanently differentiated by a process of subsequent self-development. Its creative act is not simply its own self-completion. Because it is self-complete, more than complete, it is infinite, a foison. And it may be seen to originate the world not because of defect in itself, but rather, because of excess. For to create is not to originate out of defect and to remedy self-defect. Creation is an excess of completion and wholeness.

It is this very excess that discloses the reserved indeterminacy of being and makes given being appear as a gratuitous origination. There is a sense of the beyond here that forces us to dehumanize the origin, even as we try to comprehend it on the image of original selfhood. Unlike the self, even when understood metaxologically, it does not overcome its own lack and seek wholeness by temporal succession; for it is an eternal whole, where *eternal* does not imply inert immobility but the fullness of activity which, while abiding in itself, yet creates the different. Again we see the usefulness of the analogy of agapeic otherness. This can both remain in itself in ontological security and yet be beyond itself; it can be grounded in itself and yet be available as an ontological support of the other as other, at home in its own being and yet in community with all being different from itself.

We must conceive wholeness here not as a progression from lack to positivity, or from imperfection to perfection, but rather from positivity to positivity, from perfection to perfection. If the absolute original as whole lacks nothing, as infinite, it is more than the whole that lacks nothing. It is original creation. Again we are beyond the double negation. Consider this ethical example: say a man renounces a bad way of life, opening up a new way; his negation does not constitute this new way; doing nothing bad is not the same as being good; it may be a necessary, but it is not a sufficient, condition of the latter. By contrast, being a man of goodwill does not simply consist in the freedom not to do evil things. Far more, it consists in a condition of being that is irreducibly positive. Indeed, it may be that a person of goodwill finds it *necessary* to do the good because it simply expresses his being. It is the overflow of wholeness. Such a person is not free, in the sense of arbitrary will, to choose or do evil, even though the condition of his being is one of genuinely real freedom.

Thus, the kind of wholeness at issue here is beyond the normal antithesis of freedom and necessity. These two are exclusive opposites if one is arbitrariness and the other external compulsion. But this antithesis does not capture the reality wherein freedom is self-determination—that is, inward necessity. If the absolute original is superabundant wholeness, it is not determined by necessity in the sense of some limiting lack, but it may be called necessary as being immanently self-determined. Yet its necessary being as self-determination need not be inconsistent with an openness to the free creation of the different. Its affirmative infinity may be freely creative beyond itself, even if within itself, as whole, it is both free and necessary—that is, if creative freedom is the necessary nature of its being.

Thus, we could also say that the givenness of finite being, the origination of what is, might be a free creation without thereby being capricious, might be gratuitous without being absurd. Here the notion of agapeic giving reminds us of the ancient view that *omne bonum est diffusivum sui,* as also of the view expressed in Plato's *Timaeus* and reiterated throughout the tradition from Aristotle to Aquinas and indeed by Hegel himself, that God is not envious.[20] The absolute original is not grudging of existence. Its creation of the diverse, the plural, the manifold, is no lapse from its primordial integrity, but a presentation of its bounty, its fabulous horn of plenty. Creation is not a decrease of the origin. Nor does this origin, when it overflows itself, perfect itself, for it is already perfect, pluperfect, more than pluperfect. And if the infinity of the absolute original is its originative act, its wholeness prevents this act from being a diminution, thereby conserving its overcompletion. Its rich store is not compromised by its creation of what is different, but rather takes joy in giving it for nothing.

If the absolute original originates finite being other than itself, does not this put a limit on its absoluteness, thereby compromising its unconditionality? The difficulty here, I think, lies in picturing a limit in holistic terms that are misleadingly spatial. The wholeness of the absolute original cannot be assimilated to the determinate identity of finite entities that limit each other externally. Nor is wholeness to be thought of simply as enclosed, monadic self-sufficiency. Agapeic wholeness testifies, through the unconditional value of goodwill, to a bond with otherness that is not limiting and constraining in this way. A limit regarding the absolute original has to do more with the indeterminate limit of its reserved power, which cannot be simply objectified. This limit is not that of a totality which bounds the sum of things. If we must use spatial terms, it is not inside or outside the totality of things; it is both inside and outside at once; it is everywhere—it is here, it is there, it is nowhere. If we must use holistic terms, then we must say that it is not the circumference of a circle but its center and yet not the center but the circumference; or it is the circumference and the center, for the center is out on the periphery and the periphery is at the center; or it is neither center nor circumference, for there is no center and no circumference, and there is no circle.[21]

However, we must be very guarded in the use of holistic terms. Earlier, we noted the limitations of organic metaphors with respect to agapeic otherness. Here, with the absolute original, if we let ourselves be misled by the analogy of substantival identity, we will find ourselves with a self-same unity that cannot radically originate, and hence we will make real plurality unintelligible. The only way such a unity could be conceived to originate would be if it were either less than or more than a simple identity or whole. If it were less, at most it might originate itself as a whole, itself as the identity that is initially lacking; but it could not create an other, something different. If it were more, there would be no need for it to originate itself in this sense, for it *is* itself already and does not lack; and hence it may be the ground of a different, created plurality. Since the absolute original, as infinite, is more than a whole, it may do more than create itself, may be other than self-creation.

Perhaps Hegel is the thinker who is most thoroughgoing in his attempt to take negativity into account with respect to the absolute, yet here we meet the same reduction of origination to the negation of the negation by which *the whole comes to constitute itself*. But even this is not possible, as we have seen, without a more ultimate sense of affirmative being prior to all negation. The absolute original does not constitute itself a whole by way of lack; but as more than whole, it may originate genuine otherness. There is obviously a sense in which Hegel seeks a certain unity of the whole and the infinite, even to the point of identifying them. But because of his stress on dialectical self-mediation, he shows a predeliction for wholeness. For Hegel there is a dialectic of finite and infinite and the self-mediating inclusion of finitude in infinity. Relative to the absolute original, by contrast, there is no dialectical subsumption of the finite in the infinite, because here it is more appropriate to speak of the metaxological intermediation of infinite and infinite. The dialectical sense of a monistic totalizing whole is exploded open by this pluralized sense of infinitude. And even though we speak of the absolute original as whole and infinite, there is a sense in which the metaxological view means that a sense of the openness of infinity is more primordial than any form of wholeness.[22]

On this score we might venture that there need be no dialectical necessity for the creation of the world. For an account of the world in terms of dialectical necessity, as in Hegel, tends to subordinate infinity to wholeness and makes self-relation more primordial than originative act. In the absolute original, originative act *is* self-relation, but in a sense that carries us beyond any finite sense of wholeness or identity and in a manner reminiscent of the classical view of God as uniquely one, whose essence is being itself.[23] Viewing the matter from a somewhat different angle: since the givenness of finite being might be seen as a creation, as a gratuitous origination, as an original image, the relation of the absolute original to the originated world is not to be captured by dialectical necessity. Within the absolute original itself, dialectical necessity is not adequate to the positive power of self-determination, self-origination: the self-grounding of the absolute original is not described as the whole that constitutes itself by way of negating its own lack. Between the absolute original and the originated world lies a discontinuity between the absolute original as its own whole and the world as freely created and other. If there is a "necessity" of creation, it is more metaxological than dialectical. The contingent world appears as a gratuitous origination because it intimates a necessary—that is, a self-justifying—freedom as its origin. This freedom and necessity of the origin are better imaged by agapeic otherness than dialectical self-identity.

THE ABSOLUTE ORIGINAL AS BEGINNING AND END

Let me here offer some brief remarks on the absolute original in relation to the extremes of time, namely the beginning and end, in so far as this is possible from the middle of the metaxological. The absolute original is not a beginning in any sense confined to becoming as succession. It is not an originating event that is first in becoming as a series of events. Of course, becoming may itself be seen as a kind of perpetual beginning. Yet to confine the absolute original to one event in its sequence would be to diminish it to less than becoming as a whole. The absolute original is not an *archē* lost in the dark backward of time; it is, as it were, an anarchic origin that gives time's beginning, without itself being a first moment or a temporal product. This origin is beyond becoming but is not a static eternity. Indeed, by comparison with the dynamic power of the origin, becoming can be seen to be relatively static. Becoming may give us an original image of this origin, but to move from this image to the absolute original is not to renounce the generative power of becoming and extrapolate to ungenerating being. It is to heighten this power, to think of it as unoriginated originating rather than originated originating.

Considered as a metaphysical beginning, the absolute original is not just the power to form matter or to unify form and matter as given to its originating act ab extra, like Plato's Demiurge. It is not the unitive act that relates form and matter as already there. Relative to it, form and matter—indeed, becoming as formation process—are not prior, but derivative, hence originated modes of being. That they have being at all is by virtue of this ageless origin. Nor are they just implicit in the absolute original in a way that subsequent origination makes explicit and such that the temporal process becomes the absolute original differentiating itself. We must try to think of absolute origination as limited by nothing. Relative to it, nothing would be prior; limited forms of being, no matter how dynamic, would be derivative; and without it there would be nothing. Though it is almost impossible to say what such origination would be like (we have tried to see an image of it in gratuitous origination), its radical difference from finite origination has to be granted, as it is in the traditional restriction of the notion of creation uniquely to God's action (in Aquinas, for instance).[24]

The sense of an end appropriate to the absolute original is related to the ultimate good of primordial desire, which cannot be restricted to satisfaction with determinate things. Thus the absolute original as end cannot be just a determinate limit that completes a sequential movement or a totality or temporal terminus that circumscribes a sum of events. It is foolish to imply any such temporal terminus to the process of becoming. But the absolute original is something different. It has to do with a certain qualitative presence emergent in time, but this emergence may occur at any moment or may span time; nor does it necessarily privilege any one of the dimensions of time, past, present, or future. As an end, the absolute original might be seen as an indeterminate limit, at which the point is not to come to a dead halt but to begin to create. This end is no end, because it gives the open space that solicits new beginnings.[25] This end cannot be a closure, since it is the opening up of originated being to what is ultimate. It does not promise any determinate completion, but hints at an overdetermined completion, something more than finite completion. The absolute original implies a kind of eschatology wherein its radical otherness offers, but does not guarantee, some hope of the transfiguration of time. Such an end, traditionally spoken of as the "fullness of time," suggests a kind of inexhaustible wholeness of being, in which the eternal ruptures normal time and subverts its smooth flow with a dislocating, yet fulfilling, *peripeteia.*[26]

All man's masquerades of wholeness are put into question here. This end cannot be a mere ideal that we project onto the future. We cannot adventitiously impose this ultimate end on becoming, as if we were giving a telos to time to overcome the future in its sometimes terrifying indefiniteness. Often, in fact, this end contributes to the goodness of the middle behind the backs of our quotidian consciousness. It may erupt unexpectedly in the middle, blocking our drift into somnolent life, wearing away our immersion in finite satisfactions. Like Hegel's cunning of reason, it need not harmonize with the ends we give ourselves in our projects or respect the limits we devise to regulate and domesticate the succession of becoming. Its emergence in the succession of time refers not to an indefinite future or a remote past, but to the rich elusive now that is currently in the making. It is as if we were assembling a jigsaw puzzle, and someone else, unseen, were disassembling it at the same time, but peculiarly bringing out the real pattern beyond our own botched arrangement. For every piece we connect, we think there is still a piece missing, or rather, a piece taken out. In the measure that we continue to look for the missing piece, we are frustrated, but in truth what is missing is not a piece at all.

THE ABSOLUTE ORIGINAL, HEIGHTS AND DEPTHS

Let me now remark on the absolute original with reference to the extremes of space, metaphorically expressed in terms of the height and the depth of being. The metaphor of height is closely connected with the sense of a beyond, and in this regard the absolute original might be seen as a kind of vertical transcendence. Such a vertical transcendence does not refer us to the highest member of a sequence of beings (see above on the ens realissimum), but to something that is beyond humankind and all finite beings. It is what humans and beings are *not*, what, as more, is conspicuous by its absence in finite things, what is at the same time superabundant and held back. The absolute original as height refers us to the sublimity of the originative source of what is, the infinitude sensuously suggested by the overwhelming majesty of being, which towers above us by its transcendence of finitude.[27]

As this transcendence, the absolute original exhibits a freedom from finite structure, for it is above and beyond and never identical with such structure. Because of this, the absolute original may appear absurd or irrational to structural thought. But why should the fact that we cannot capture the sublime in finite structure make it absurd? Here something is essentially hidden and absconding to finite thought, not because of any vacuity but because of its inexhaustibility. In being overdetermined, this transcendence overflows finite structure. Our choice here is not between the irrational and what can be encompassed by finite reason. Indeed, the absolute original as height can be seen as offering an openness in being for human freedom that itself cannot be finitely bounded. The nonidentity of the absolute original with the finite sustains the open space for freedom, draws freedom forth and upward. Because of this openness, finiteness in human existence cannot itself be finitely closed up. Moreover, it is not true that, because the absolute original is absolute, there is nothing left for human beings to create. Least of all, as our previous discussion of the sublime indicated, is the world an inert, fallow, mechanical thing.[28]

The absolute original as depth is a metaphor for the ground of being. Interestingly, the Latin for "high," *altus,* can also mean "deep," just as the sublime carries traces of the abysmal, the subliminal. As a vertical transcendence, the absolute original is beyond a univocal either/or; it is double, both high and deep. It requires a metaxological both/and. As height, it is transcendent to the world; as depth, it is its immanent ground. But this ground, even in its immanence, maintains its difference. It is intimate to the being of things yet recedes into a reserve that no finiteness can exhaust. We are not entirely at a loss for some sense of this grounding activity, however, for the originative power disclosed in the process of becoming is an original image of this primordial grounding. As a poiēsis, becoming embodies original power and, like the poem or the sublime, may be a sensuous, charged suggestion of its ground. Becoming is an original process, but, as metaxologically intermediate, it images a more primordial ground, the absolute original.

This ground, or, better, this grounding, is the profound upsurge of the power of being, that most intimate constituent of beings without which they would be nothing. Hence this ground is supporting, but not in a way that is reductive of the otherness of finitude. (Again it is interesting that *altus* is from the verb *alere,* whose meanings include "to support," "to maintain," "to raise up," "to cause to grow or increase," "to strengthen.") Finite things are independent; they are there. But this thereness is not absolutely self-supporting. Finite things evince a constitutive dimension of nothingness, being inherently marked by the possibility of not-being, as we see in becoming as a process of coming into being and also passing away. Yet, as dynamically there, they intimate a ground that is a creative support and not an inert stasis. The fact that finiteness is not absolutely self-grounding points to an asymmetry between it and the absolute original. But this asymmetry is what makes possible the metaphysical space for real difference. It makes genuine plurality possible. It also supports the space wherein originated being may itself become original. To say that the absolute original is the ground is to say that all finite being is shot through with its own dynamic orientation toward absoluteness, toward its own potential wholeness and participation in infinity, for which all creation groans.

The point might be put in a way that reiterates the imagistic, aesthetic dimension and at the same time responds to the insufficiency of finite form. In a word, the absolute original, understood as a metaphysical metaphor, is what we might call *a post-Romantic symbol*. I use the terms as Hegel uses them in his philosophy of art, but this particular combination of terms allows a certain non-Hegelian twist. Hegel classifies the types of art in terms of the Symbolic, the Classical, and the Romantic.[29] Very broadly, we find the Symbolic in, say, Egypt's pyramids (Egypt, for Hegel, is the "land of symbol," and the Sphinx the "symbol of symbols"). In the Symbolic, the finite self is swamped by the awful power of an indefinite divinity or the illimitable power of nature in its otherness and exteriority. Finite selfhood is not yet developed to full spiritual proportions. In Classical art—which, for Hegel, means par excellence the art of Greece—the sense of spiritual individuality has been more fully developed, and in the formed wholeness of Classical beauty, self and sensuous otherness find their balance in a harmonious whole. Hegel's predeliction for formed wholeness (the third degree of concreteness in our discussion, corresponding to dialectical self-mediation) comes out in his aesthetic preference for Classical art.

Finally, in Romantic art, the sense of the inward infinity of the self has developed explicitly, culminating after the Christian era in modern interiority. The result, for Hegel, is a new disproportion, reminiscent of the Symbolic; only now the infinitely inward self swamps sensuous otherness, thereby reducing it to finiteness. Hegel is very guarded regarding both the Symbolic and the Romantic disproportions, because of his stress on dialectical self-mediation and on that wholeness which dialectically sublates finiteness into infinity. The view elaborated here, by contrast, makes possible a certain celebration of this disproportion. When I speak of the absolute original as a post-Romantic symbol, I wish to preserve this infinite inwardness of the self but to obviate the destructive consequences of efforts by the self to assert absolute sway over otherness, which has clearly been part of the project of modernity ever since Descartes willed humankind to become the "masters and possessors of nature."[30]

I agree that there is no going back behind Romantic inwardness or modern selfhood to some primitive beginning in terms of an immediate symbol.[31] Such a sense of origins would yield the aesthetic infinitude of the sublime without self-consciousness, and hence be only another form of flight from human difference, another nostalgia for an absorbing god. Nor can we return to Greek wholeness or Classical harmony, again as if we could get behind modern self-consciousness. The absolute original has nothing to do with a return to origins in any sense of a regression along a temporal sequence, nor does it project a return of the origin in some future utopia. The sublime as symbolic intimates a different dimension; and the absolute original as height and depth, as transcendence and ground, has nothing to do with any canceling of human self-consciousness. Granting modern self-consciousness, our sense of infinite interiority (the aesthetic version of which is suggested by Romantic inwardness), we must grant the need for wholeness, but also, and perhaps more important, the sense of infinity in otherness.

The absolute original, as a post-Romantic symbol, emerges *beyond* a dialectical self-mediation of the infinite with finiteness. It emerges from the metaxological intermediation of more than one infinity, the interior infinity of the original self and the suggestion of another infinity emergent in being itself. As the reader will notice, the requirements of wholeness, infinite inwardness, original selfness, and so on developed in part 1 answer to a dialectical move beyond the merely indefinite, equivocal symbol in Hegel's sense; whereas the notions of otherness, the metaxological, the sublime as aesthetic infinitude, and so on developed in part 2 answer to a move toward a positive sense of overdetermined being, overwhole being. Taken together, these two allow us to speak of the absolute original as a post-Romantic symbol.[32]

In speaking of the absolute original, we are dealing with an ultimate question. We are trying to "picture the whole," to use a common phrase that indicates the imagistic, aesthetic aspect of the issue. No more than religious representation can philosophical concepts escape this need for imaging.[33] What we must add here, however, is that the sublime, agapeic otherness, and the absolute original are metaphysical metaphors that ultimately break beyond any framed, whole picture. Hence there is no delimited whole that we can frame or encompass. A post-Romantic symbol is a paradoxical effort to picture the whole that confesses the breaking open of all framed wholes. It is image making that must also be iconoclastic. For a post-Romantic symbol is an effort to picture an infinitely open and overflowing wholeness. Thus, in the very act of imaging, it must call its own imaging into question, lest the image be idolatrously identified with the absolute original itself. It is always an effort, never an absolute achievement, an effort that, even when it succeeds, is also the confession of its own failure.[34]

THE ABSOLUTE ORIGINAL AND THE ABSORBING GOD

The inadequacy of trying to think about the origin on the model of a closed whole implies that the absolute original cannot be conceived as an absorbing god. At best, an absorbing god might be an encompassing whole in which what is different is defined in terms of the absorbing god's self-differentiation into parts. Here there can be only *one* original, within whose wholeness everything finite is a part, and whose origination hence cannot be the creation of the really distinct. The absolute original, by contrast, does not originate parts in respect of its creation of finite things; it creates a different original, thus setting up an asymmetrical relation, but also the possibility of metaxological intermediation, between the source and the created. What is created is not a part of the self-origination of the absolute original, for finite being is not the fragmentation of the beginning that, after dispersing itself into parts, must subsequently be reintegrated by the temporal process into the source again. An absorbing god tends to make the movement from the origin to the finite creature a *degeneration,* as in some Neoplatonic thought concerning the *fall* of the One into manyness or, in Hegel's case, in the necessary *self-alienation* of the Idea into the realm of finiteness. This degeneration or fall or self-alienation must subsequently be taken back again by the absorbing god and restored to the origin, in the way that a part is assimilated to the whole. With the absolute original there is no assimilation of part to whole in this sense. Indeed, the language of parts and whole is insufficient, for finite being is no mere part, but a unity of being that may be original in itself.

With the absorbing god, otherness tends to be seen as the dualistic opposition of part and whole, a dualism to be resolved by the reappropriation of the part by the whole. But the relation of created being to the absolute original cannot be captured by this dualistic opposition of part and whole; rather, it points to a metaxological plurality of differently original centers of being. Dualism springs from a misleading sense of the origin. For if the origin is overdetermined, there is no need for origination to be a degeneration or fall or self-alienation of the whole into parts. If the absolute original is overwhole, the kind of plurality it originates need not dissolve into such an opposition of dispersed parts. Difference need not be divisive, nor need wholeness be absorbing. Nor is a retreat to some lost unity appropriate here. This would be the futile effort to reverse the entire process of diversification and singling out that we find in becoming, like desire in flight from otherness into static eternity. This would make the emergence of the different indistinguishable from the issue of the absurd.

An absorbing god must ultimately mean that originating activity and what is originated are illusory. It becomes impossible to make sense of why this initial whole should fall apart in the first place, much less why it is necessary for it to traverse a course of degeneration and reintegration. By contrast, the absolute original does not alienate itself or fall apart in its origination of the world, since it does not constitute its own wholeness by way of bringing the world into being. It does not need the finite world as a kind of dialectical detour just to be or become itself. Put more succinctly, theogony is not identical with cosmogony in the absolute original. The absolute original looses from itself what it creates. It does not bring finite things into being within its own wholeness, as if this wholeness were a kind of cosmic womb that refused to part with anything in that radical breach in which otherness is born. Rather, the absolute original, as an excessive infinity, is just the giving, the releasing, and the letting be of real otherness.

Hence self and world are not parts of the absolute original, but original unities, given a difference that is irreducible. Since an absorbing god entails a logic of part and whole, identity tends to dominate difference, the same proving more basic than the other. But the absolute original does not subordinate the other to the same, the different to the identical. If we approach it purely as a whole, we are likely to end up with, in Hegel's terms, the identity of identity and difference. However, it we see it both as an infinite whole and as overdetermined power of creation, then it reveals the difference of identity and difference. The sense of otherness here is fundamental, in the same way that the metaxological relation is more ultimate than the dialectical. The absolute original is a paradigm of the metaxological in agapeically giving the other its freedom and in supporting the other's distinctiveness in a pluralized relation between originals. Of course, monists who tend to an absorbing god as the ultimate principle do not deny diversity outright. But the kind of diversity they acknowledge tends to attenuate any fundamental sense of positive otherness. The absorbing god is symptomatic of their nostalgia for a unity that would end difference. With the absolute original, the point is rather to affirm an original difference that is an end in itself, and yet whose overwholeness is consummated in community.

THE ABSOLUTE ORIGINAL, MAN, AND THE WORLD

Dualism finitizes the absolute original by letting humankind and the world bound it. Monism overcomes this finitization only by absorbing the finite self and world into an absorbing god. Thus dualistic opposition begets monistic absorption. But since the first is not adequate to the fullness of difference, the second is not consonant with the fullness of relation. Metaxological pluralism is beyond both this dualistic opposition of the finite and the infinite and this monistic absorption of the finite in the infinite. It pluralizes infinity and wholeness in such a way that otherness may be an end in itself and the richest relation may involve a community of originals. Let me now conclude with a brief description of how man, the world, and the absolute original might constitute such a community.

Suppose we start with the originated world. As becoming, this world is also originating; it may generate an open plurality of particular things. As a process of positive othering, its becoming initiates new beginnings. The diversification it produces is not just a dispersed manifoldness; it individuates beings in a process of singling out (see chapter 4). This is especially true with human beings. Here, difference becomes originating and free. Here, too, a qualitative openness in being appears. In the metaxological interplay of the human self and becoming, in which both are original and open, the overdetermined being of the absolute original may be mirrored. So we are not trapped by a dualistic either/or between finite being as an indifferent nothing (as is supposedly the case with nihilistic Platonism) and finite being as an idolized all (as with a supposedly yea-saying Nietzscheanism). We do not deny the world or man to affirm the absolute original or deny the absolute original to affirm man or the world. A pluralized affirmation, a yes to all together, is necessary.

In the wake of Nietzsche and the seeming eclipse of eternity in modernity, we must insist that affirming the absolute original involves no *contemptus mundi* or rancor toward finiteness. The point is to renew self and world within this pluralized affirmation. There cannot be any return to origins if this blots out difference in some primordial, homogeneous unity. Nor must we situate the world and the self as limited parts to be incorporated in one overarching whole. We are caught in the open space between whole and whole, original and original, infinite and infinite. So, too there is no escape from the difference between self and world. Though we cannot be freed *from* this difference, we may be freed *by* it; for it may offer, as it were, the possibility of a purgatorial release. In existing in and weathering its metaphysical stress, we may be guided toward the ground of difference, the absolute original. Like Lear, we learn the truth by facing the extremes, by exposing ourselves to feel as wretches and divinities feel. The absolute original creates outward, and we live in the open externality of creation. There, the absolute original neither absolves us from ourselves nor shelters us from otherness; rather, it solicits from us that positive finitude that ripens in gratuitous origination. The pluralized yes calls for agapeic goodwill toward being.

The picture that ultimately emerges, then, is of a certain plurality of wholes, others, infinities, and originals. First, the absolute original, as whole, is self-relating, but, as infinite, creates the different. Second, what is created, the finite world in its otherness, is becoming, hence original too, and, as infinite succession, yields a manifold of particular wholes. Third, with time, the process of becoming issues in the self as a free difference, as the power to gather a temporally dispersed manifold into an open, dialectically self-relating wholeness. The indefiniteness of becoming as succession becomes the positive indeterminacy of the human being's intentional infinitude, an openness to otherness in new, self-conscious form. With this, and fourth, the human being's metaxological relation with otherness opens beyond finiteness to the absolute original as the ground of being. Such an opening can never be a conquering of otherness, since the difference of the absolute original is ineradicable. At best, the human self, in its own gratuitous origination, may spark across the gap of world and absolute original. The self is an intermediate original, and the ultimate difference may be mediated, but not obliterated. Yet the self's gratuitous origination and the agapeic otherness it sometimes manages to exemplify may provide a metaphor for the absolute original as whole and infinite. Even here in such metaphors we find a sense of irreducible difference. The overall picture cannot be of a linear, continuous movement from an origin to an end, nor yet of a continuous circular motion whose end returns to its beginning. Ultimately, there is no absolutely adequate image or picture, because every line is always disrupted, and every circuit always opened.

Let me put the matter one last way, using the four possibilities of the univocal, the equivocal, the dialectical, and the metaxological as themselves metaphysical metaphors, for both the immanent reality of the absolute original and its relatedness to the created world. *Within* the absolute original, the univocal points us to its identity with itself; but since this is no inert self-sameness, the equivocal points us to its immanent self-differentiation; since, further, this self-differentiation is no dispersion, the dialectical points us to its self-relating wholeness; but since, further still, this wholeness is overwholeness, the metaxological points us to a community of infinites in agapeic otherness. This is the matter from the side of the infinity of the absolute original as an immanent overwholeness. *Between* the absolute original and the created world, the univocal suggests to us the affinity between finite being and its ground; but since this affinity is not unambiguous, the equivocal brings home to us their difference; since, further, this difference is not a dualistic opposition, the dialectical allows of its mediation from the side of immanence; but since, further still, this mediation is intermediation, the metaxological allows for the mediation of this difference from the side of the otherness of the transcendent. This is the matter from the side of the infinity of the absolute original as excess creation. If we take these two sides in their togetherness, we may articulate some mediated sense of the metaxological community of being.

There is never an immediate, direct access to the absolute original in the world or man. We are always brought home to the otherness of the absolute original and to our own difference. So we must refrain from any claims to ultimate explanation. What I have tried to provide in this work is a kind of periphrastic philosophical image, culminating not in absolute knowledge, but in the acknowledgment of a radical enigma. Unavoidably, our language drifts toward an untrue, structural fixation of what is ultimate. I have tried to minimize this drift by discerning the metaphor in the structure, thereby turning this limitation to some positive use. For our limits may be an indirect image of the ultimate otherness, a kind of ontological salutation of what is always beyond us. Facing into this final difference, one may consent to the community of

being and seek to be divided oneself no longer. For we become pat-
terned after what we love as ultimate.

If we run the course of our metaphysical metaphor, the "circuit" will
come round, bringing us back to the middle again. The enigma we now
acknowledge, however, is not the unarticulated lack of our first beginning. We lack what is beyond us, but in the radically positive sense that
this work as a whole tries to articulate. Even now there is no closure,
for we are always in the middle, meeting again the ceaseless charge to
renew thinking about the beginning. To be is to be in suspense—that
is, suspended in the metaxological. In this always returning, never to
be abandoned, middle, the absolute original remains this charged enigma, present yet absent, immanent yet transcendent, intimate yet other,
whole yet never encompassed. Again, this is not our downfall, but just
our difference. Paradoxically, this enigma precludes the mystification
of human existence in the middle by bringing home to us both our limits
as positive finitude and our unlimited reaching as intentionally infinite.
This deepens, rather than dissolves, the peculiar dilemma of man, that
finite infinite that does not coincide with himself, who, even were he
sufficient *unto* himself, would not be sufficient *for* himself. For here what
is enigmatic is not a rationalization of ignorance too lazy to root out its
own lack. It has nothing to do with a lack that we ourselves could will
away. The world in its otherness is opened out, and we cannot will its
closure. The overdetermined power of being invades us within and
surrounds us without. We encounter a limitation, the confession of
which need occasion no lamentation. Again, it is not enough just to say
brusquely that the enigma is there and then go on as before, as if it
made no difference. The talent is not for burial or for rusting, but for
our ripe, originating return.

Notes

INTRODUCTION

1. Thus, Parmenides' view of nonbeing as radically other than being, and hence barred from inclusion in philosophical *logos*, is one of the first instances of philosophical diffidence regarding irreducible difference. Of course, difficulties with this uneasy relation to the other have occupied philosophers from Plato, through Hegel, down to Sartre. Not surprisingly, there are strong Parmenidean tendencies in Sartre's ontology, though it is man as nothingness (via Hegel's negativity) who becomes the other *(pour-soi)* of being *(en-soi)*. The problem of otherness is treated by the Eleatic Stranger in Plato's *Sophist* (e.g., pp. 257ff.), in which nonbeing is seen as the other but not as the opposite of being. The issue of dialectic and "logocentrism" here centers on the Stranger's effort to encapsulate the other by means of *diaeresis*, a strongly analytical method. There is, however, a different, more concrete dialectic in Socrates' maieutic dialogue, in which the other is not an abstract concept, but the living individual. These two kinds of dialectic (diaeresis, as logical analysis, and Socratic dialogue, as seeking truth in conversation between the philosopher and the other) are *both* found in Plato and should make us uneasy about any charge of logocentrism. On this doubleness in Plato, see my "Plato's Philosophical Art and the Identification of the Sophist." See also Stanley Rosen, *The Limits of Analysis*, pp. 156ff., and *Plato's Sophist: The Drama of Original and Image*, esp. pp. 1–57. On Hegel and ancient dialectic, see H.-G. Gadamer, *Hegel's Dialectic*, chap. 1. Some commentators see Hegel as trying to include the law of contradiction within the law of identity. See M. Heidegger, *Identity and Difference*, for a discussion of Hegel and the principle of identity. On Hegel and contradiction in relation to the ancient problem of nonbeing, see Rosen, *G. W. F. Hegel: An Introduction to the Science of Wisdom*, esp. chap. 4.

2. The beginning was actually with the later Schelling, whose "positive" philosophy sought to go beyond his own early position and Hegel's purportedly "negative" philosophy. Kierkegaard, accorded by many the honor of being the first existentialist, attended the later lectures of Schelling, agreeing with Schelling's desideratum, but becoming disillusioned with its implementation. Schelling's importance is beginning to be recognized again. See, e.g., Alan White, *Schelling: An Introduction to the Science of Freedom*, and Werner Marx, *The Philosophy of F. W. J. Schelling*. But it was not only thinkers like Feuerbach and Marx who saw Hegel as bringing philosophy to a certain end; so did the poet Heine, who said: "Our philosophical revolution is concluded; Hegel has closed its great circle" (*Philosophy and Religion in Germany*, p. 156).

3. I am thinking here of Jacques Derrida's *Margins of Philosophy* and Heidegger's notion of the "unthought" in *Identity and Difference*.
4. Existentialism develops the search for what Kierkegaard (against the so-called objectivism of Hegelian rationalism) called "the subjective thinker." On philosophy and nonphilosophy, see Vincent Descombes, *Modern French Philosophy*, chap. 1. The generation of the 1930s in France saw in Hegel's dialectic the salutation of otherness, whereas from around 1960, thinkers have tended to see only its domestication. On nonphilosophy, see Alan Montefiori, ed., *Philosophy in France Today;* and Richard Kearney, *Dialogues with Contemporary Continental Thinkers.*
5. The Anglo-American version of concern for the nonphilosophical is related to the break with idealism in its British form (which tended to be flabbier than Hegel himself), starting with Russell, Moore, and James, and moving through the Wittgensteinian distrust of theory and suspicion of philosophy as a sickness and ending with ordinary language analysis.
6. See Gadamer, *Hegel's Dialectic*, chap. 5, on Hegel and Heidegger; also Jacques Taminiaux, *Dialectic and Difference: Finitude in Modern Thought*, esp. chaps. 3 and 4.
7. Descombes, *Modern French Philosophy*, chap. 1, discusses the influence of Hegel (via Kojève's lectures of the thirties) on Sartre, Merleau-Ponty, and Bataille, among others. On Hegel and the nineteenth century, see Karl Löwith, *From Hegel to Nietzsche;* on Hegel and recent German thought, see Rüdiger Bubner, *Modern German Philosophy*, esp. chap. 3, and Herbert Schnädelbach, *Philosophy in Germany 1831–1933*. On the Hegel revival among English-speaking philosophers, see H. S. Harris, "The Hegel Renaissance in the Anglo-Saxon World Since 1945." The pragmatists' break with Hegel, having taken a detour through Anglo-American analysis, seems to have come full circle; and with Richard Rorty a joining of Hegel and pragmatism is again emerging. Thus, in *Consequences of Pragmatism*, p. 224, Rorty diagnoses the dilemma of Anglo-American philosophy today in terms of the question "Who is going to teach Hegel?" Rorty's Hegel is a radical historicist Hegel, a Hegel without the absolute. It is a Hegel laundered through analytical thought, through Heidegger's "overcoming" of the tradition and through recent post-Heideggerian thought, a rather wan encyclopedist philosopher—encyclopedist not in Hegel's but in Rorty's sense of a ragbag thesaurus of interesting philosophical pictures, someone you can rely on for an interesting angle in the "conversation of mankind" (see Rorty's *Philosophy and the Mirror of Nature*, chap. 8). For a more serious view of Hegel in relation to the issue of time and eternity, see Rosen, *G. W. F. Hegel*, pp. 128–40. Rorty might seem to confirm some of Rosen's suspicions in *The Limits of Analysis* (pp. 153, 170), that analysis will succumb to some form of post-Heideggerian deconstruction.
8. Hegel's challenge might thus be seen as analogous to the challenge of Heidegger to the stream of thought that takes its bearings from phenomenology. Like Hegel, Heidegger was profoundly self-conscious regarding the history of philosophy, as well as penetrating in his dwelling with certain central thoughts. See Werner Marx, *Heidegger and the Tradition*. Gadamer might be viewed as trying to mediate between Hegel and Heidegger, in that he develops the Heideggerian emphasis on historicity while attempting to restore important aspects of Hegel's thought—in aesthetics, for instance. See, e.g., *Truth and Method*, pp. 87ff.
9. See Clark Butler, "Hermeneutic Hegelianism"; also Alan White, *Absolute Knowledge: Hegel and the Problem of Metaphysics;* White sees Hegel's logic as a system of categories, though he does not exclude a different task for philosophy (somewhat in the mode of the later Schelling). See too my "Hermeneutics and Hegel's Aesthetics."
10. Hegel, *Science of Logic*, p. 50.
11. This view is associated with Kojève's interpretation in *Introduction to the Reading of*

Hegel; for a recent work sympathetic to Kojève, see Barry Cooper, *The End of History: An Essay on Modern Hegelianism.*

12. See André Glucksmann, *The Master Thinkers,* pp. 119ff., where this standpoint is polemically applied to many thinkers, starting with Fichte. The results are initially provocative, but subsequently flattening and insipid. The polemic against the "master thinkers" is rammed home with an overkill in the *argumentum ad hominem,* verging on the *argumentum ad baculum* (were that possible in a book). Indeed, one begins to wonder who is more infected by will to power, the author or the master thinkers.

13. Friedrich Nietzsche, *On the Genealogy of Morals,* 3, 25. On Nietzsche, Platonism, and nihilism, see M. Heidegger, *Nietzsche, Volume I: The Will to Power as Art,* pp. 151–61. For an antidialectical, anti-Hegelian Nietszchean stance, see Gilles Deleuze, *Nietzsche and Philosophy,* pp. 8ff. and chap. 5. On Nietzsche and Hegel and the will to power, see my review of *Hegel's Letters, The Owl of Minerva* 17, no. 2 (1986): 204–08. On the importance of dialectic in German literature and its destructive consequences for Nietzsche, see Peter Heller, *Dialectics and Nihilism,* e.g., p. 80, where Nietzsche is said to be a Hegel without Hegel's absolute, a dialectician "deprived of all faith in an enduring and harmonious condition of being." As indicated in note 1 above, it is unfair to reduce Plato to simple logocentrism. The critics of Plato seem to agree with Whitehead's famous statement: "The safest general characterization of the European philosophical tradition is that it consists of a series of footnotes to Plato" (*Process and Reality,* p. 63). But whereas Whitehead implied a compliment to Plato in this statement, these critics imply a condemnation—though the issue is not without ambiguity, since the Plato of dialogue still tends to be respected, while the Plato of dualism tends to be rejected. For a sympathetic post-Heideggerian reading of Plato, see Gadamer, *Dialectic and Dialogue: Eight Hermeneutical Studies on Plato.* On Plato's provocative ambiguities regarding philosophy and art, see Iris Murdoch, *The Fire and the Sun: Why Plato Banished the Poets;* also J. Moravcsik and P. Teinko, eds., *Plato on Beauty, Wisdom and the Arts,* esp. chap. 4.

14. In the *Symposium* and the *Phaedrus,* Plato was very clear about the unstable ambiguity of human desire, of the possibility of both the ennoblement and the debasement of man through *eros.* Mirroring eros's double nature as mixing *poros* (resource) and *penia* (poverty), it may yield man's receptivity to the highest good or else become the boundless, unbridled desire of the tyrant. Both extremes emerge from desire's restlessness, from its dangerous doubleness or intermediate character. See Rosen, *Plato's Symposium;* also John M. Rist, *Eros and Psyche,* chap. 2. For the negative and positive sides of man's uneasiness, in both the ancient and the modern world, see Marcel, *Problematic Man,* pp. 67–144.

15. *Art and the Absolute: A Study of Hegel's Aesthetics.* There I try to bring a generous hermeneutic to Hegel's thought; on art and philosophy, see chap. 2, in which I argue that Hegel's subordination of art is complexly qualified and presupposes philosophy's openness to art. See also chap. 5, where I take up the issue of dialectic in relation to deconstruction, situating both relative to Nietzsche and Heidegger, and their respective relations to univocity and equivocity.

16. See *Art and the Absolute,* chap. 4. On the totalizing pretensions of the supposed antitotalizers, see my review article of *The Irish Mind,* ed. R. Kearney, in *Philosophical Studies,* vol. 31, where I make some remarks on logocentrism and reverence for otherness in the tradition. On efforts to preserve dialectic in Merleau-Ponty, see Descombes, *Modern French Philosophy,* chap. 2. Even Derrida grants the distance and proximity of dialectic and his own *différance* (see, e.g., *Margins,* pp. 13–14).

17. Heidegger, among others, tends to see all of modernity as the offspring of such a project of mastery; though, more questionably, he extends the line of origin back to Greek philosophy, totalizing (again, I believe, questionably) the entire Western tra-

dition as now a more hidden, now a less hidden, will to power. On the intertwining of the modern subject's mastery of an objectified nature and the reduction of man himself to an object amenable to technical manipulation (by the seemingly opposite modern "materialisms" of capitalism and communism), see William Barrett, *The Illusion of Technique;* also Marcel's critique of technical, functional man in *The Mystery of Being,* vol. 1, chap. 2.

18. Of course, the univocal, the equivocal, and so on have an august ancestry, since Aristotle spoke of the many senses of being (*to on pollachōs legetai;* see *Metaphysics,* 1004b ff.). I might note here that, though in the present work, I will insist strongly on man's crucial importance, this implies no post-Kantian reduction of metaphysics to philosophical anthropology, as will be evident later. We might also note the importance of these concepts in the Middle Ages with respect to analogical predication concerning God. They also figure in recent thought—that of Ricoeur and Derrida, for instance, with respect to the whole issue of polysemia, where we tend to find denunciations of univocity in favor of an equivocal polysemia. Similar issues are at stake in analytical philosophy with respect to the question of whether the plurality of ordinary meanings can be reduced to one proper univocal sense, as in technical, formal systems like logic or mathematics. On analogy and metaphor, see especially Carl Vaught, *The Quest for Wholeness,* pp. 178–82. Vaught seeks to develop a complex sense of plurality and wholeness, rather than a merely equivocal polysemia after the manner of the Derrideans.

19. It would take a whole book to substantiate this properly. The notion of a rich between is relevant to all forms of philosophy, such as phenomenology and hermeneutics, that seek to transcend the traditional opposition of subject and object. The between is also crucial for all conversational models of philosophy, whether Rortian edification or the emphasis on dialogic models in, for instance, Habermas or Apel. On this, see Bubner, *Modern German Philosophy.* The nonclosure of the between is obviously not irrelevant to the deconstructionist's concern with difference, though I believe that dialectic and the metaxological go beyond an alternating to-and-fro between univocity and equivocity. I also believe that the metaxological approach addresses the problems of dialectic in a more affirmative fashion than is generally found in the negative dialectics of the Frankfurt school. I will try throughout to indicate the differences and convergences of my view with other contemporary views.

20. In his *Apology for Poetry,* Sidney says that the poet "thrusteth into the middest." In saying that the philosopher speaks out of the middest, I imply a different, reflective directionality to philosophical thought, coupled, of course, with a proper skepticism regarding abstraction. Mark C. Taylor, in *Erring: A Postmodern A/theology,* makes much of the notion of the middle. He mixes Hegelian, Nietzschean, and Derridean notions, not always doing justice to the differences between Hegel and the others. On the middle as a divine milieu, see pp. 112ff.; also interestingly he cites this assertion from Nietzsche, where Zarathustra is talking about the ring of eternity: "The middle is everywhere (*die Mitte ist überall*). Bent is the path of eternity" (pp. 114–15). Taylor seems so intent on avoiding univocity that he tends to lean toward equivocity (e.g., pp. 173ff.), where, echoing Derrida, he says that ends and origins are unacceptable. How one can have a middle without an end and origin is not faced, as one would expect from one who has written extensively and with great sensitivity on Hegel. Dialectical thought in Hegel, as Taylor well knows, is much more than a mere oscillating interplay between univocity and equivocity.

21. It is not only the Nietzschean style of genealogy that assumes an a priori of suspicion here. As Ricoeur reminds us, Freud and Marx, the two other "masters of modern suspicion" display the same a priori. These masters of suspicion, having debunked

the nineteenth-century superego, now, as fathers of modern culture, seem to have taken up residence in the vacant superegos of some twentieth-century intellectuals.

22. On this, see Karl Löwith, *From Hegel to Nietzsche;* on the Young Hegelians, Lawrence Stepelevich, ed., *The Young Hegelians,* pp. 1–15. Stepelevich rightly points out the line of continuity from Young Hegelianism down to the Frankfurt school. Bubner develops the same point in connection with Adorno (*Modern German Philosophy,* chap. 3). See also John Toews, *Hegelianism: The Path Towards Dialectical Humanism 1805–1841.*

23. The famous madman passage concerning the death of God is found in Nietzsche's *The Gay Science,* sec. 125. On the death of man, see M. Foucault, *The Order of Things,* pp. 385–86. On the tabooed nostalgia for origins, see Charles Guignon, *Heidegger and the Problem of Knowledge,* pp. 236ff.; also Allan Megill, *Prophets of Extremity: Nietzsche, Heidegger, Foucault, Derrida,* chaps. 3 and 4. The term *ontotheology* is introduced with a certain reluctance, since it seems to set off an almost programmed reaction in some post-Heideggerians, thereby short-circuiting the "openness" so vaunted by these thinkers. Instead of the logos of Occidental metaphysics speaking through them, the texts of Heidegger now speak. One would think that ontotheologians were as plentiful as blackberries in a ripe fall, but these bushes are very bare, and hence the air of unreality about the rhetoric.

24. Thus I do not think that the question of origins is a sickness to be cured by therapy, or that it is due to the bewitchment of language, à la Wittgenstein. See Ricoeur's remark regarding Freudian genealogy: "But psychoanalysis has no access to problems of radical origin, because its point of view is economic and only economic" (*The Conflict of Interpretations,* p. 145). Ricoeur goes on to ask for a hermeneutic of the religious imagination, implying that Spinoza, Schelling, and Hegel were more profoundly acquainted than Freud with its significance for radical origins.

25. On the affinity of philosophy and religion in Hegel, see my "Hegel, Philosophy and Worship," also "Hegel and the Problem of Religious Representation." I have discussed the affinity of art and philosophy in *Art and the Absolute,* esp. chap. 2. It remains an important question why some thinkers today readily admit this affinity of philosophy with art, while regarding any affinity with religion as immediately suspect. Readiness for the aesthetic combined with reluctance for the religious is a revealing mixture.

26. I imply no empty *Jenseits* of the kind against which Hegel inveighed. On the *meta* as beyond yet in the midst, see my "Memory and Metaphysics." See chap. 4 below and n. 5 of that chapter on hermeneutics and the metaxological.

27. Augustine, in Platonic vein, sometimes speaks of the soul being alone with itself and God. I imply no such "aloneness" in the sense of a solipsistic abstraction from the otherness of being. See my "Augustine's *Confessions:* On Desire, Conversion and Reflection." On "inwardness" in Augustine and Husserl as a mode of being rather than a kind of being, see Erazim Kohák, *The Embers and the Stars: A Philosophical Inquiry into the Moral Sense of Nature,* esp. pp. 205ff. Hegel has sometimes been viewed in a kind of Augustinian light, in that his *Phenomenology of Spirit,* for example, seems driven by a similar restlessness for the absolute. But in Hegel one does not find the Augustinian celebration (at least the Augustine of the *Confessions*) of the enigma of divine otherness or of the otherness of the self as an unmastered, inward abyss. In this respect there is an exemplary lack of totalitarian closure in Augustine, a sense of the enigma and incompleteness of the self and an affirmative openness to mystery. This is an Augustine who is as much postmodern as premodern.

1 DESIRE, LACK, AND THE ABSORBING GOD

1. The concept of the self as active is undoubtedly one of the major emphases of post-Kantian thought. At this stage of our discussion, I imply no commitment to what

some have seen as the too strongly voluntaristic side of philosophy after Kant—from Fichte, through Kierkegaard, Marx, Nietzsche, pragmatism, on into contemporary existentialism. Human activity need not be voluntaristic, if this means subordinating otherness to the will of the self, as we will see later. See George Santayana, *Egotism in German Philosophy*, for a perceptive, though too polemical, account, which traces the sources of this aspect of voluntarism back to Leibniz's concept of the monad. Since positivism, there has been increasing recognition by analytical philosophers of the knower as active. For articles critical of the spectatorial view of Cartesianism, see the April 1965 issue of the *Monist;* also L. W. Beck, *Actor or Spectator;* and Tom Rockmore, *Fichte, Marx and the German Philosophical Tradition*, which shares the recent philosophical distaste for Cartesian dualism while exploring the similarities between Fichte and Marx in terms of Aristotle's notion of activity as *energeia*. Charles Taylor's *Hegel* brings out some of Hegel's relevance to the theory of action (esp. chap. 20).

2. Temporality is intertwined with many of the central problems of post-Kantian thought, including that of the self, since for Kant, time is one of the fundamental a priori forms of our experience. This theme is obviously crucial after Nietzsche—in Bergson, in Husserl's meditations on inner time consciousness, in Heidegger's *Sein und Zeit.* See chap. 4 below. On Hegel and historicity, see my "Hegel, History and Philosophical Contemporaneity"; also *Art and the Absolute*, chap. 4.

3. See the recent comprehensive study of love's multiple interpretations by Irving Singer, *The Nature of Love.* I imply no criticism of the psychoanalytic view here. For present purposes of philosophical clarification, I plot an emergence of difference within desire, emphasizing the most salient considerations in an admittedly idealized portrait. Psychoanalysis gives us one picture of the tangled particularities of desire's unfolding.

4. Supporting a teleology of desire implies no denial of what, after Pascal, we might call the inconstant, elusive stirrings of the heart. Still, we do attempt to give these meaning and cannot completely avoid the effort to situate them teleologically. Even the experience of radical absurdity is greeted with the cry "To what purpose?" These stirrings may float free of our efforts to make sense of them, but the effort is a basic exigence, nevertheless. Even when we cannot harmonize them with a particular teleological view, we are still impelled to see things as whole as we can. Sometimes, of course, great art will articulate these stirrings better than philosophy, and with a kind of open teleology that does not tyrannize over otherness. Consider here Kant's strange phrase concerning the aesthetic in the *Critique of Judgment:* "purposiveness without a purpose." See chap. 2 below.

5. This may be one reason why despair and love can be both extremely close and ultimately foreign. Love might be seen as a positive fulfillment of desire, one that inverts the inversion of despair, hence one that has to accept within itself the possibility of despair, without being destroyed by it.

6. Consider the emphasis in contemporary psychological thought on the progressive emergence of self from an initial narcissistic immediacy, in which self and other are not separated definitively, infantile desire being permeated by an inarticulate sense of the unity of the whole. The hold of this first womb without difference may never be entirely effaced and may resurface in a nostalgia for that "oceanic" feeling, in which difference will again be assuaged and the pain of otherness melted; this ties in with the notion of an absorbing god, discussed below. On the issue of immediacy for epistemology, see my "Collingwood, Imagination and Epistemology." For a thoughtful comparison of Kierkegaard's analysis of desire and the stage of aesthetic immediacy with Freud's treatment of infantile desire in the oral stage, under the dominance of the pleasure principle, see Mark C. Taylor, *Kierkegaard's Pseudonymous Authorship*, pp. 131ff., esp. pp. 140–41. For Freud's treatment, see *The Ego and the Id.* Of course, ultimately, there is no isolated self, for even here, desire is our entrance into com-

munity. The body cries out to another; more important, the infant smiles spontaneously at the approach of a human face. On the metaxological community as the
ultimate, concrete context of selfness, see part 2 below.

7. On the self's restless noncoincidence in Augustine, see my "Augustine's *Confessions:
On Desire, Conversion and Reflection.*" On Hegel's sense of the self's noncoincidence
in terms of the Unhappy Consciousness, see my "Hegel, Philosophy and Worship."
For a very perceptive treatment of Sartre in relation to Hegel, see Klaus Hartmann,
Sartre's Ontology, pp. 126–48.

8. This theme is very well treated, for instance, in Maurice Merleau-Ponty, *The Structure
of Behaviour* and *The Phenomenology of Perception;* also by J. P. Sartre in *Being and Nothingness,* part 3, chap. 2.

9. Relative to this distinction, see, for instance, Aquinas, *Summa Theologiae,* I–II, Q. 1,
art. 8, and Q. 2, art. 7, where the discussion of desire bears on man's ultimate end.

10. This tension between the whole and the infinite will run throughout this book, right
into our efforts in part 3 to venture a metaphysical metaphor for the ground of being
in terms of the idea of the absolute original. I will criticize any notion of a bounded
whole or absolutely determinate totality, though I will defend a different, seemingly
contradictory notion of an open whole.

11. This is evident, for example, in Hegel's distinction between *Verstand* and *Vernunft,*
the former being the analytical understanding that inevitably bogs down in antinomies
and contradictions, the latter the synthetic reason that gathers dialectical oppositions
within a more embracing perspective. See *Enzyklopädie der philosophischen Wissenschaften
im Grundrisse,* §§79–83; also my "Hegel, Philosophy and Worship," pp. 11–17. I am
not saying that dialectical reason exhausts the issue. Here also the affinity of philosophy
with art and religion is important. Whereas Hegel does not simplistically subordinate
art to philosophy (see *Art and the Absolute,* chap. 2), the view that I will develop later
involves a sense of the aesthetic that presents a recalcitrant otherness to dialectical
thought. Hence I prefer to speak of metaphysical metaphors, rather than speculative
categories (see chap. 7 below on the sublime as the aesthetic infinite and chap. 8 on
the absolute original as a metaphysical metaphor).

12. The importance of imagination in *all* knowing follows from Kant's doctrine of transcendental imagination. See my "Collingwood, Imagination, and Epistemology"; also
Richard Kearney, *Poétique du Possible,* pp. 22ff. The issue of metaphor and philosophy
is important in recent Continental thought—for instance, in Derrida's "White Mythology: Metaphor in the Text of Philosophy," also collected in *Margins,* pp. 207–71;
also Ricoeur's *The Rule of Metaphor,* esp. chap. 8, entitled "Metaphor and Philosophical
Discourse." It is bound up with the relationship between philosophy and poetry, an
issue as old as Plato, but one that is also very important in Schelling, Hegel, Nietzsche,
and Heidegger, to name but a few. See *Art and the Absolute,* chap. 2.

The difficulty of discourse about desire is the tendency to think of language as
extraverted onto finite things, as indexical in a simple, nominalistic way. But, since
it involves the dynamic articulation of experience, desire can neither be thinglike nor
be fixed by simple indexical reference. It must be named in a more complex, mediated
manner. Although this involves going beyond the univocal sense of language (which
tends to see words as tags, ostensive designators, and the world as a nominalistic aggregate of particular facts), it need not end in mere equivocation. Metaphor is related
to the dialectical and the metaxological in affording us a different, richer sense of
unity and difference in the community of being and language. Part of the difficulty
here is not unrelated to the central difficulty of modern consciousness as it surfaces
in Romantic art: how to communicate a seemingly inexhaustible content through a
finite expression. On this, see *Art and the Absolute,* chap. 6.

13. As Aristotle says in the *Ethics* (1104a1 ff.), we must look for as much precision as the

subject matter allows. Our choice is not between Nietzschean dithyrambs and some kind of anorexic analysis. On trying to find a way between *technē* and sheer *poiēsis*, see E. Kohák, *The Embers and the Stars*, pp. 49ff. Here we find a good discussion of the necessity of metaphor in philosophy; metaphor need not be just some deviation from literal use; reality itself may be metaphorical (p. 55). Perhaps because of his starting point in Husserl, Kohák tends to oppose seeing and speculation. This is to accept the post-Cartesian denigration of speculation as "idle theory," just as Descartes rejects the ancients for their "useless" theories. But, in fact, ancient *theoria* implied a seeing, a watching in a noninterfering way. Speculation, as found in German idealism—e.g., Hegel—implies a rebirth of ancient theoria in a post-Kantian context (see my, "Hegel, Philosophy and Worship," pp. 11–17). The term *speculare* is itself tied to images of seeing. Thus, speculative thinking need not imply the construction of idle theories (as it seems to for Husserl), but rather, a rational openness to *die Sache selbst*. Certainly Hegel would have no quarrel with the phenomenologist's cry *zu den Sachen selbst*.

14. The notion of an absorbing god is also relevant to contemporary discussion of otherness and the supposed predeliction of the philosophical tradition for unity, sameness, and identity. To some extent the absorbing god names a tendency in metaphysics originating in Parmenides' sense of being, one that has been renewed in the modern age perhaps by Spinoza. Of course, all the great thinkers sought to reconcile unity with plurality, the one with the many. But the shadow of the absorbing god may still hover in the background. Spinoza's influence on modern thought, via Jacobi, Fichte, Schelling, Hegel, down to Sartre, is sufficient indication of this. F. H. Bradley's absolute (see, for instance, *Appearance and Reality*, chap. 26), has some echoes of the absorbing god, the emphasis being on the inclusion of the differences found in finite experience within an all-encompassing, comprehensive whole that itself cannot be known fully. Bradley, of course, was influenced by German idealism and also by Spinoza.

For the Spinozistic influence on Fichte and the early Schelling, see Alan White, *Schelling*, pp. 21ff., where the annihilation of finite selfhood in an absolute beyond all determination is discussed. Many of the characteristics we have noted regarding the absorbing god are evident here. The issue involves man's restless, infinite striving, the satisfaction of which tends to be conceived in terms of the suppression of finite determinacy. Thus, too, the solution is beyond all articulation and hence involves a strangely empty fulfillment. This same point could be made about Schopenhauer's view of "salvation." We might also think of Hegel's tart comment on Schelling's absolute as the night in which all cows are black. But Hegel himself does not entirely escape the shadow of the absorbing god, for his thought tends to be guided by a concept of the whole, albeit a very complex concept. Obviously I am in agreement with views that emphasize man's infinite restlessness. What we need, however, is a concept of absoluteness that differs from that of an absorbing god in not suppressing finitude, in allowing an appropriate human wholeness, one that neither reduces the difference of the finite nor the otherness of the absolute. We will see later how the metaxological can help us here.

Perhaps the first contemplated "parricide" of Parmenides occurs in Plato's *Parmenides* (241d). On a recent "parricide of the Greek father Parmenides" and a reopening of the infinite spaces of Jewish otherness, see Derrida, *Writing and Difference*, chap. 4, entitled "Violence and Metaphysics: An Essay on the Thought of Emmanuel Levinas."

15. As is well known, Nietzsche criticizes philosophy after Plato, as well as ascetic Christianity, on this score. Nietzsche himself is not entirely unambiguous concerning the tension between affirmation and the temptation to self-extinction, as the dissolution of individuality in Dionysian intoxication clearly reveals. Schopenhauer's under-

standing of the will, his search for salvation in the ascetic desire to suppress desire, his concern to extinguish the *principio individuationis,* are all marks of the philosophical approach we find in the notion of the absorbing god. Schopenhauer liked to reaffirm the pessimistic "wisdom" of Marsyas: best is not to be born at all, to be nothing; second best is quickly to die. Nietzsche repeats this in *Birth of Tragedy* (sec. 3). Though he later repudiated Schopenhauerian pessimism, the ambiguity of his continuing devotion to Dionysus is clear: after all, Silenus, who utters the above wisdom, is the companion of Dionysus. We need not accept uncritically Nietzsche's somewhat caricatured picture of Plato. I think that Nietzsche's view of Plato was more influenced by Schopenhauer than is granted by many commentators. In Schopenhauer many so-called Platonic dualisms become systematized, almost streamlined, thus making easier Nietzsche's "deconstruction."

We need not deny that a similar ambiguity might be said to exist in Plato in the tension between philosophy as articulating the eros of reason *in* the metaxu and philosophy as the prolonged practice of death in the *Phaedo,* and hence as an escape *from* the metaxu, though, again, one cannot ignore the dramatic context of the *Phaedo*—i.e., Socrates' impending death. In the notion of the absorbing god, we find the complex doubleness, dangerous doubleness, of desire, its tension between *eros* and *thanatos,* in Freud's terms. Humans are often curiously enticed by thoughts of self-extinction; but as long as desire persists, eros wins out over thanatos. This is not to deny that a certain kind of self-abnegation may sometimes be the prelude to a greater affirmation where something greater than the human self is at stake. Thus, there may be sacrifices and noble renunciations that are the very opposite of nihilistic.

2 DESIRE AND ORIGINAL SELFNESS

1. What is at stake is not a return to some impossible pure immediacy, an aesthetic version of which we sometimes find in the predeliction of some modern art for primitivism. Origin need not be some "back-there" beginning that an impotent nostalgia pines for. It may be emergent in the middle, in the metaxological; hence some mediation is unavoidable. The difficulty is to go through and beyond self-mediation to an original otherness that is there in the middle all along. On modern art and primitivism, see Karsten Harries, *The Meaning of Modern Art,* pp. 95–108.

2. Cartesianism is currently in bad repute in both Anglo-American and Continental thought. Earlier this century, Husserlian transcendental phenomenology and existential phenomenology tried to appropriate the Cartesian starting point, in both cases profoundly reinterpreting it. This story is one of the essential episodes in contemporary philosophy, and although it is now generally thought to be one that is finished, the issue is hardly so simple.

3. For a recent, wide-ranging defense of modernity, see Hans Blumenberg, *The Legitimacy of the Modern Age.* On Romantic subjectivity and the aesthetic dilemmas of modernity, see *Art and the Absolute,* chap. 6.

4. There is renewed interest in the Romantics today. See the remarks of Claude Lefort, in *Philosophy in France Today,* ed. A. Montefiori, p. 90.

5. This is related to the traditional Aristotelian notion of being, according to which *to be* means to be a determinate something *(tode ti).* See *Metaphysics* 1006b.

6. We will see more clearly later why we need not assent to the self as Sartrean nothingness or entirely to Hegel's superior understanding of the self as self-relating negativity.

7. The problem of synthesis is central in Kant and German idealism, as it is also in Husserl and his successors. The literature is vast. But see Ralph Walker, *Kant,* and my

review thereof in *Philosophical Studies* (Ireland) 27:364–69; Erazim Kohák, *Idea and Experience*, and my review thereof in *Philosophical Studies*, (Ireland) 28:362–67; also Piotr Hoffman, *The Anatomy of Idealism: Passivity and Activity in Kant, Hegel and Marx*, and my review thereof in *Philosophical Studies* (Ireland) 30:335–38.

8. The middle referred to here is that of dialectical self-mediation, rather than metaxological intermediation. See Introduction.

9. The reader will forgive my belaboring the obvious. But since the fact of self is questioned so often, it seems necessary to insist on its ontological stubbornness. This, of course, is only a first step. In subsequent discussion I will explore what I take to be the concreteness of both the self and the other. My strategy is not to begin by offering an encapsulating definition of concreteness, but to try to unfold its meaning progressively. In a sense this entire essay is an effort to speak of what is concretely "there." I have discussed the issue of concreteness in relation to Hegel in *Art and the Absolute*, chap. 2. What I mean by concreteness diverges from both the empiricist and the Hegelian views (but see below, chap. 6).

10. Lord Shaftesbury: "We have undoubtedly the honour of being originals" (A. Hofstadter and R. Kuhns, eds., *Philosophies of Art and Beauty*, p. 252). Here we have some prefiguring of later notions of "creativity" and so on.

11. This is well recognized in the contemporary view of the human being as project in Heidegger's *Sorge* (a post-Nietzschean version of Platonic eros) and in the transcendence of Sartre's *pour-soi* (a humanization of Hegel's self-relating negativity). It is related to the emphasis on *Streben* in German thought. Indeed, in Spinoza's *On the Improvement of the Understanding* attention is drawn to the fact that we image an ideal self. Even in the seemingly fragmented chaos of modern art, an ideal self is not entirely evaded (see, Harries, *The Meaning of Modern Art*, pp. xii–xiii, 45, 95). In ancient thought the emphasis tended to be on human mimesis of exemplary archetypes—ideas in the Platonic sense. Modern man wants to project the ideal out of the resources of his own originality; ancient man seems to have granted the givenness of exemplary ideals to which he submits to become himself. But the necessity of the ideal, however interpreted, is inescapable in both.

12. Thus Rimbaud: "Je, c'est un autre." This immanent otherness of the human self, its lack of Cartesian transparency to itself, its sometimes startling depths, is a major theme of contemporary culture, in psychoanalysis and modern art, for example. See Harries, *The Meaning of Modern Art*, pp. 119–30.

13. Examples of exploration of the self in flight from itself are, most notably, the young Augustine's anxious quest for happiness in things outside himself, Pascal's "diversions" calculated to help one avoid facing oneself, Kierkegaard's sense of the person secretly in despair of itself, Sartre's bad faith, and Heidegger's vision of *Dasein*'s flight into the anonymity of *das Man*.

14. The notion of an immanent standard is indicated ethically, for instance, in Kant's famous reference to "the moral law within," which, together with the starry skies above, seems to have filled him with a kind of metaphysical astonishment. Hegel's *Phenomenology of Spirit* might be seen as a heroic working out of the dialectical tension between an immanent standard of truth and the partial truths that we mistakenly take as actually absolute: the ideal standard is both regulative, hence capable of facilitating human self-correction, and constitutive, for it articulates the kind of being we are.

15. At this stage we are limited to an ideal considered as immanent in the self. A different sense of the ideal, as other, is not precluded. The point is that there may be something absolute about the human person without the person being *the* absolute. We move through the ideal as immanent to the absolute as other. Something analogous is at stake when Augustine asks about the life of the soul, given that the soul is the life of the body; or when he asks in *De Libero Arbitrio* if the soul can itself be the creator

of the standard of truth that it finds within itself. The issue concerns the *ontological* weight of the ideal as other. We also encounter this issue in Anselm's efforts to move from the idea of perfection to the being of perfection. The ontological status of perfection and infinity (the possibility of their being radically other to the finite self) is also at stake in Descartes's proof of God in *Meditations on First Philosophy* (Third Meditation): is the absolute ideal a projection of the imagination, an invented idea, or is it grounded in being, even though it is brought to light only through the self's searching of its own being? This second kind of question will be more directly our concern in parts 2 and 3.

16. That man can come to expressly affirm *that he is*, and further celebrate the metaphysical givenness of being makes one shudder at the privilege of this mode of self-present being. One recalls Pascal referring to man as a thinking reed, who, as thought, is somehow greater than the universe. This is hardly an incitement to hubris. On the contrary, it recalls man's middle being, intermediate between misery and grandeur: an all in relation to nothing, a nothing in relation to the all, an intermediate between the infinitesimal and the infinite.

17. This brings to mind Kant's view of the imagination as the enigmatic root out of which stems sensibility and understanding as distinct faculties (*Critique of Pure Reason*, A77–78; B103–104); also Heidegger's claim that Kant drew back from unfolding the full implication of the doctrine of transcendental imagination (*Kant and the Problem of Metaphysics*, p. 167).

18. Thus, for instance, Heidegger's notion of Dasein points to the self as being there, but never in the manner of other facts within the world, which fall under the category of *Vorhandenheit;* which is not, of course, to deny the human being's facticity, but to bring out its distinctive character.

19. The poet Gerard Manley Hopkins, who in fact subscribed to a Scotistic sense of *haecceitas*, gives excellent expression to this: "Each moral thing does one thing and the same: / Deals out that being indoors each one dwells; / Selves—what goes itself; *myself* it speaks and spells, / Crying *What I do is me: for that I came.*" The reader will recall Hopkins's notions of *instress* and *inscape*. My use of the term *selfscape* is a mutation on Hopkins's *inscape*. For an attempt to provide a philosophical discourse about individuals after Hegel, see Brian Martine's *Individuals and Individuality.*

20. See R. Bubner, *Modern German Philosophy*, p. 26, where Husserl's belief that he is the heir to Kant's transcendental philosophy is criticized; because of its basis in Cartesian belief in clear and distinct givenness, Husserl's thought is opposed to Kant's sense of the unknowableness of the thing in itself. Some Derridean criticisms of Husserl are anti-Cartesian in the sense of rejecting univocal presence and moving toward something reminiscent of the Kantian unknowable, only here this is described in terms of absence and *différance*. Although I agree with the critique of univocal presence, I see unacceptable equivocations in the pure Kantian unknowable, or pure absence. But while I agree with the Hegelian critique of the Kantian unknowable, I do not think this need commit us to Hegel's absolute knowing. In criticizing univocal presence, we need a more complex sense of presence, one not just patched with a questionable, parasitic equivocal absence, but a rich, overdetermined sense that at the same time resists the hubris of totalitarian encapsulation.

21. Augustine, *Confessions* 4. 14. The *Confessions* are pervaded by the abysmal nature of the self, as well as by paradoxes of proximity and distance, intimacy and unfathomability. We are reminded of Nietzsche, who, in speaking of those who "know" themselves, said that each of us is furthest away from ourselves. Here too we think of memory as concrete ideality. As Augustine saw (*Confessions* 10. 8, for instance) with astonishment, memory could contain a world within, yet be beyond us. See my

"Memory and Metaphysics." For one of the most thoughtful and thorough explorations of the self in recent writings, see Paul Weiss, *Privacy.*

22. See n. 7 above.

23. I have discussed this in terms of classical empiricism, the twentieth-century notion of the sense-datum, and Collingwood's "Kantian" view of perception in "Collingwood, Imagination and Epistemology." Against the empiricist view of the mind as a *tabula rasa* and of the self as passively determined by external impressions, I defend the mediating activity of the knower. In terms of the notion of the original self, it makes little sense to speak of a tabula rasa, except perhaps as a minimal metaphor for human openness to otherness.

24. Think here of the way Hume shakes off philosophical perplexity and the skeptical impasse produced by his guiding assumptions; a glass of wine and the conviviality of backgammon are sufficient to restore normal, commonsense concreteness (*A Treatise of Human Nature,* book 1, part 4, sec. 7). "Woolliness," a critical standard used by some analytical philosophers, is itself a very "woolly" concept, I would say. Instead of being a strict univocal standard, its use (often to put down philosophical views that are not understood) is riddled with equivocalness.

25. Think here of Hume (*Treatise,* book 1, part 4, sec. 6), who speaks of the self as "nothing but a bundle or collection of different perceptions, which succeed each other with an inconceivable rapidity, and are in a perpetual flux and movement." On a "process" experience of self, see William James ("the present thought is your only thinker"), *Principles of Psychology,* vol. 1, pp. 321ff.

26. There is an interesting connection here between Nietzschean perspectivalism and Hume's psychic flux. Nietzsche's Dionysianism dissolves the individual in a more primordial flux, though Nietzsche, a thinker of extremes, hardly shares Hume's conservative (I am tempted to say dull) respect for common sense. Nietzsche is far more radical as a thinker of flux, including the flux of self, to the point of becoming lost in the labyrinth and devoured by the Minotaur, some commentators might say. (Indeed, one of his last, mad letters to Cosima Wagner contains a reference to Ariadne.) But sheer flux is incompatible with his perspectivalism, properly speaking. On Nietzsche and Ariadne, see *Selected Letters of Friedrich Nietzsche,* p. 346, esp. n. 240.

27. See, in this connection, Paul Ricoeur on Freud, *The Conflict of Interpretations,* pp. 160–76.

28. One can grant, though, that Freud's famous statement "Where id is, there will be ego" (*Wo Es war, soll Ich werden*) might be seen as a psychoanalytic version of the civilized teleology of the libido. There is still the metaphysical question. There may no longer be any need to dethrone any Victorian God the Father in our superego (that throne seems empty); rather, we should interrogate the triumvirate Marx, Freud, and Nietzsche, the three "masters of modern suspicion" who, albeit in the name of tyrranicide, have taken possession of the throne. Of course, the unconscious is inevitably an ambiguous, if not equivocal, notion, and in other versions of depth psychology is amenable to a more religious interpretation.

29. The literature is extensive. See n. 7. Vincent Descombes, *Modern French Philosophy,* and Rüdiger Bubner, *Modern German Philosophy,* include excellent discussions of the issue both in the form it took earlier in the century and in the manifold forms it takes today.

30. On the issue of concretizing the transcendental ego after Kant, see, for instance, Jürgen Habermas, *Knowledge and Human Interest;* for some representative writings on the split after Husserl regarding the interpretation of intentionality and the matter of transcendental idealism, see Joseph Kockelmans, ed., *Phenomenology: The Philosophy of Edmund Husserl and Its Interpretation.* On the issue in Anglo-American thought, see Richard

Rorty, "Epistemological Behaviorism and the De-Transcendentalization of Analytical Philosophy."

31. As is well known, Kant claimed to be awakened from his "dogmatic slumbers" by the disturbance caused by the skeptical results of Hume's empiricism. Similarly, Husserl sought to avoid the charge of "psychologism" and the skeptical relativizing of truth by historicism. On psychological and transcendental subjectivity, see Husserl, *Formal and Transcendental Logic*, sec. 99.

32. I am thinking here of Kant's view, expressed in the *Critique of Pure Reason*, that, in the final analysis, all concrete content for valid knowing must be derived (as in empiricism) from sensuous intuition; hence, in Kant's famous phrase (A51, B75), concepts without intuitions are empty. However, in the other half of this statement (intuitions without concepts are blind) we see Kant's recognition of the need for something more than the merely empirical—for instance, categories of understanding to give form to the otherwise indeterminate formlessness of merely empirical appearance.

33. Consider the language of *rupture* involved, for example, in Husserl's move from the natural attitude to the transcendental sphere. On the problem of mediating between these two, see Timothy Stapleton, *Husserl and Heidegger*, chap. 1. The problem is analogous to the Platonic problem of moving beyond the cave from *doxa* to *epistēmē* and to Hegel's problem in the *Phenomenology* of journeying from the natural attitude of sound common sense to the philosophical stance of absolute knowing. Certainly for Hegel, there cannot be a radical rupture here, for the whole point is to establish the immanence of the absolute within the natural attitude, albeit not always explicitly recognized as immanent. On this, see Joseph Flay, *Hegel's Quest for Certainty*.

34. On Husserl's so-called Cartesianism, see his *Cartesian Meditations* and *The Idea of Phenomenology*. On the transcendental unity of apperception as the pure "I think" accompanying all representation, see Kant, *Critique of Pure Reason*, and its treatment of the transcendental deduction.

35. On Max Stirner and the Young Hegelians, see L. Stepelevich, ed., *The Young Hegelians*, pp. 335ff. Santayana touches some raw nerves regarding subjectivism in the German tradition in *Egotism in German Philosophy*. Sartre comes close to vulgarizing himself in *Existentialism is a Humanism*.

36. This metaphysical openness of desire is quite clear in Platonic eros. It is also evident in Heidegger's Sorge. On the difference between these, see Stanley Rosen, *Nihilism*, esp. chap. 5.

37. Think of numerology raised to genuinely philosophical significance in Peirce's Firstness, Secondness, Thirdness. See Martine, *Individuals and Individuality*, chap. 3.

38. Consider here Sartrean existentialism, where the implication seems to be that the human essence is entirely protean. This view is a reformulation of the modern concern with man as essentially a self-making animal. Without denying that the self is active, we have tried above to understand its activity as ontologically rooted, thus avoiding the ontologically uprooted nothingness of the Sartrean self, and what I previously called the mania for unanchored originality. Human essence, I am arguing, is anchored in a prior sense of being. Undoubtedly, man can make a "second nature" for himself, as it has been put traditionally; but in the pursuit of human wholeness, this second nature must not be entirely unanchored. Nietzsche is right to point to an indeterminacy in man when he speaks of him as the unfinished animal; but without ontological anchoring, this indeterminacy is easily converted into an insatiable lack of being (witness man as Sartrean nothingness) that nothing at all can satisfy; hence man's own efforts at self-grounding through his own original power inevitably come to nothing, and (recalling the contradictory annihilation of desire in the absorbing god) we come to the Sartrean conclusion that "man is a useless passion."

39. It is more appropriate to talk of "affinity" than "identity," since the latter notion might

easily collapse into univocal sameness, whereas the former retains the essential dimension of openness. In part 1 we are looking at this openness from the side of the self. When in parts 2 and 3 we consider it from the side of the other, we will see the metaxological nature of this affinity.

40. Although Husserl talks of "bracketing" being, Stapleton, in *Husserl and Heidegger*, argues that Husserl (like Heidegger) is dealing with the question of being: the transcendental realm as the realm of absolute being. The issue is controversial. Even the "later" Husserl, supposedly replying to Heidegger with the notion of the *Lebenswelt*, continues to define *transcendental* in terms of cognition (*The Crisis of the European Sciences and Transcendental Phenomenology*, sec. 20). On the eidos ego in Husserl, see T. Adorno, *Against Epistemology*, chap. 4, esp. pp. 222ff.

41. The language of transcendental phenomenology tends to be a language of the "not," in that we are asked to prescind totally from the psychological (psychologism), perform an *epoché* wherein we "bracket" and neutralize the natural world, "suspend" and "put in parenthesis" the "natural attitude," and explore for "pure" transcendental subjectivity in the "residuum" left over. One is sometimes reminded of Aristophanes' caricature of Socrates in the *Clouds:* the abstracted thinker suspended above the stage, above the real drama of existence. The difficulty with the not that separates the transcendental from the merely factical and natural is how to explain the *movement between* these poles. Our emphasis on the power of being manifested in desire tries to speak to this and runs counter to any pure self-reflection. For all self-reflection, if it reflects on itself incisively, will, in the long run, encounter desire as the "engine" of its articulation, and with this the original power to be that pitches us out of an ideal purity into the rough world of being. Nor are we denied the possibility of ascent from the relative to the ultimate. But any real ascent cannot turn its back on concrete being or fail to try to appropriate the dynamism of its own movement. Another image of abstracted ideality is Swift's picture of the Laputans in *Gulliver's Travels*. Of course, these thinkers in Laputa needed the periodic reminder of flappers (who would strike them on the head with bladders, a comic example of Peircean Secondness), to return them to their ground in the world of being.

42. Recent critics of the tradition of metaphysics claim that this tradition is captive to a whole series of dualisms, moving back and forth between various binary oppositions such as the real and the ideal, the sensuous and the spiritual, and so on. I agree that opposites are pervasive throughout the tradition and also that some traditional positions sometimes tend to "flip" from one side to the other, not always with appropriate self-consciousness of the fact or of their own embeddedness in such an oppositional context. I do not think, however, that we can just jettison these oppositions and step outside philosophy, as some Heideggerians and post-Heideggerians seem to demand. The tradition includes thinkers (I need but mention Plato and Hegel) who were tremendously self-conscious about the difficulty of dualistic opposition, and who in different ways tried to attain philosophical positions beyond such oppositions—for instance, Plato's doctrine of eros, which seeks to bind up the whole against the often caricatured Plato of dualism, or Hegel's notion of dialectical thinking. We do need to become as self-conscious as possible of the dualistic oppositions informing philosophical thought. But we must think through these opposites to a more profound understanding of the meaning of being, one that does justice to the dialectical approach and, perhaps more important, to the respect for otherness that we find in the metaxological view.

43. Perhaps it is clear now why a doctrine of categories is not the first requirement of the present essay. In the normal sense, categories are logical forms of thought, formal means of logical synthesis, derived structural determinations that define specific forms of thought in relation to finite entities. Undoubtedly, analysis of such categories is

necessary. But instead of looking at logical forms, we have looked at forms of activity in order to retrieve the central eros of their being, relative to which determinate categories are originated forms. Our concern with desire as a metaphysical openness to being means that there is always something more than the finite determinations of logical categories, an excess, or surplus, that extends beyond and overflows such forms.

44. Regarding the gap (like the Platonic *chōrismos*) between the empirical and the transcendental and the flipping from the empty formal ego to a grosser concreteness, consider, for instance, Hegel's critique of what he took to be the empty formalism of Fichte's ego, inherited from Kant (whose moral teaching Hegel also criticized on the same score of formalism). The same formalism of the ego was passed on in aesthetics, in the debunking negativity of Romantic irony, whose hollowness Hegel variously criticized—for instance, in *die schöne Seele* and in the emptiness of Schlegel's irony (see my *Art and the Absolute*, chap. 6). Hegel himself is a deeply searching critic of the flip that occurs with empty formalism. But his Left Hegelian successors have not always had his dialectical balance, and their debunking, negative, deconstructive use of dialectic evinces something of the recoil from what they saw as the empty formalism of idealism toward materialism, historicism, and in some cases irrationalism (see Stepelevich, ed., *The Young Hegelians*). Heine (*Philosophy and Religion in Germany*) tells very well the story of this development, at least some of its earlier episodes. A twentieth-century version of the same flip has followed the Heideggerian and existentialist critique of Husserl's transcendental phenomenology. Some of Heidegger's own successors have turned deconstructive weapons against Heidegger himself, accusing him of still being bound to the so-called metaphysics of presence. The widespread use of the language of absence recalls what I said above concerning the vacancy left by the vanishing of the pure, formal, transcendental ego. The deconstructionist criticism tends to see in the transcendental ego a univocal presence or identity beyond the flux of consciousness. The deconstructionist rightly finds no such simple identity or univocal presence, but sometimes leaps from this to a critique of *all* presence, all concepts of identity, all notions of the self. He appeals instead to ideas like absence and emphasizes the equivocal difference he finds in language. The view defended in this essay denies that presence can be reduced to univocal identity or that difference is exhausted by equivocalness. Even at the outset, when we considered the conversion of lack within desire (chap. 1), we saw the impossibility of maintaining univocal identity and sheer absence.

45. Consider Dostoevski's *Underground Man* (one who does not *want* to escape Plato's cave?) as a concrete existential instance of the flip into the irrational. He alternates between vacuous, idealistic dreams of "the beautiful and the sublime" and brutal, base concreteness; between empty, swelling ideality and bitter, sour facticity; between the extremes of either wanting to be a hero or wallowing in the mud, so he tells us. He displays a mixture of Kierkegaardian irrational faith and Sartrean nausea, mainly the latter. He embodies Dostoevski's reaction to the German idealism and romanticism that exerted considerable influence in Russia in the second quarter of the nineteenth century (see Isaiah Berlin, *Russian Thinkers*, pp. 114–49). In fact, the Underground Man reminds us of an existential version of Hegel's Unhappy Consciousness, blending together master and slave, sadist and masochist, bully and humiliated man. Dostoevski helps us to see (as does Hegel) that if one develops what is latent in the beautiful soul, it becomes, in fact, the ugly soul.

3 DESIRE'S INFINITUDE AND WHOLENESS

1. Ancient Epicureanism, for instance, serves to caution us on this point. So much so that sophisticated versions of Epicureanism, such as that of Epicurus himself, embody

an ethics that is essentially a rational safeguard against the ambiguities of immediate gratification, rather than a permission to indulge spontaneous desire. There is a similar suspicion of univocal desire, perhaps, in Freud's recognition that narcissistic, infantile desire must be weaned from the pleasure principle and learn to mediate its fulfillment in accordance with the reality principle.

2. Kant's criticism of "eudaemonism" can be seen as a criticism of the good defined in terms of a combination of immediate desire and the rationalization of self-interest by the calculative intellect. Utilitarianism, after Kant, tends to involve the same combination, situated within the complex context of society and the plurality of competing self-interests therein. Just as Kant as a transcendental philosopher explored a sense of self more radical than that of empiricism, so also his sense of human beings as moral is more profound than the utilitarian understanding of desire. In both spheres of course, Kant is haunted by the problems of formalism and dualism. His critique of eudaemonism is not altogether adequate, I believe, to Aristotle's sense of moral wholeness. See my "Phronesis and the Categorical Imperative." Gadamer has recently made an important effort to restore the notion of *phronēsis* (*Truth and Method*, pp. 278ff.); see also Alasdair MacIntyre, *After Virtue: A Study in Moral Theory*.

3. This mentality is ably criticized by Marxists, though one need hardly be a Marxist to demand demythologization of idolized things.

4. See S. Kierkegaard, *Either/Or*, vol. 1, pp. 35–110, and Albert Camus, *The Myth of Sisyphus*, pp. 51ff. For a Freudian interpretation in terms of an impossible infantile regress to the mother, see Otto Rank, *The Don Juan Legend*. The bibliography on the legend in that volume indicates something of the interest of nineteenth-century artists (including Baudelaire and Byron) in the theme. This is not unrelated to the aesthetic possibilities of desire, as Kierkegaard, taking some of his cues from Mozart's *Don Giovanni*, recognized. On Nietzsche and what he calls "The Don Juan of the Mind," see Eric Heller, *The Artist's Journey into the Interior*, p. 195.

5. On the theme of *Streben nach dem Unendlichen* in the nineteenth century, see M. H. Abrams, *Natural Supernaturalism*, pp. 215–17. Here we find revealing instances (in Fichte, Schiller, Hölderlin, Blake, Wordsworth, and Coleridge) of aspiration to which no worldly object can correspond, of discontent with every partial object. We find the modern dissatisfaction with classical perfection and often a preference for the boundless over the bounded. Goethe, of course, was no devotee of mere formless restlessness: *in der Beschränkung zeigt sich erst der Meister* ("in limitation only is the master manifest"). See also Peter Heller, *Dialectics and Nihilism*, pp. 297ff.

6. Hegel criticizes the Beautiful Soul in both the *Phenomenology* and the *Aesthetics*. Equivocal desire is perhaps not unrelated to Romantic irony, which, relative to the preciousness of its own inwardness, devalues and denigrates everything external. There is here a refusal to come to terms with finitude, a refusal in which there is little difference between desire and despair. Every merely determinate object is something to be surpassed, leading to an endless negation of all externality by a rampant inwardness, a tyrannous subjectivity. We have a spurious self-sufficiency, a subjectivity that grows hollow because it is really monological, not dialogical. This attitude can be as much political as aesthetic, as the Young Hegelians make clear. And there is a line of inheritance from the Young Hegelians down to the negative dialectics of the Critical school, in which, not surprisingly, we meet a similar commingling of aesthetics and politics. Sometimes the negative dialectics of the Critical school strikes us as a philosophical *doppelgänger* of Young Hegelianism (see R. Bubner, *Modern German Philosophy*, p. 175). See my *Art and the Absolute*, chap. 3, on aesthetics and politics in the Left Hegelian tradition, and chap. 6 on the excessive subjectivity of Romantic inwardness.

7. Robert Jay Lifton, in *History and Human Survival*, has spoken of the contemporary

self as "protean man." One might surmise that this protean man is often without a hidden name or identity. As with equivocal desire, we here have desire playing at being desire, playing with the possibilities of passion, yet fearful to limit possibility by commitment to a definite actuality. Playing with possibility thus allows of infinite evasion. Rather than the divine Proteus, we are reminded of the possessed young man of Gadarene whose name was Legion, a perverse parody of divine infinity.

8. Some commentators have found a questionable ambiguity here in Kierkegaard's emphasis on truth as subjectivity, in the implication that an absolute passion may be a passion for the absolute. This might seem to justify equally a frenzied fanaticism for a finite objective, distortedly desired with demonic zeal, and a genuine passion for the unconditioned. Not that I am accusing Kierkegaard of this intent; it is a matter, rather, of the adequacy of his manner of articulating the issue.

9. Intentionality, a matter of importance to medieval scholastics, resurfaces in contemporary philosophy with the influence of Brentano on Husserl. Consistent with the notion of self developed in chap. 2, it need not be confined to epistemic functions. Intentional infinitude tries to point to the primordial eros in man, which serves as a radical openness to otherness. Against any closed self-transparency, desire finds itself thrust out of monadic inwardness by a power of being it cannot entirely subordinate to its own will. We may subsequently mediate this power and come to direct it. But there remains an unappropriated dynamism, never entirely subject to conscious mastery.

10. Thomas Hobbes, *Leviathan*, book 1, chap. 11. See Schopenhauer, *The World as Will and Representation*, vol. 1, pp. 149, 164–65, 321. One need not deny that human beings often view things in this light. Desire's essential ambiguity allows deformed possibility. Well in advance of Hobbesian restlessness or Romantic inwardness, Plato saw unbounded desire as one of the fundamental problems, the problem of the tyrant. The dialogues provide many pictures of this: for example, Thrasymachus, as advocate of power without justice, settles for uncritical acceptance of debased desire and takes the fact of deformed selfhood as absolute, without any adequate reflective sense of desire's orientation toward the ideal. For Hobbes (following Thrasymachus and followed by Nietzsche), power is more primordial than justice; whereas for Plato, justice is more primordial than power. For the latter, justice is no mere human projection, but manifests a condition of being.

11. Kierkegaard points to this self-mediation in the move from the aesthetic to the ethical. On "uneasiness" in Augustine and Pascal, see G. Marcel, *Problematic Man*, pp. 90–100; also Romano Guardini, *Pascal for Our Time*, chap. 2.

12. I am thinking in particular of the phenomenological doctrine of intentionality in Husserl and the almost immediate modification of epistemic intentionality into a more encompassing notion in, for instance, Sartre's notion of transcendence and Heidegger's *Sorge*. Critics of phenomenology's concept of intentionality are uneasy with what they fear is an unacceptable sense of appropriating power hidden in epistemic intentionality. Whether this fear is justified or not, the view I develop is not committed to such dominating power, as will become clearer later.

13. I have tried to develop these notions in "Memory and Metaphysics."

14. In regard to intentional infinitude and the desire to be everything, we are reminded of Aristotle in *De Anima* (e.g., 431b2ff.) telling us that "somehow the soul is everything," or Aquinas (e.g., *Summa Contra Gentiles* II. 98) speaking of the mind as *potens omnia facere et fieri*. One thinks also of Hegel in the *Phenomenology* (chap. 5) speaking of reason as the conscious certainty of being all reality. Undoubtedly, part of the difficulty here is that humans set themselves up as whole in opposition to the infinite otherness that envelops them, trying to subject it to their own self-mediation. I am not arguing for this at all. The above statements need not be read as expressions of the will to power;

rather, they can be taken as ambiguous pointers to the implicit affinity or community of humans with all of being. They point to our astonishing, yet humbling, grandeur within this community.

15. We will consider positive finitude more fully in parts 2 and 3.

16. See my "Plato's Philosophical Art and the Identification of the Sophist."

17. See chap. 2 above for a discussion of the transcendental ego. On the deconstructionist shift from presence to absence, see V. Descombes, *Modern French Philosophy*, chap. 5.

18. See the discussion of agapeic otherness and goodwill in chap. 7 below.

19. *Art and the Absolute*, esp. chap. 5. The intertwining of the aesthetic and the question of wholeness is an important theme after Kant, one that is not always divorced from the desire to renew in modernity something of classical Greek harmony. After Kant, with his view of the aesthetic idea as straining for a completeness nowhere to be found in nature, we find Schiller trying to overcome human duality and Schelling and Hegel recognizing, albeit in different ways, the absolute dimension of art. Later, Schopenhauer and Nietzsche accord crucial importance to art in the metaphysical economy of human life. Heidegger and hermeneutical thought, especially that of Gadamer, pursue a similar possibility. Even Marxist thought—that of Marcuse and Adorno, for example—is not immune from the vital appeal of the aesthetic.

20. The enjoyment of being in such resting places is not unrelated to the ancient contemplative comportment toward being instanced in theoria. Ancient theoria derived from the sense of joyful vigilance that the *theoroi* brought to the sacred games and festivals. It is thus unlike modern, post-Cartesian theory (theory as the product of the subjective mind), with its connotations of spectatorial alienation from being. This contemplative comportment is close to art; and indeed this is part of why Hegel saw something absolute in both. One thinks of Plato in the *Theaetetus* (155d) speaking of *thaumazein* ("wonder") as the feeling (*pathos*) of the philosopher and echoes thereof in Aristotle, at the beginning of the *Metaphysics* (982b10ff.), where philosophy's marveling astonishment before being is granted, even in its kinship with *muthos*. On the ludic, sacral basis of civilized being, see J. Pieper, *Leisure: The Basis of Culture*. The ontological significance of play was suggested by Schiller and Nietzsche and has been developed more recently by Gadamer.

21. On wholeness as between fragmentation and completion, see the introduction to Carl Vaught's excellent *The Quest for Wholeness;* also my review thereof in *Philosophical Studies* (Ireland) 29:332–36.

22. *Art and the Absolute*, passim.

23. Many twentieth-century aestheticians are antimimetic, carrying forward, often without realizing it, some of the implications of Kant's transcendental imagination. The complexity of the problem of otherness is not always thought through, and what we sometimes get is a naive exultation at breaking with a naive realism. For a defense of mimesis, see G. Graff, *Literature against Itself*. The issues are complex, but I do not think that mimesis (understood here as an opening and likening to otherness) is to be jettisoned. Nor do I reject the sense of human originality, as I indicated in the previous chapter. On the insufficiency of breaking with a simple realism, see chap. 5 below.

24. In relation to the gathering together of unity and manyness, see Nietzsche's view that philosophical greatness must be "capable of being as manifold as whole, as wide as full" (*Beyond Good and Evil*, sec. 212). Nietzsche's approach to wholeness is ambiguous, in that, on the one hand, he recognizes the need for a certain balance of the Apollonian and the Dionysian, whereas, on the other hand, the Dionysian seems more primordial than the Apollonian. His sense of human promise carries some admiration for the Greek *kalokagathia* (as we see in his depiction of thinkers in *Philosophy in the Tragic Age of the Greeks*) as well as for the heroic artistic creators of the Renaissance.

Very loosely, his Apollonian corresponds to what we are calling wholeness, whereas his Dionysian is more directly related to the infinite restlessness of desire. We need both, but in Nietzsche the dark, inchoate, formless ferment of the Dionysian sometimes drowns the sunlike serenity and bounded measure of the Apollonian. As I have tried to present it, we need more than a dualism of Apollo and Dionysus (these remind us of Schiller's *Formtrieb* and *Stofftrieb*) and more than the reduction of one to the other. Concrete wholeness must itself be the embodiment of the energy of being that wells up in the infinite restlessness of desire and that desire's self-mediation tries to articulate in a form which does not diminish dynamism. Instead of a duality, we need something like the trinity of Ariel, Caliban, and Prospero. Prospero is the artful magician, the artificer whose intimacy with airy spirit and lordship of cunning dross makes him an agent of transformation and reconciliation.

25. Images of fire are pervasive in the language of desire: thus we burn with desire, are ablaze with it, inflamed by it; desire is enkindled, flares up, sets us on fire, puts us in heat. Fire is also a common image for the divine, as in Heraclitean fire or Pentecostal fire. The Prometheus myth, imaging man's reception of the fire of the gods, can help us make a point that is counter to a very common use to which the story has been put. Those who set up Prometheus as the paradigm of the superman, the human superhero whose defiance of the gods defines man's freedom, miss a subtlety present in the original myth. Prometheus puts into their hands, we might say appositely, an axe to grind. Armed with this, they proceed to forget that Prometheus is a thieving Titan (not a human superhero) who gives the fire to mortals. Man, creature of the day, receives this gift; he does not originally seize upon it himself. Those who indiscriminately identify Prometheus with the prototypical free man circumscribe the idea of freedom to the negative form of resistance, in a way that is not fully warranted by the myth they use as justification. Shaftesbury (who said, "We have the honour of being originals") gave us the more nuanced view when he described the artist as a "just Prometheus under Jove", (cited in *Philosophies of Art and Beauty*, ed. A. Hofstadter and R. Kuhns, p. 240).

4 DESIRE, TRANSCENDENCE, AND STATIC ETERNITY

1. As we shall see below, however, this notion is perhaps more Eleatic than strictly Platonic. Or better, the dualistic diagnosis tends to be Platonic, whereas resort to an immutable eternity in response to dualism tends to be Eleatic. Obviously Plato (in the *Sophist* most clearly, in the discussion of the possibility of life and movement in the forms) was both attracted to and dissatisfied with the Eleatic One. Even Parmenides, though a monist regarding the unity of being, is a strange, inconsistent dualist in subscribing to a difference between the Way of Truth and the Way of Seeming.

2. The stress on time might be traced to Kant's view of time as a necessary a priori form of our experience. The insistence on history is strong in Hegel and his successors. Its importance in the twentieth century is evident in Husserl's *The Phenomenology of Internal Time-Consciousness* and Heidegger's *Being and Time*. The significance of historicity is further developed in hermeneutical philosophy—for instance, in Gadamer's *Truth and Method*. Here I might comment on some affinities and differences between the metaxological and hermeneutical approaches. Hermeneutics insists on the context-bound nature of interpretation. We have no ahistorical privileged view but are always emmeshed in a web of meanings, in the interplay of subject and object. The metaxological view is sympathetic to this emphasis on the between and to the criticism of the abstraction of Cartesian solipsism present in the hermeneutic approach. We are always in the middle and have no vantage point in a static eternity from which we

can survey the whole. But even though we have no privileged perspective outside time, within the middle and out of the middle certain manifestations of ultimacy may come to appearance. Hermeneutics has sometimes been criticized here as unable to avoid the charge of relativism. Regardless of the justice of this charge, the metaxological middle, I will argue, testifies to the articulation of human desire as an eros seeking to rise above sheer relativity and conditionedness. The philosophical difficulty is how to do justice in reflective discourse to the fullness already at work in the concrete. The desire for the unconditioned articulates itself within the middle, yes, and so it is impossible to leap outside time. But within the middle there may be an emergence from within human experience of its own ultimate dimension. I agree with hermeneutical thought that human finitude is not to be denied, but neither is our infinite restlessness. Philosophical interpretation always carries something of the dense ambiguity of its own originating context, even while clarifying the texture of this ambiguity. The search for wholeness and absoluteness within the middle need not deny the situatedness, limitation, and openness of man's being. The impossibility of univocal or dialectical closure and the importance of the aesthetic are other points of affinity between hermeneutical thought and the metaxological view we are developing. On these issues, see my "Hermeneutics and Hegel's Aesthetics."

3. Even Nietzsche has Zarathustra exclaim: "All joy wills eternity, wills deep, deep eternity (*tiefe, tiefe Ewigheit*)." See my "The Child in Nietzsche's Menagerie." Nietzsche is not himself a Last Man ("What is longing, asks the Last Man, and blinks; what is a star, asks the Last Man, and blinks"). The tepid historicism of some post-Nietzscheans sometimes makes one wonder whether his disciples have not betrayed Nietzsche's own longing, having learned little from his warning regarding the uses and abuses of history and having enfeebled his eros for eternity.

4. Of relevance here is Zeno's argument regarding the flight of the arrow (see G. S. Kirk and J. E. Raven, *The Presocratic Philosophers*, pp. 294–95). One point of this Eleatic argument is to show the impossibility of movement if reconstructed in accordance with a univocal logic. If we try to rationally reconstruct movement in this way (each point in flight must be a static "now," a univocal punctual instant, nothing but itself alone), then the "flow" of the flight, its becoming or movement, dissolves into a maelstrom of equivocations. The static now, the self-identical instant, under the dominance of the univocal assumption is taken as the standard of being, which the equivocal flight cannot meet. See also *Parmenides* 127d–128e on this sense of the instant.

5. See previous note. One might add here that, though the equivocalness of becoming seems to be established by logical argument and its univocal ideal for Parmenides and Zeno, this logic is often only the bright side of a more ambiguous eros. We need to get to this eros to comprehend fully the roots of the abstractly logical. We might use Pascalian terms here by saying that univocal logic feeds on *l'esprit de géométrie*, whereas human beings as desiring creatures of ambivalence and contradiction call for *l'esprit de finesse*. We might also note the inseparability of these two, even in Parmenidean being, in that the sense of logical unity gains some of its strong power through its alogical echoes of a mystical vision of the unity of the whole. It is this complex ambiguity of desire that we must understand in relation to static eternity.

6. This emphasis on guilt and fallenness is to be found not only in certain Gnostic doctrines, but in more orthodox religious views and in the injunction to "overcome the world." One finds traces even in Heidegger's sense of Dasein's "fallenness" and in Sartre's talk of the human being as "condemned" to be free. Obviously the opposing power of time is nowhere more evident than in the brute, recalcitrant finality of death. Relative to this, one might see Socrates' will to free the soul from the body and liberate the eternal in man from time as a response to time as equivocal; the immortal soul is the ideal self beyond change into which desire dies by philosophically opposing

time as the opposing power. Human salvation thus becomes deathless identity. One might also note that aspects of Schopenhauer's views—the futility of time, the duplicity and absurd meaninglessness of striving without end, human desire understood as participation in becoming's futility—fit with a sense of becoming as equivocal process. The artist, or more completely, the saint, escapes the wheel of Ixion, the saint by negating desire through an asceticism that flees the wearying cycle of coming to be and perishing. See Schopenhauer, *The World as Will and Representation*, vol. 1, pp. 266–67. On pure will-less knowing in art, see p. 196: "We celebrate the Sabbath of the penal servitude of willing; the wheel of Ixion stands still." See also vol. 2, p. 480, where Schopenhauer's praise of the Eleatic concept of immobile being and the *nunc stans* reminds one of the metaphysics of presence. Schopenhauer has an interesting view of original sin: guilt is inherent in just being.

7. This is a misinterpretation of the origin of difference which we discussed in part 1 in terms of the self-differentiation of the original self. Here in part 2 we have the added complexity of the ontological origin of difference in otherness itself.

8. See Kirk and Raven, *The Presocratic Philosophers*, pp. 270–71.

9. Thus, Parmenides speaks of a total whole, not unlike the absorbing god, which is *epei nun estin homou pan, hen, sunexes* (ibid., p. 273). Echoes of this are found in Boethius's view of eternity as a *totum simul* in *De Consolatione Philosophiae*, which is echoed in turn by Aquinas in *Summa Theologiae*, I, Q. 10, where characteristics like immutability and uniformity figure prominently in the discussion of God's eternity. Relevant to our focus on desire, notice that Boethius is concerned with *consolation*, not just abstract logical consistency.

10. Consider here the element of Parmenidean stasis in Absolute Beauty in Plato's *Symposium* (210e ff.). Like Eleatic being that is *agenēton*, it is said to be ever existent, neither coming to be nor perishing (*aei on kai oute gignomenon oute apollumenon;* 210e8–9), but always existing unto itself alone and being uniform (*alla auto kath' hauto meth' hautou monoeides aei on;* 211b1–2). This is obviously not to say that Plato has to be reduced to an Eleatic, for his views are richer than this one strand. I merely point to one, albeit important, tendency.

11. We may perhaps find here some justification for the contemporary critique of the so-called metaphysics of presence, which is said to favor univocity of being over the equivocity of becoming, Parmenides' Way of Truth over the Way of Seeming. This critique might be said to be vehemently anti-Parmenidean, though I believe it has an immoderate tendency to reduce the whole tradition of metaphysics to a core of pure Eleaticism. As I implied before (chap. 1, n. 15), I think Nietzsche's criticism of the tradition is more applicable to Schopenhauerian Platonism (with its praise of Eleaticism and its tendency to be a metaphysics of presence) than to the more many-sided "Platonism" of Plato himself. See J. Derrida, *Margins*, p. 40, where classical metaphysics of presence is said to reduce the temporal "now" to "the intemporal kernel of time"; also Henry Staten, *Wittgenstein and Derrida*, p. 19, where time is discussed as the "not now"—that is, as reduced to nonbeing, to nothing. Staten very well connects the critique of deconstruction with the traditional Aristotelian notion of eidos as univocal presence and the Husserlian transcendental ego as transparent self-presence. See my remarks on the transcendental ego with respect to the same question of form in chap. 2 above.

12. This is literally the language of eternal being as *auto kath' hauto*. One is reminded also of Kierkegaard's treatment of God's unchangeableness in terms of the image of the mountain (*Edifying Discourses*, pp. 239–53). The image of dead stone reminds us of the catatonic god. I know that this image is also intended to conjure up the thought of the enduring, and I have no quarrel with this intention, only with the unfortunate connotation of deadness. I agree that process thought touches a sensitive nerve in

the traditional conception of impassive divinity. Below I hope to make clearer that it may be possible to preserve the transcendence of the divine without retaining some of the difficulties of traditional dualisms. Here we might ask whether Schelling's *Indifferenzpunkt* is not a catatonic god (since a "point" implies a unity contracted into itself, and "indifference" implies a unity beyond difference that repels manyness). I know that Schelling wished to defend an originative ground; but does the language of the Indifferenzpunkt help or hinder us? With respect to the criticism of static eternity in terms of descent which follows, see Hegel's criticism of Schelling's Absolute as the night in which all cows are black. The point at issue is the vanishing of articulate difference. On Schelling and eternity, see Michael Vater's discussion in his translation of Schelling's *Bruno*.

13. This desire to make the transcendent absolutely determinate can be looked at in terms of either unity or multiplicity, but this does not affect the present point. In terms of unity, and putting the point in terms of religious representation, we are given one god who is a determinate being among other determinate beings, albeit the highest— that is, we have determinate monotheism; or, if philosophical reflection is dominant, we are given a univocal conception of the unity of being. Looking at it in terms of manyness, we might find a multitude of determinate divinities—determinate polytheism; or, if reflection is to the fore, we get a multiplicity of something like univocal universals, forms in a Platonic manner. Whether conceived in terms of unity or multiplicity, however, the difficulty is the connection between absolute determinacy and creative origination. Here we might consider Aristotle's question: in what sense can the Platonic eidos be a cause? The forms do not seem to be *archai kinēseōs:* they are not sources of change or efficient causes, but only final or formal causes; they do not initiate change, but only regulate change initiated elsewhere. (See *Metaphysics* 990b18, 991a9, also 1071b15 on movement and eternal substance.) Of course, we must remember that Aristotle tends to an extreme transcendent view of Platonic forms, which accentuates the chōrismos in a manner helpful to the highlighting of his own doctrine of immanent form.

14. Consider the following from Peter Heller, *Dialectics and Nihilism,* p. 48: "According to Jacobi the idea of a perfect Being enjoying its own unchangeable and complete perfection was repellent to Lessing: 'He associated with it a notion of such infinite boredom that he felt sick at the very thought of it.' " This is a common feeling in modernity and, in our terms, displays a conjunction of equivocal desire and static eternity that leads to the rejection of eternity and the dissipation of desire. I stress that, in criticizing static eternity, I do not intend to defend such a view. My point is rather to insist on a richer sense of desire and originative transcendence. In this regard, one can sympathize with contemporary "antifoundationalism," if the foundation rejected is a dead ground. I do not believe that we need be antifoundational, however, if the "foundation" is properly dynamic, if the grounding origin reveals the energy of being as this comes to manifestation in the process of becoming itself.

15. As will be seen in later chapters, my purpose is not to subordinate being to becoming, but to discover in becoming a more originary sense of being, one that is recalcitrant to an exclusively dialectical comprehension (see chaps. 5 and 6), one that is more than the abstract indeterminate beginning of Hegel's *Logic*. The deeper penetration of becoming reveals a metaxological, not just a dialectical, sense of being. My point is not simply to reject Hegel, but to move through the dialectical.

16. When Plato in the *Timaeus* (37d6 f.) calls time a moving image of eternity, this is often taken to mean that Plato sees movement as subordinate to stasis; but, of course, a moving image might also mirror, just in its movement, the originative energy of eternity and thus itself be an original image. On the difficulty of distinguishing image

from original in Plato, see Stanley Rosen, *Plato's Sophist: The Drama of Original and Image.*

17. But see chap. 6 for more detailed discussion of the thing and its concreteness. In speaking of becoming as othering, the stress is not on the otherness of some static substratum, but on othering as an activity, a dynamic process.

18. See n. 6 above. Schopenhauer sees the futility of sheer striving without end and seeks some equilibrium in the end. Art may provide us with a Sabbath from ceaseless becoming. Later in this work (see chaps. 6 and 8) I will discuss a sense of the aesthetic as a poiēsis of a creative origin without the nihilistic weariness in the face of becoming that wants to be extricated from time.

19. The sense of external becoming here might be thought of in terms of the Greek notion of *phusis*, as the process of coming to be and passing away, arising and being annulled, one that manifests an immanent source of origination and that cannot be reduced to a nominalistic aggregate or sum of things. Thus, also a sense of being born is present in the word *natura*. See Aristotle's *Metaphysics* 1014b16ff., where the connection of phusis with genesis and growing is suggested (though Aristotle's etymology has been thought fanciful). What is at issue is *natura naturans*, the activity of naturing.

20. See, for instance, Hegel, *Enzyklopädie*, secs. 23 and 405; also n. 6 above.

21. For qualification of this protean nature, see chap. 3, n. 7. I imply no simple teleology of nature in terms of our place within becoming, as I indicate in chap. 7 in relation to the unsheltering effect of the sublime and in chap. 8 in relation to the decentering of all anthropomorphic projections in relation to the absolute original. Yet we are undoubtedly singular in a strong sense. This is perhaps the element of truth in nominalism: the real is the individual. But the individual emerges in a process of becoming singular. This process is not simply an aggregate of fixed, pregiven singles, but a dynamic activity of determinate individuation. This does not commit us to any understanding of individuality as *isolated* from relations with others. In chap. 6 I speak of nominalism and particularity.

22. Think here of Rilke's celebrated lines in the "Ninth Duino Elegy": *Erde, ist es nicht dies, was du willst: unsichtbar/in uns erstehen?* ("Earth, is not this what you want: invisibly/To arise in us?").

23. The image of time as a child is Heraclitean: "Time is a child playing draughts" (frag. 12). It is also used by Nietzsche in *Thus Spoke Zarathustra* (see my "The Child in Nietzsche's Menagerie"). But my use of the image coincides with neither of these.

24. In relation to the above affinity, we might here think of a possible likening between desire's infinite restlessness and the infinite succession of things that becoming generates; or between man's ceaseless search for a ground of being and the power of becoming to transcend all particularity. We might think of the human self, like external becoming, as instancing sameness and lack of self-sameness, a unity diversifying itself, yet a manifold crying out for integrity, but trying to achieve this in an ever fuller interiorized way.

5 DESIRE, KNOWING, AND OTHERNESS

1. See my "Collingwood, Imagination and Epistemology" for a discussion of immediacy in contemporary British treatments of perception.

2. See the citations in chap. 1, n. 1; also in chap. 2, n. 8.

3. On concreteness and philosophy, see my *Art and the Absolute*, chap. 2.

4. I deal with this more fully in chap. 7 in relation to agapeic otherness.

5. For a discussion related to our concern with the intermediate, see Paul Ricoeur, "The Antimony of Human Reality and the Problem of Philosophical Anthropology," in *The*

Philosophy of Paul Ricoeur, pp. 20–35. Ricoeur explicitly mentions the metaxu, though he is primarily concerned with *thumos* in the *Republic,* rather than *eros* in the *Symposium.* His concern with transcendental synthesis in Kant, as well as the dialectical interplay of finite and infinite in Pascal, Hegel, and Kierkegaard, is clearly related to the themes of this essay; though, as I indicate in chap. 7, I am concerned not merely with a dialectic of finite and infinite, but with a metaxological intermediation between man as intentionally infinite and otherness as a different, irreducible infinity. I find myself very sympathetic to Ricoeur, though in fact I had already developed the themes of the present work before I read his insightful discussion.

6. G. W. F. Hegel, *Phänomenologie des Geistes,* p. 27; *Phenomenology of Spirit,* p. 17. The translations of Hegel given here are my own, although I have consulted both the Baillie and the Miller translations. For the reader's convenience, I will cite the page number(s) in Miller's translation, as well as in the original German. I might remark that Hegel's concern with knowing, in being essentially dynamic, might be seen as a post-Kantian, transcendental concern with eros. Hegelian knowing, like Platonic eros, is inspired by a passion for the absolute, a drive for the unconditioned.

7. *Phänomenologie,* p. 80; *Phenomenology,* p. 59.

8. *Phänomenologie,* p. 87; *Phenomenology,* p. 65.

9. *Phänomenologie,* p. 21; *Phenomenology,* p. 11.

10. *Phänomenologie,* p. 21; *Phenomenology,* p. 11.

11. *Phänomenologie,* p. 20; *Phenomenology,* p. 10; emphasis original.

12. *Phänomenologie,* p. 32; *Phenomenology,* p. 21.

13. *Phänomenologie,* pp. 32–33; *Phenomenology,* pp. 21–22. I do not mean to narrow the astonishing wealth of the *Phenomenology* to just the issue of self-mediation. Yet this issue is crucial and, I believe, the source of much suspicion (whether justified or not) of Hegel. For some representative discussion of the *Phenomenology,* see Merold Westphal, ed., *Method and Speculation in Hegel's Phenomenology;* also Joseph Flay's exhaustive *Hegel's Quest for Certainty.* Let me also add that I am focusing on the movement from consciousness to self-consciousness, and that one must grant that when Hegel talks of spirit (*Geist*), he is concerned with more than *one* self-consciousness. The fullness of a historical community comes into play here. But one has to say that Hegel still characterizes Geist in terms of complex, dialectical self-mediation: spirit mediates its relatedness with itself in its own otherness. This is clear in the preface to the *Phenomenology* (e.g., pp. 14–15, Miller trans.), throughout the work, and in its culmination in absolute knowing. I might also mention that this movement from otherness as "beyond" is also at stake in the very important shift from the religious *Vorstellung* to the philosophical *Begriff:* the Begriff more adequately interiorizes the otherness of the divine so is no longer burdened for Hegel with dualistic opposition; whereas the *Vorstellung* does not complete the movement from the immediacy of consciousness to the self-mediation of self-consciousness. The position I try to defend is more than immediacy, dualistic opposition, and dialectical self-mediation. But for a sympathetic reading of Hegel on religion, see my "Hegel and the Problem of Religious Representation." I take up the issue again in relation to Hegel's notion of the absolute in chap. 8.

14. This is clearly implied by Hegel's crucial notion of a dialectical Aufhebung, for this entails a movement toward a unity that at a higher level subsumes what at lower levels of multiplicity is discordant and opposed. Let me repeat that the Hegelian Aufhebung does preserve difference even in the act of surpassing and encompassing it, but the crucial issue is the kind of difference. Thus, in the *Logic* (Miller trans., pp. 417–18) we find a section on "Absolute Difference." This is a brilliant, concise discussion of difference as *both* itself and identity. But my point remains. Hegel's "Absolute Difference" is still dialectical difference in the sense of being *self-mediating* difference,

self-relating difference: the identity of difference is *its own* identity, just as the difference of identity is also *its own* (i.e., identity's) difference. Dialectical self-relation, dialectical self-mediation, is the truth of both absolute identity and absolute difference for Hegel.

For a defense of Hegel's dialectic against the decomposition worked by deconstruction, see my *Art and the Absolute,* chap. 5. In relation to the criticism of dialectic, see Joseph Flay's claim that Hegel identifies intelligibility with totality (*Hegel's Quest for Certainty*); in the language we have used, metaxological intermediation points to an otherness that is intelligible, but not so in terms of a closed, totalized self-mediation.

15. One always has to be extremely guarded in dealing with thinkers like Hegel (see the Introduction to this essay; also my *Art and the Absolute*). I do not think the philosophical point is simply conditional on a sometimes questionable eagerness to "overcome" Hegel. The thing itself is what matters, which in this case means the effort to give a philosophical account of the metaxological. One sometimes wonders to what extent Hegel intends something like the metaxological, albeit using the language of self-mediation. My point is that the language of self-mediation is not sufficient.

16. On dialectic and speculative Vernunft, see *Enzyklopädie,* secs. 79–83; also my "Hegel, Philosophy and Worship." In justice to Hegel, one must also say that his understanding of otherness, even within the context of dialectical self-mediation, does not simplistically evidence the totalitarian violence that has often been charged against it. Thus in his discussion of the Begriff in the *Logic* (Miller trans., p. 603), he says: "The universal is therefore *free* power; it is itself and takes its other within its embrace, but without *doing violence* to it; on the contrary, the universal is, in its other, in peaceful communion with itself. We have called it free power, but it could also be called *free love* and *boundless blessedness;* for it bears itself towards its other as towards *its own self;* in it, it has returned to itself." Within self-mediation, no violence to otherness need be perpetuated. Thinkers who criticize Hegel for totalitarian violence are often influenced by Nietzsche. Consider, by contrast, what Nietzsche says of the will to power in *Beyond Good and Evil,* sec. 259: "Here one must think radically to the very roots of things and ward off all weakness of sensibility. Life itself is essential assimilation, injury, violation of the foreign and the weaker, suppression, hardness, the forcing of one's own forms upon something else, ingestion and—at least in its mildest form—exploitation."

17. This is a tendency one often finds in practitioners of post-Heideggerian deconstruction. Significantly, such thinkers often take the criticism of the Hegelian Aufhebung as their point of departure, which reflects their fear of closure. In my view their response is at a level of philosophical discernment that is lower than Hegel's, not beyond it. See my *Art and the Absolute,* chap. 5, for an extended discussion.

18. See my "Plato's Philosophical Art and the Identification of the Sophist." Here we also see the proximity or affinity between dialectic as dialogue and the metaxological. If we take the latter seriously, however, it may mean remapping entirely our relations to otherness.

6 DESIRE, CONCRETENESS, AND BEING

1. Previously I referred to Parmenidean being, in relation to both the absorbing god and static eternity. I have been critical of the reduction of difference to sameness. But perhaps one might read differently Parmenides' profound statement: *to gar auto noein estin te kai einai.* The issue turns on the interpretation of *auto.* Instead of reading this as a univocal identity or a dialectical identity in difference, we might perhaps read it as a metaxological community.

2. Regarding ostensive definition, one thinks of the Wittgensteinian critique of pointing

as seeming to give us immediate, univocal certainty about a thing without the mediation of identifying descriptions, or perhaps of Hegel's critique of sense certainty
in the first chapter of *Phenomenology of Spirit.*

3. This tendency also existed in early twentieth-century British discussion of pure sense-
data, which, of course, were treated in terms inspired by classical empiricism. Collingwood's critique in *The Principles of Art* is telling, as is his critique in the *Autobiography*
of what he calls, following Berkeley, the "minute philosophers." See my "Collingwood,
Imagination and Epistemology." It is appropriate here to say that knowledge of otherness is not a question of looking through the "veil of ideas" to things "out there."
This attitude has dominated much philosophy since Descartes and has been ably criticized recently by Richard Rorty in *Philosophy and the Mirror of Nature.* We have seen
already that knowledge of otherness does not involve joining together a dualistically
opposed "subject" and "object." The modes of identification and degrees of concreteness at issue in the present chapter are metaxological intermediations within the
community of being that is *always* between the self and the other. They relate to the
coming to express articulation of the community of being that is there.

4. Hegel, *Phenomenology of Spirit*, chap. 2.

5. Although the individual existent is primary substance for Aristotle, he nevertheless
says: "That which 'is' primarily is the 'what,' which indicates the substance of the thing"
(*Metaphysics* 1084a14). Again, the identity of a thing is inseparable from its essence
(see, for instance, *Metaphysics* 1031b18 ff.); though for Aristotle, *ousia* is not a merely
static essence, but involves the form of a process of becoming (*Metaphysics* 1015a10).
See Joseph Owens, *The Doctrine of Being in the Aristotelian Metaphysics;* also Curt Arpe,
Das Ti En Einai bei Aristoteles.

6. This question remains controversial. In Continental thought, one thinks of the legacy
of Husserl's *Wesensanschauung*, his notion of categorial intuition, an issue not irrelevant
to structuralism and the deconstructive critique of poststructuralism. In analytic philosophy, the question of Locke's real and nominal essence continues (see S. P. Schwartz,
ed., *Naming, Necessity and Natural Kinds*). For a perceptive discussion of traditional
Aristotelian eidos, the Husserlian transcendental ego, and criticism thereof in deconstruction and Wittgensteinian analysis, see Henry Staten, *Wittgenstein and Derrida,*
pp. 1–27.

7. The sense of dynamic form here is related to the notion of becoming as othering
that was discussed in chap. 4. See Aristotle's *Metaphysics* (1015a10, for instance) where
form, or essence, is identified with the end of a process of becoming. On Hegel on
form and forming, see my *Art and the Absolute*, chap. 5. One can sympathize with the
Wittgensteinian critique of the so-called essentialist fallacy, if essence is identified with
a rigidified eidos. But one cannot agree with the implication of sheer plurality without
connection sometimes enjoined by Wittgensteinians. Does not Wittgenstein's "family
resemblance," or notion of "forms of life," reintroduce a more open sense of essence?
Aristotle saw the relation of "family" and "form" in connection with "genus"—dynamic
form again is also implied in relation to *gens*, generation (see, e.g., *Metaphysics* 1024a28).

8. Aristotle *De Anima* 3. 8. Notice how Aristotle talks of intellect *(nous)* as the form of
forms *(eidos eidōn)*, and sometimes uses *logos* and *eidos* interchangeably (*De Anima*
412b10–413a3; *Metaphysics* 1039b20 ff.) This, I suggest, is not unrelated to the present
point concerning knowing as an indeterminate openness to otherness. It need not
imply any reduction of the otherness of the other. We see this also in the word *intellect*,
a word derived from the Latin *intellegere (inter-legere*, "to read between"; cf. *dialectic*
as *dia-legein);* for, if we stress the *inter*, there need be no domination of difference.

9. This is a pervasive theme in the opening chapters of the *Phenomenology.* One thinks

also of Hegel's inaugural lecture at Heidelberg (he repeats the point in his Berlin inaugural lecture), in which he praises the courage of knowledge and says that the initially hidden essence of the world cannot resist its power. Of course, Hegel has been seen as hubristic on this score. I will return to this issue later. In *Art and the Absolute*, chap. 2, I tried to do justice to Hegel's sense of the emergence of the inherent unity and universality of the particular thing in its concreteness.

10. We might here think of the critique of Platonic essentialism in Aristotelian and Tho- mist thought or the critique of Hegelian panlogism and essentialism by post-Hegelian existentialists; or we might think of the critique of Husserlian essentialism by many twentieth-century Continental thinkers. These are crucial episodes in ancient and medieval thought, in modern and contemporary philosophy. I am not here setting myself up as an adjudicator, but merely pointing to a knot of philosophical ambiguity that needs to be unraveled. Regardless of whether Plato or Hegel or Husserl were essentialists, the philosophical point is the adequacy of essence to account for full concreteness.

11. Hegel, it might be argued, tries to unite all these possibilities in an extraordinarily complex discourse. He also points beyond form to the forming power, though in places he implies that he has articulated the totality of forms that exhausts the possibilities of the forming power. (In chap. 8 I will develop a different sense of the forming power.) The issue is not unrelated to Hegel's view of being as an empty indeterminacy, as set forth at the beginning of the *Logic*. Hegel goes on to show that this beginning in indefinite immediacy must be explicitly mediated. It is not to be denied that Hegel returns to being at the end of the *Logic*, where the Absolute Idea is the final category; this does not reveal a sense of empty being, but rather, being as the intensive and fulfilled totality (*Logic*, p. 842). Note, however, that totality is the telos, the end that offers the full self-mediation of immediate being. The whole tends to dominate the infinite; self-mediation is stressed over intermediation. The metaxological offers a different sense of being and beginning, namely, an indeterminacy that is entirely positive and no mere indefiniteness, one not to be enclosed in totality. The openness of the beginning remains in an open-ended end.

12. See n. 7; also Collingwood, *The Idea of Nature*, chap. 3.

13. Consider, for instance, *Summa Theologiae*, I, Q. 4, art. 1, ad 3: *ipsum esse est perfectissimum omnium: comparatur enim ad omnia ut actus. Nihil enim habet actualitatem, nisi inquantum est: unde ipsum esse est actualitas omnium rerum, et etiam ipsarum formarum*. Of course, there is a view of contemporary Thomist scholarship, defended by Etienne Gilson, among others, that maintains that Aquinas is more radically "existentialist" than Ar- istotle, who remains "essentialist" in this respect; that even though primary being is individual substance, the primary sense of *ousia* remains *eidos* (see n. 5). Aquinas's notion of *esse* cannot be reduced to *eidos*, as the above citation makes clear. On Aquinas in relation to Heidegger's charge of *Seinsvergessenheit* (the oblivion of being) with respect to the tradition of metaphysics, see John Caputo's excellent *Heidegger and Aquinas*. For helpful discussion of some of the differences between Aquinas and Hegel in re- lation to being, see Denis Bradley's "Thomistic Theology and the Hegelian Critique of Religious Imagination," *New Scholasticism* 49, no. 1 (winter 1985): pp. 60–78.

14. I will return to this in chap. 8 in relation to the givenness of being.

15. See my "Memory and Metaphysics."

16. If we articulated the various mixtures of the four modes of identification and degrees of concreteness, we might approximate something like a typology of philosophical positions. Of course, we would have to consider the multiple interplays between self and other, the oscillations between one level and another, and the fine shadings of their merging and distinguishing.

7 DESIRE, OTHERNESS, AND INFINITUDE

1. We might recall here the tendency of the Greeks to think of the unlimited *(to apeiron)* in terms of the indefinite and the possibilities of chaos, as well as the Greek predilection for bounded wholeness. We might think of Aristotle's sense of the absurdity of the infinite regress or the fact that Plato's Demiurge in the *Timaeus* is subject to limit *(peras)* in terms of the eidē. *To apeiron* is the indefinite to be determined by eidos. Think of the bounded wholes of Greek sculpture. Here too we find awareness of the fine line separating the possibilities of human wholeness from the chaos of the Furies or the wild abandon of Dionysus or the willful, boundless desire of the tyrant (recognized by Plato). Below we will remark on the same predilection for wholeness in Hegel, even after the advent of Christianity, with its infinite inwardness, both in his aesthetic preferences and his philosophical view that the true is the whole. On the ancient preference for bounded wholes, see M. Foss, *The Idea of Perfection in the Western World,* pp. 14ff.

2. See A. Koyré, *From the Closed World to the Infinite Universe.*

3. For a discussion of Bruno in the context of the inauguration of modernity, see Hans Blumenberg, *The Legitimacy of the Modern Age,* pp. 549–96; see also the discussion of Nicholas of Cusa in relation to the importance of the notion of infinity, pp. 483–547.

4. Hegel, *Science of Logic,* pp. 137–56. I agree with Hegel's critique of the "bad infinite," but, as will become increasingly obvious, I believe that what is needed is more than a dialectical Aufhebung of the finite into the infinite. It demands metaxological intermediation between different kinds of infinitude. See the introduction to this essay, where I remark on the defense of finitude in post-Hegelian thought.

5. See chap. 4 on the positive possibilities of becoming, chap. 6 on "kinds" in relation to the third degree of concreteness.

6. This is related to the first sense that Aristotle gives to *phusis* in the *Metaphysics* (1014b17 f.). Though philologists quarrel with Aristotle's etymology, the philosophical point is nevertheless illuminating.

7. This is not entirely unrelated to the criticism of mechanistic views of nature and of the Cartesian will to be its "master and possessor" that we find in the contemporary ecological sense of the community of nature. If nature is an ecological community, we require, as it were, a kind of *pietas* of thereness. I would add the qualification, however, that neither organic metaphors nor the monistic sense of nature as a kind of absorbing god adequately capture the metaxological sense of community and the otherness and openness it defines, especially in relation to the human self as emergent freedom. See the qualification on organic metaphors in the discussion of agapeic otherness in chap. 8.

8. In chap. 3 we discussed a form of desire—namely, equivocal desire—that corresponds to indefinite sequential passage. Remember too (as discussed in chap. 4) that external becoming as coming to be and passing away cannot be reduced to equivocal process.

9. See chap. 3 above, as well as part 1 generally; also my "Memory and Metaphysics."

10. From Gerard Manley Hopkins's sonnet entitled "God's Grandeur." See also his "That Nature is a Heraclitean Fire."

11. Concerning the closeness of absolute being and nothing, God and the void, we might think of traditions of apophatic theology that, despite the sometimes ambiguous emphasis on the negative, are inspired by a positively saturated sense of the divine mystery.

12. The image of the moth, nocturnal creature, reminds us of Aristotle's image of the bat in sunlight, which Aquinas repeats, of Hegel's owl at twilight, and of the dazzling blindness effected by the illumination of the Platonic sun into which we must not look directly.

13. Heidegger's notion of the ontological difference between the being of Being and the being of beings has been the subject of much discussion. Perhaps the present distinction between these two senses of limit is not unrelated to it, though the present discussion is more Hegelian than Heideggerians are likely to be comfortable with and less shamefacedly respectful of so-called ontotheology.

14. Resistance, of course, is more characteristic of modern subjectivity, in which it is epistemologically related to the idealistic emphasis on the active nature of the knower and politically manifested in modernity's infatuation with the rhetoric of revolution and revolt. Resignation is more characteristic of, say, ancient Stoic acceptance and the recognition of the place of the human self within an order that will never be entirely the product of that self's will. The view that I am developing here tries to avoid the ontologically unanchored infinite restlessness of modern subjectivity, as well as the abject finitude that is merely overwhelmed by the otherness of being. It affirms finitude, having passed through desire's infinite inwardness, yet tries to place it appropriately within the otherness of being. On the ancient sage and human metaphysical unease, as well as the responses of what we might call post-Pascalian man, see G. Marcel, *Problematic Man*, pp. 65ff.

15. There is a rough correspondence between the triad (1) immediacy, (2) self-mediation, (3) intermediation and the quadruplicity (1) the univocal, (2) the equivocal, (3) the dialectical, (4) the metaxological. The asymmetry disappears if we remember that the univocal and the equivocal are two sides of the same orientation to the immediate. Their cross-relation, taking into account the three senses of infinitude being discussed, could then be represented thus:

(1) Immediacy	Infinite Succession	The Univocal / The Equivocal
(2) Self-mediation	Intentional Infinitude	The Dialectical
(3) Intermediation	Actual Infinitude	The Metaxological

16. For convenience, when I speak subsequently of the third form of infinity, I will refer to it as "the infinite."

17. See, for instance, Kant's doctrine of aesthetic ideas in *The Critique of Judgment*, sec. 49; aesthetic ideas are representations of imagination that occasion much thought, without any definite thought being entirely adequate, however. We might also consider Keats's notion of "negative capability" as a kind of aesthetic version of Aristotle's nous poiētikos in its openness to otherness. We might think, too, of the sense of wonder that the artwork releases, a sense that resists contraction or fixation in merely analytical concepts.

18. Kant's discussion of the sublime recognizes the discord and disequilibrium between human powers and the overwhelming majesty of nature. Nevertheless, he tends to see the sublime in terms of "subjective" feelings. Moreover, these feelings are even more subjective than those aroused by the beautiful, where form supplies an element of the objective. Though Kant relates the sublime to what he calls the Idea of Reason, he does not go far enough, failing to see that the sublime points to something constitutive of concrete being, something not merely subjective, but possessed of ontological weight. Hegel recognized something of this, but his predilection for beauty as harmonious wholeness made him wary of Symbolic and Romantic art, both of which exhibit disproportions of form and content, finite and infinite, and both of which are more properly sublime than beautiful, because they reveal a more, an excess. I agree with Hegel's ontological emphasis but, in line with the distinction between the third and fourth degrees of concreteness, see the sublime as of utmost importance regarding the finite and infinite in this sense: that it manifests a more not completely subsumable within a dialectical Aufhebung, though allowing of metaxological intermediation. Interestingly, Hegel's most extensive discussion of the sublime, in his *Aesthetics* (vol. 1,

pp. 362–77), is developed in the context of the Symbolic art form and in connection with Jewish transcendence. In the elevation of Geist over external nature, Hegel sees an advance over Oriental pantheism; nevertheless, he is not satisfied with the otherness of the divine and the otherness of nature in its opposition to the finite self. Otherness, whether of God or of nature, has not yet been aesthetically overcome. Greek art overcomes the resultant disunion in his view. For Hegel, Greek wholeness is clearly aesthetically superior to Jewish transcendence. The whole wins over the infinite. This is also relevant to the appropriate sense of the absolute, as we will see in part 3, in relation to what I call a "post-Romantic symbol," for example. See also my *Art and the Absolute*, chap. 6, on Hegel and the ontological weight of aesthetic beauty.

19. See the collection of articles on the sublime in *New Literary History*, vol. 16, no. 2 (Winter 1985).

20. Schopenhauer, *The World as Will and Representation*, vol. 1, p. 204. Schopenhauer, perhaps because of his dependence on the legacy of Kant, tends to a certain subjectivism in dealing with the sublime, his acknowledgment of the objective side of the matter remaining on the level of the third degree of concreteness in terms of the crucial importance he assigns to the Platonic Idea. He goes beyond the third degree and the Platonic Idea only in the case of music, which he sees as a *direct* copy of the Will itself. We find a celebration of the sublime in "deep-vallied Desmond" in a poem entitled "Gougane Barra" by the early nineteenth-century Cork poet J. J. Callanan. In his poem "The Recluse of Inchydoney," the poet identifies himself with the place and the landscape, identifying himself as the "wild voice of Desmond." On this, see Robert Welch, *Irish Poetry from Moore to Yeats*, chap. 2, esp. pp. 60–61.

21. I have had previous occasion to remark on the importance of Kant's doctrine of transcendental imagination for modern thought. Schelling was one of the first to give a strongly ontological significance to this doctrine in connection with the metaphysical meaning of the aesthetic. Coleridge's doctrine of primary imagination as the prime esemplastic power can also be seen to have ontological significance, especially if we keep in mind his view of finite creation as a repetition of the eternal "I am," as suggested in his *Biographia Literaria* (chap. 13). One of the crucial issues at stake in connection with the sublime is just this, its resistance to complete subjectivization: what is unmastered here reveals the recalcitrance of the power of being to complete humanization; yet in this recalcitrance is revealed its kinship with the original power of the human self.

22. On this, see chap. 2, n. 45 above; also my *Art and the Absolute*, chap. 6.

23. The unsheltering effect of the sublime and the ambiguity of the daimonic are not unrelated to the unsheltering experience of Nietzsche's madman in the wake of the death of God. Consider the images in this famous passage from *The Gay Science* (sec. 125): "Do we not stray as through infinite spaces?" Significantly, the preceding section is entitled "In the Horizon of the Infinite" and reveals Nietzsche's awareness of both the releasing and the terrifying power of the infinite. We are reminded of Pascal, but without the consolation of Christianity, and of Bruno's "heroic furor," but now ontologically unloosed from any moorings in a harmonious condition of being. I want to say that humanity may be more radically unsheltered by the sublime than Kant sometimes allows in his tendency to moralize the sublime, yet not so unsheltered as to preclude any sense of homecoming to being in the intrinsic worth of its thereness, a homecoming that the Nietzschean unsheltering seems to bar.

24. See Martin Buber, *Between Man and Man;* Gabriel Marcel, *The Mystery of Being*, vol. 1, chap. 9; Albert Camus, *The Rebel*, e.g., pp. 250ff.; M. Heidegger, *Being and Time*, div. 1, sec. 4; J. P. Sartre, *Being and Nothingness*, part 3; and E. Levinas, *Totality and Infinity*. I believe that Levinas's emphasis on the ethical meaning of the face to face is very important, but I disagree with his dualism of being and the good. Our present

concern is precisely with the goodness of being—the being there of the good man in agapeic otherness. Levinas is responding to a sense of moral neutrality in being, which he claims to find in Heidegger. Marcel, I believe, comes closer to the ontological weight of the "we are" without sacrificing its ethical significance.

25. Hegel, *Phenomenology of Spirit*, pp. 111ff. Toward the end of the *Phenomenology*, Hegel points to the infinitely open reciprocation of free spirit in the act of forgiveness. As Merold Westphal very relevantly suggests (*History and Truth in Hegel's Phenomenology*, pp. 226–27), it is not altogether clear how this turnabout from previous antagonistic relations is possible on the terms of an erotic conception of dialectic. For Hegel the life-and-death struggle between master and slave was very important, and Hegel liked to repeat that the fear of the Lord is the beginning of wisdom. J. Taminiaux has discussed the relationship of Hegel and Hobbes to this issue, in *Dialectic and Difference*, chap. 1. Death for Hobbes tends to be essentially an external threat, whereas for Hegel its significance is tied up with man's interiorization in spirit of the power of the negative. But again, there are different ways of recognizing the negative. Gratuitous origination before the sublime and agapeic otherness are two such responses that consent to our proper finitude and are thus to be distinguished from the will to power that refuses finitude. Hobbes's Leviathan reminds one of a man-made—that is, artificial—absorbing god. Hence Hobbes calls Leviathan a "mortal god."

26. In relation to agapeic otherness, we might think of Kant's "Kingdom of ends" as a moral community of persons. See too Josiah Royce's "Beloved Community." See E. Kohák, *The Embers and the Stars*, pp. 124ff., on the category of "person" as ultimate. On Kant's goodwill and Aristotle's character, see my "Phronesis and the Categorical Imperative."

27. On the violence of the eye, see Sartre's famous discussion of "the Look" in *Being and Nothingness*, part 3, chap. 1, sec. 4. One thinks of Milton's Satan in *Paradise Lost*: ". . . round he throws his baleful eyes,/That witnessed huge affliction and dismay/Mixed with obdurate pride and steadfast hate" (book 1, ll. 56–58). In contrast, one might think of how the unsheltered openness of lovers before each other can be a being at home with each other, or how the genuine act of forgiveness can be radically unsheltered yet reconciling; or one might see Christ's death as a radical unsheltering that is given up for an other.

28. As Aristotle rightly says (*Ethics* 1168a28 ff.), it is altogether appropriate that the good man should love himself. Part of the problem of self-will, of course, is accepting oneself, forgiving oneself for not being a god.

29. Of course, many commentators have detected something like this distended desire as infecting the entire will to power of modernity. See William Barrett, *The Illusion of Technique;* also my review of it in *The Independent Journal of Philosophy* 3 (1979): 148–49.

30. We might think here of Nietzsche's discussion of *ressentiment* in *The Genealogy of Morals*, book I, sec. 10. Ressentiment is the outgrowth of an inner lack, secretly vengeful of the other in its positive being, vengeful toward it as possessing superior, intrinsic worth. Ressentiment debases the value of the other to compensate for an inwardly lacking self. Max Scheler, in *Ressentiment*, has defended some forms of Christianity against Nietzsche's denunciations. One sometimes comes across interesting twists on the theme of ressentiment in a kind of left-wing inversion of the supposedly bourgeois ressentiment. Consider, for instance, this exchange between Sartre and Simone de Beauvoir. De Beauvoir: "When I first met you you had what you called an aesthetic of opposition. You thought it just as well that a very great part of the world should be detestable, that there should be a bourgeoisie, that there should be . . . in short, a world to loathe." Sartre: "Yes . . ." (S. de Beauvoir, *Adieux: A Farewell to Sartre*, p. 378).

31. This implies a judgment in favor of Plato and Aristotle, rather than Hobbes and Spi-

noza. There is, of course, the complexity in Spinoza that, while holding to a Hobbesian self-interest in understanding human desire, he nevertheless says in the *Ethics* that love is the only way to break through the closed circle of hatred. It is unclear, however, where the necessary agapeic openness can come from if desire is exhausted in Hobbesian self-interest. This reflects a general tension in Spinoza between the ancients and the moderns.

32. See chap. 3 above, where I talk about a prior integrity of being with regard to the self. It is a similar prior integrity of being that must here be acknowledged with respect to the other. What is involved is a certain honoring of otherness.

33. An image expressing the fourfold possibilities in regard to the univocal, the equivocal, the dialectical, and the metaxological might be as follows. The univocal is a clenched fist, a unity closed in on itself. The equivocal is two hands spread apart, the fingers of each splayed wide, thrusting away in a movement of separation. The dialectical is the hand of one enclosing the other. The metaxological is two hands entwining, clasped in reciprocal friendship.

34. Organicist models of community, of course, are common in idealist social and political theories; they tend to evolve from consideration of the problem of the place of the individual within the larger whole. See D. D. Raphael, *Moral Philosophy*, chap. 8, and my review thereof in *Philosophical Studies* (Ireland) 29:317–18.

35. The difference between the third and fourth degrees of concreteness is again revealed here. The issue also relates to the debated question of whether Hegel's dialectic allows for a letting be of the other in its otherness, an otherness that is not just *for* the self. Consider these two ways of trying to know the other. In the first (corresponding to dialectical comprehension of form), I say: "I know what you are saying." In the second (corresponding to the metaxological affirmation of being), I say: "I know what you are saying, but an irreducible difference still remains; yet, I acknowledge you as other." This further acknowledgment of otherness is crucial. It is not the grasp of a *what*, but the affirmation of one *who* is in his very being justified in his own right, and not simply by me. This acknowledgment is a knowing, without being reducible to the dialectical comprehension of form. It is a kind of ontological salutation of the rightness of the other as other. It is born in a free consent to a difference. A knowing, this acknowledgment is also an unknowing: I may not dialectically comprehend, but I accept, I consent, I affirm, this otherness. Such acts of acceptance of what is beyond are vital. Moreover, to accept the other as beyond is not just to say that the other is out there, like the empty Jenseits that Hegel attacked; for the beyondness of the other is right there before me, absolutely there.

36. This, of course, is part of the appeal of the Romantic "return to Nature." Romantic thinkers have often been caricatured as hopelessly lost, as pining "Beautiful Souls." But Romanticism was in many respects an extraordinarily robust movement of the human spirit. See M. H. Abrams, *The Mirror and the Lamp* and *Natural Supernaturalism;* also my *Art and the Absolute*, chap. 6.

37. Modern Europe has been charged with fulfilling this destiny in the death camps and the Holocaust, by Camus in *The Rebel* and, more recently, by André Glucksmann in *The Master Thinkers* (see Introduction, n. 12), to name but two examples. I find unacceptable what seems to be a sheerly univocal accusation against the Western tradition; for in that tradition I see as much reverence for otherness as violence toward it.

8 DESIRE AND THE ABSOLUTE ORIGINAL

1. Plato *Parmenides* 130c7ff. One thinks too of Heraclitus's supposed response when a visitor came upon him in his everydayness; here too are gods. On this, see Aristotle

De Partibus Animalium (1.5.645a17). Aristotle is talking about the beauty of the perishing phenomena of nature, in contrast to the imperishable divine; but he enjoins
us not to recoil with aversion from the humbler things. Here one thinks too of Rilke's
belief that a certain naming of things, a certain saying of "jug," "house," "tree," could
be one of the highest human attainments.

2. Aquinas *Summa Theologiae*, Q. 47, art. 1. The possibility of the glorification of plurality
entailed by the doctrine of creation seems to me to escape the charge of reductive
ontological nostalgia often leveled against the tradition of metaphysics, or ontotheology.

3. Something of this is involved in Aquinas's third way, in the contrast between necessary
and possible (contingent) being: part of the question turns on whether the *being* of
contingency can be accounted for in terms of the totality of contingent beings. Some
commentators, Copleston for instance, have spoken of a "vertical" causality. One can
agree with the Kantian interrogation of ambiguities in the notion of "cause" if we
think of the latter as a finite determinate origin. But it seems to me that Aquinas is
clearly trying to think a radically different sense of origin.

4. Consider Marcel's helpful distinction between "problem" and "mystery," for instance,
in *Being and Having*, pp. 185–86.

5. In *Against Epistemology*, Adorno criticizes the search for origins. His targets are immediacy, the primitive or original, self-transparency, the assured self-identity of subjectivity, and so on. Unfortunately, the whole tradition tends to get boxed into this
one mold: dominance of identity with the secret fascistic will to power in the form
of spiritual lordship over the world. "The enemy, the other, the non-dialectical. . . .
Fascism sought to actualize the philosophy of origins" (p. 20). I agree with the critique
of pure immediacy and see transcendental subjectivity as problematic. I also agree
that dialectic risks disrespecting otherness. But I think that the tradition of philosophy
has been more complex in regard to otherness than is allowed by Adorno's Left-
Hegelian simplification. It is also unacceptable to identify origins with immediacy,
as I have argued throughout. To conflate origins with fascism is to identify a degenerate realization with the essential promise of a possibility. In regard to origins,
Adorno's negative dialectics anticipates post-Heideggerian deconstruction à la Derrida, though the latter tends to have a more explicitly cultural, rather than political,
agenda.

6. This is one of the fundamental difficulties with religious representation, of course;
idolatry consists in wrongly identifying the image with the original. See my "Hegel
and the Problem of Religious Representation."

7. Here one sympathizes with the critique of any "objectifying proof" of God. But perhaps traditional "proofs" need not always be interpreted thus. They might instead
be seen as certain meditations on the metaxological, and hence not ontotheological,
if by this we mean a kind of Wolffian rationalism that imposes a grid of abstractions
on the divine. If, by *ontotheology*, one wishes to acknowledge a certain kinship of religion
and philosophy, however, one might reconsider the metaxological between in terms
of the otherness of nature as the ontological context of the cosmological "proofs";
likewise, Kant's moral "proof" and the ontological "proof" might be reconsidered in
terms of a metaxological interpretation of the inward abyss of self and its recalcitrant
otherness.

8. Hence Plato's reminder of the tentativeness of his explorations, his open acknowledgment that accounts of origins and ends have an unavoidable element of the likely
story (e.g., *Timaeus* 29c4ff.).

9. In *Tractatus Logico-Philosophicus* 6.44, Wittgenstein puts the point thus: "Not what the
world is, but that it is, is the mystical."

10. Parmenides' *estin*, and Heidegger's *es gibt* are not irrelevant here. See John Caputo,
Aquinas and Heidegger, on Heidegger in relation to Aquinas's esse. Aquinas is not an

ontotheologian in Heidegger's sense, which implies a forgetting of the difference between Being and beings. Nor is the present discussion ontotheology in that sense.
But, with Aquinas and also with Hegel, one may grant a certain affiliation between
religious and philosophical concerns; and if the term *ontotheology* implies that affiliation,
then the present work is not programmatically averse to ontotheology. See my remarks
in the Introduction. Caputo ably defends Aquinas, but in chap. 5 he claims that Heidegger more truly thinks what it is that gives the difference of Being and beings: the
differentiation itself, the difference (*Austrag*) that gives the ontological difference
(*Differenz*). The present discussion of the absolute original is clearly concerned to think
what it is that gives this difference, and my emphasis on the metaxological is not incompatible with Heidegger's sense of the between (see Caputo, *Aquinas and Heidegger*,
p. 160). But I am unsure about Caputo's and Heidegger's claim that Aquinas was
not concerned with thinking about what it is that gives the ontological difference.
The issue is too large to deal with adequately here, but let me make these points.
Heidegger tends to see *creatio ex nihilo* on the model of Greek making. This, I believe,
is a fundamental distortion. Creatio ex nihilo is not the imposing of form on preexisting matter, as, say, with Plato's Demiurge; it points to a radical origination that is
bound by nothing. Now Aquinas's *ipsum esse* might be seen as a philosophical name
for Being as radically originative in this sense. Moreover, creatio ex nihilo gives an
irreducible difference between God and finite created being; the sense of *ens creatum*
as "standing outside" its originating "cause" indicates this irreversible outside, this
irreducible otherness. In our terms, it may indicate an asymmetrical relationship between the absolute original and originated being, a relationship that is not reducible
to dialectical mutuality, moreover. So also, creatio ex nihilo might be seen as indicating
an agapeic origin that gives difference in the sense of the metaxological—metaxological
between itself and finite being, metaxological relative to the community of finite beings.
Aquinas does not say all this, but I think it is not incompatible with his views, especially
if we grant the disjunction between creation and fabrication in the sense of Aristotle's
technē.

Heidegger regards Hegel as an ontotheologian, but there are crucial differences
between Aquinas and Hegel. For Hegel the world of finite being is a disclosure of
the absolute, but their relation is not radically asymmetrical, nor is an irreducible
otherness given. I believe that Hegel was also trying to think what it is that gives the
difference (*Austrag*), but that he did so in terms of dialectical self-mediation, so that
the origin exhaustively determines itself and its otherness in its self-disclosure. There
is no radical otherness between it and finite being and hence no "withdrawal" in Heidegger's sense or "transcendence" of Aquinian character. The present account of the
self's place in metaxological otherness as possibly metaphoric of the absolute original
is sympathetic to these latter emphases.

11. Plato, *Symposium* 205b10ff. Consider also Thales' phrase (reported by Diogenes Laer-
tius) for the world as *poiēma theou*.
12. On the regulative ideal as a subjective, formal postulate, see the *Critique of Pure Reason*,
Transcendental Dialectic, chap. 3, esp. sec. 7 and appendix. It is very important to
notice how Kant's entire discussion moves between the poles of the ens realissimum
and the regulative ideal; sometimes it seems as if the regulative ideal is merely the
ens realissimum but projected only as a subjective, formal postulate.
13. On Hegel's critique of the Kantian "ought to be," see, for instance, the *Enzyklopädie*,
sec. 60; on the "bad infinite," see *Science of Logic*, pp. 137 ff. There, Hegel also criticizes
the ought (pp. 131ff.).
14. Heidegger's critique of the metaphysics of presence is perhaps especially applicable
to positions dominated by the univocal sense of being, as here with the ens realissimum. As should be clear, I agree with certain aspects of the critique of univocity

but disagree with the Heideggerian tendency to totalize the tradition of philosophy as univocal logocentrism. The metaxological involves forms of presence and logos, but not forms reducible to the univocal.

Concerning the indefiniteness of Kant's regulative ideal, we find a certain equivocation and vacillation in that Kant is caught between realism and idealism, otherness and selfhood, and does not always reconcile the two. Thus, in the *Critique of Pure Reason*, there can be no theoretical proof of the existence of God or the soul as substance; for here we are at the ontic level of being and the scientific knowledge of nature in its exteriority. But in the Second and Third Critiques we find this no balanced by a somewhat equivocal yes, in that they try to suggest, in a complex way, some actual sense of the thereness of the unconditional. Here we are not just dealing with finite things in exterior nature. The Second Critique points to some sense of the unconditional in humans as moral. In his treatment of the aesthetic and the teleological, Kant tries to tease out some sense of the whole, but in an affirmation so hedged with qualification that we easily become lost. As so often with Kant, one has the feeling of two steps forward, one step backward. Many commentators who see only destructive results in the *Critique of Pure Reason* fail to do justice to this affirmative movement forward.

Hegel tries to drive a way through Kant's equivocal vacillation between realism and idealism, and dialectical self-mediation is said to be constitutive of the very life of the absolute. I will take this up below. Hegel risks an exaggerated extrapolation from the being of the self as dialectical mediation and does not do justice to the sense of otherness that we have defended in relation to metaxological intermediation. Compared to many versions of traditional theism, Hegel's strategy is very powerful. Yet his dialectical sense of selfhood and otherness make his strategy different from the one we have followed.

15. One might mention here the tendency to identify theogony and cosmogony in idealistic and pantheistic appropriations of Spinoza's *causa sui*: God needs to become, and his self-becoming cannot be separated from the becoming process of the created world. But these are characteristics of an erotic absolute. Schelling's appropriation of Spinoza also exhibits some of these characteristics. On this, see Werner Marx's *The Philosophy of F. W. J. Schelling*, pp. 64ff. and 83ff. Let me also mention two important atheistic versions of erotic absolutes, namely those of Schopenhauer and Nietzsche. Schopenhauer explicitly calls the *genital organs* the focal point of the Will, which for him is the primordial ground of all becoming (*The World as Will and Representation*, vol. 1, p. 203, also 330). Moreover, all willing arises from lack, from deficiency (p. 196). Thus, the primordial Will is a dark, blind striving which struggles to release itself from the suffering self-insistence of desire in bondage to coming into being and passing away; hence as primordial beginning, the origin lacks the peace it strives to effect through what is essentially an erotic struggle to transcend eros. Notice the importance of the Platonic Idea in relation to the healing peace of art for Schopenhauer.

We find an appropriation of Schopenhauer's Will in Nietzsche's Will to power. We find a clear example of an erotic absolute in Nietzsche's *Birth of Tragedy* (see part 3), where he speaks of the primal one (*das Ureine*) that through suffering and contradiction, creation and destruction, seeks its *own redemption* via the process of becoming. (We might note the revealing language that studs the *Birth of Tragedy*—e.g., in sec. 17—regarding the pain of the eternal lust for life, indeed language of the maternal womb.) In contrast to Schopenhauer, however, Nietzsche came to deny any Platonic peace beyond the erotic struggle, absolutizing the becoming of the Will to power in the figure of Dionysus. It is no accident that such an absolute ends up looking like an absorbing god, for Apollonian individuation seems to be swallowed up by the Dionysian Will to power. Of interest here is Nietzsche 's description of the world as a "monster of energy" (*The Will to Power*, p. 550; entry dated 1885). Here the positive self-becoming of the Will to power has the character of a cosmic circle. It reminds us of the Parmenidean One, only now energized by Heraclitean becoming, in its eternal arising and dissolution. It is impossible for the philosophically attuned ear not to hear certain Spinozistic, even Hegelian, echoes here.

16. Hegel, *Science of Logic*, pp. 82ff.

17. See chap. 6 for the previous discussion of "being is." I repeat that, understood in the proper light, this need not be seen as a hollow tautology. Erazim Kohák has an insightful discussion of the traditional belief that being and nothing are not convertible (*The Embers and the Stars*, pp. 57ff.). He also comments on some of the moral implications of the asymmetry of being and nothing; should we make them convertible, certain nihilistic consequences are possible in relation to relativism and historicism (p. 58). Hegelianism is not mentioned, though some forms of post-Hegelian thought give evidence of just these difficulties (on p. 59, he mentions Heidegger on *Sein* and *Zeit*). On Hegel's negativity and the crucial question of how the negation of the negation is at all capable of producing positive content, see Stanley Rosen's critical discussion in his *G. W. F. Hegel*, pp. 276ff.

18. Aquinas, *Summa Theologiae*, I, Q. 25; see also H. P. Owen, *Concepts of Divinity*.

19. Jacques Derrida says: "The motif of homogeneity, the theological motif *par excellence*, is decidedly one to be destroyed" (*Positions*, pp. 63–64). There may be some element of truth in this if we are dealing with something like an absorbing god, though even here there are complex ambiguities that are not to be destroyed. But the view is decidedly crude if our philosophical sights are on more sophisticated notions of the divine. Derrida's remark is symptomatic of the deconstructionist's horror of tabooed univocity. Ironically, a peculiar totalitarian ambition seems to inform Derrida on this issue in his "appropriation" of the tradition of philosophy. Consider: "A noun is proper when it has but a single sense. Better, it is only in this case that it is properly a noun. Univocity is the essence, or better, the *telos* of language. *No philosophy, as such, has ever renounced this Aristotelian ideal. This ideal is philosophy*" (*Margins*, p. 247; emphasis added). How can one respond philosophically to such totalizing, reductive claims? If one does respond, one is immediately indicted by that very fact on the charge of univocity. Philosophers get caught in something like a Cretan liar paradox if they claim to even try to think beyond univocity. But, of course, there are philosophers (I do not say "philosophy, as such") who think deeply beyond univocity. Is it perhaps Derrida himself who, in the heel of the hunt, reduces philosophy as such to a univocal core, namely, the ideal of univocity itself?

20. Plato *Timaeus* 29e2–3. See A. Lovejoy, *The Great Chain of Being*, for the reiteration of this view throughout the tradition. Chap. 11 of Lovejoy's classic work contains discussion very relevant to what I am calling an erotic absolute, especially in relation to Schelling.

21. See Aristotle *Physics* 264b10 ff. on circular motion as the most perfect. The image of the circle is pervasive in Hegel's thought; indeed the *Logic*, p. 842, is described as the circle of circles. This relates to Hegel's sense of being as a dialectically self-mediating whole.

22. In *Totality and Infinity*, Levinas seems intent on defending the ultimacy and recalcitrance of infinity relative to any totalizing concepts. I agree with the stress on infinity but do not think we need pit it against the notion of the whole in such a dualistic contrast. Levinas does not always distinguish precisely enough the different senses of infinity. One of the lines of argument throughout this book has been that a more open sense of wholeness is absolutely necessary and need not be vulnerable to the totalizing charge.

23. On the "dialectical creation" of nature in the going forth of the Absolute Idea into externality, see the controversial passages at the end of Hegel's *Logic*, pp. 843–44.

On the identity of being and essence in the God of classical theism, see Owen, *Concepts of Divinity*.

24. Aquinas, *Summa Theologiae*, I, Q. 45, art. 5. This radical difference of God's creative act should serve as a warning against any reduction to human fabrication, understood as the imposition of form on matter. See n. 14 above in connection with Heidegger's ontological difference. On the radical nature of creation as traditionally understood, see Langdon Gilkey, *Maker of Heaven and Earth*. Human creative acts, understood as gratuitous origination, image this more radical origination, insofar as such originative acts, even in the face of the radical negativity of death, may create for no reason beyond the goodness of creation. I am cautious about using the term *creativity* with respect to humans, since contemporary use of the term tends to be somewhat mindless. See my remarks in part 1 regarding the modern mania for originality. In a way I am trying to find some middle ground between the traditional absolute restriction of creation to God and the modern, indiscriminate, indifferent application of the notion.

25. An end that is no end may seem like a contradiction, but I am here thinking of something like Kant's "purposiveness without a purpose" *(Zweckmässigkeit ohne Zweck)* in the *Critique of Judgment*.

26. See my "Memory and Metaphysics"; we might think also of Plato's *exaipnēs* (e.g., *Symposium* 210e3ff.), the instant of illumination in *noēsis*, or Kierkegaard's "moment," to name but two examples. See Søren Kierkegaard, *The Concept of Anxiety*, pp. 85–88; also David Humbert, "Kierkegaard's Use of Plato in his Analysis of The Moment in Time," *Dionysius* 7 (1983): 149–83. On the theme of transfiguration in Hegel, see my *Art and the Absolute*, chap. 6.

27. See G. Marcel, *The Mystery of Being*, vol. 1, pp. 39ff., where he speaks of the ineradicability of some sense of high and low for humans as incarnate beings. These are categories of "lived experience" that we cannot do away with, despite the flattening of existential dimensions that happens, say, in mathematical physics. The only way these might be changed is if our actual mode of insertion in the universe were altered.

28. Some thinkers like Sartre, Merleau-Ponty, and Camus imply some such dualistic either/or between human and divine creativity: either one or the other, not both; and they opt for human creativity. The questionable tendency here is the treatment of finite being as absolutely determined if God exists; that is, there is a confusion of the self-determination of the divine with a rigid, necessitarian determinism in the course of finite being. This is a version of a confusion noted previously: to treat as identical the absolute original as whole and the creation of the world or, alternatively, to identify the becoming process of the world with the self-determination of the divine. Here we find the shadow of Hegel's dialectical self-mediation or, better, the shadow of a Spinozistic absorbing god, where clearly the self-determination of God is identified with the necessarily determined structure found in nature. This necessitarianism is tied up with the univocity of substance in Spinoza. Sartre's ontology also has obvious Spinozistic overtones. And, of course, Sartre, Camus, and Merleau-Ponty seem to accept from Nietzsche, somewhat unquestioningly, the antithetical dualism, or oppositional either/or, between God and human creativity. In his overblown will to human creativity, Nietzsche cannot tolerate any transcendent creator. In this, we again see a fragment broken off from the Hegelian legacy. For this attitude can be seen as simply a carrying through of the logic of Left Hegelianism as initially expressed by Feuerbach, Bauer, Ruge, and Marx, among others. These thinkers see God as the illegitimate extrapolation of human creativity, interpret the difference between God and man as an opposition to human creativity, and will to restore to man what previously was attributed to God alone. On this, see L. Stepelevich, ed., *The Young He-*

gelians; John Toews, *Hegelianism;* Karl Löwith, *From Hegel to Nietzsche;* and my *Art and the Absolute,* chaps. 3 and 4.

29. On Hegel and these three types of art, see my *Art and the Absolute,* chap. 3. The religious nature of the issue is also discussed there.

30. Descartes, *Discourse on the Method,* part 6.

31. On modern art, primitivism, and immediacy, see Karsten Harries, *The Meaning of Modern Art,* pp. 95–108. On modern philosophy and the search for origins in immediacy, see T. Adorno, *Against Epistemology.*

32. In the Introduction I described this essay as a kind of Augustinian odyssey embarked on after Hegel. What I am calling a post-Romantic symbol is related to this. This, it should be clear, has nothing to do with any merely reactionary return to the past.

33. On this, see Carl Vaught, *The Quest for Wholeness,* esp. chap. 4 in connection with Hegel; also Donald Verene, *Hegel's Recollection: A Study of Images in the Phenomenology of Spirit.*

34. Hegel's unease with the disproportions of Symbolic and Romantic art and his predilection for the harmonious wholeness of Classical, Greek art reflects his more general tendency to understand infinity in terms of a dialectically self-mediating whole. See Hegel's *Science of Logic,* p. 149, where he says that *the circle* is the proper image of the true infinity that is bent back on itself and, in distinction to the line, is closed. That is, despite his critique of what I am calling the absorbing god, Hegel is not entirely free of its influence. Consider the very important discussion of Spinoza in Hegel's *Lectures on the History of Philosophy,* vol. 3, pp. 252–90. Spinoza is said to be the real starting point, indeed, the testing point, of modern philosophy. Hegel says: "You are either a Spinozist or not a philosopher at all" (p. 283), and again: "To be a follower of Spinoza is the essential commencement of all philosophy" (p. 257). Or again: "The difference between our standpoint and that of the Eleatic philosophy is only this, that through the agency of Christianity concrete individuality is in the modern world present throughout in spirit" (p. 258). This last quotation is clearly relevant to what I am calling a post-Romantic symbol. But what follows from the latter is the breaking open of the Eleatic whole by the infinite inwardness of Christianity. It is impossible to seamlessly reconcile this inwardness with a Parmenidean absorbing god. Quite the contrary, we are forced to question all closed wholes and to develop a different sense of the absolute original. On the absorbing god, see chap. 1 above, esp. n. 14.

While Spinoza's manner of articulating the matter makes it difficult to avoid an absorbing god, there is no need to deny his greatness as a thinker; one may agree with many of his views. He especially helps us to see the limitations of dualism and of merely external relations; he has a penetrating view of each being's *conatus essendi,* the inherent affirmation of its being manifested by each being, as well as a deep understanding that hatred cannot be conquered with hatred. One must especially respect his sense of the ultimate togetherness of things, a togetherness that Spinoza interprets in terms of a monism of the whole, a togetherness that I have tried to reinterpret in terms of a metaxological community of originals.

Bibliography

Abrams, M. H. *The Mirror and the Lamp*. New York: Oxford University Press, 1953.
———. *Natural Supernaturalism*. New York: Norton, 1971.
Adorno, T. *Against Epistemology: A Metacritique*. Trans. W. Domingo. Cambridge, Mass.: MIT Press, 1983.
Aquinas, Thomas. *Basic Writings*. Ed. A. Pegis. New York: Random House, 1944.
Aristotle. *Basic Works*. Ed. Richard McKeon. New York: Random House, 1941.
Arpe, Curt. *Das Ti En Einai bei Aristoteles*. New York: Arno Press, 1976.
Augustine, St. *Confessions*. Trans. W. Watts. Cambridge, Mass.: Harvard University Press, 1968.
Barrett, William. *The Illusion of Technique*. New York: Doubleday, Anchor Books, 1978.
Beck, L. W. *Actor or Spectator*. New Haven: Yale University Press, 1976.
Berlin, Isaiah. *Russian Thinkers*. New York: Penguin, 1978.
Blumenberg, Hans. *The Legitimacy of the Modern Age*. Trans. R. M. Wallace. Cambridge, Mass.: MIT Press, 1983.
Bradley, F. H. *Appearance and Reality*. Oxford: Oxford University Press, 1893.
Buber, Martin. *Between Man and Man*. Trans. R. G. Smith. London: Collins, 1947.
Bubner, Rüdiger. *Modern German Philosophy*. Trans. Eric Matthews. New York: Cambridge University Press, 1981.
Butler, Clark. "Hermeneutic Hegelianism." *Idealistic Studies* 15 (1985): 121–36.
Camus, Albert. *The Myth of Sisyphus*. Trans. J. O'Brien. New York: Vintage, 1955.
———. *The Rebel*. Trans. A. Bower. New York: Vintage, 1956.
Caputo, John. *Heidegger and Aquinas: An Essay on Overcoming Metaphysics*. New York: Fordham University Press, 1982.
Collingwood, R. G. *An Autobiography*. Oxford: Oxford University Press, 1939.
———. *The Idea of Nature*. Oxford: Clarendon Press, 1945.
———. *The Principles of Art*. Oxford: Clarendon Press, 1938.
Cooper, Barry. *The End of History: An Essay on Modern Hegelianism*. Toronto: University of Toronto Press, 1984.
De Beauvoir, S. *Adieux: A Farewell to Sartre*. Trans. P. O'Brian. New York: Pantheon, 1984.

247

Deleuze, Gilles. *Nietzsche and Philosophy.* Trans. H. Tomlinson. New York: Columbia University Press, 1983.

Derrida, Jacques. *Margins of Philosophy.* Trans. A. Bass. Chicago: University of Chicago Press, 1982.

———. *Positions.* Trans. A. Bass. Chicago: University of Chicago Press, 1981.

———. "White Mythology: Metaphor in the Text of Philosophy." Trans. F. C. T. Moore. *New Literary History* 6 (Autumn 1974): 5–74.

———. *Writing and Difference.* Trans. A. Bass. Chicago: University of Chicago Press, 1978.

Descartes, R. *The Philosophical Writings.* Trans. J. Cottingham, R. Stoothoff, and D. Murdoch. Cambridge: Cambridge University Press, 1985.

Descombes, Vincent. *Modern French Philosophy.* Trans. L. Scott-Fox and J. M. Harding. New York: Cambridge University Press, 1980.

Desmond, William. *Art and the Absolute: A Study of Hegel's Aesthetics.* Albany: State University of New York Press, 1986.

———. "Augustine's *Confessions:* On Desire, Conversion and Reflection." *Irish Theological Quarterly* 47, no. 1 (1980): 224–33.

———. "The Child in Nietzsche's Menagerie." *Seminar* 5 (1981): 40–44.

———. "Collingwood, Imagination and Epistemology." *Philosophical Studies* (Ireland) 24 (1976): 82–103.

———. "Hegel and the Problem of Religious Representation." *Philosophical Studies* (Ireland) 30 (1984): 9–22.

———. "Hegel, History and Philosophical Contemporaneity." *Filosofia Oggi* 4, no. 2 (1981): 211–26.

———. "Hegel, Philosophy and Worship." *Cithara* 19, no. 1 (1979): 3–20.

———. "Hermeneutics and Hegel's Aesthetics." *Irish Philosophical Journal* 2 (1985): 94–104.

———. "Memory and Metaphysics." *Seminar* 3 (1979): 21–31.

———. "Phronesis and the Categorical Imperative." *Philosophical Studies* (Ireland) 27 (1980): 7–15.

———. "Plato's Philosophical Art and the Identification of the Sophist." *Filosofia Oggi* 2, no. 4 (1979): 393–403.

Flay, Joseph C. *Hegel's Quest for Certainty.* Albany: State University of New York Press, 1984.

Foss, M. *The Idea of Perfection in the Western World.* Princeton: Princeton University Press, 1946.

Foucault, M. *The Order of Things.* New York: Random House, 1970.

Freud. S. *The Ego and the Id.* Trans. J. Rivière. New York: Norton, 1963.

Gadamer, Hans-Georg. *Dialectic and Dialogue: Eight Hermeneutical Studies on Plato.* Trans. P. C. Smith. New Haven: Yale University Press, 1980.

———. *Hegel's Dialectic.* Trans. P. C. Smith. New Haven: Yale University Press, 1976.

———. *Truth and Method.* Translation edited by G. Barden and J. Cumming. New York: Seabury Press, 1975.

Gilkey, Langdon. *Maker of Heaven and Earth.* New York: Doubleday, 1959.

Glucksmann, André. *The Master Thinkers.* Trans. Brian Pearce. New York: Harper and Row, 1980.

Graff, Gerald. *Literature Against Itself: Literary Ideas in Modern Society.* Chicago: Chicago University Press, 1979.

Guardini, Romano. *Pascal for Our Time.* Trans. Brian Thompson. New York: Herder and Herder, 1966.

Guignon, Charles. *Heidegger and the Problem of Knowledge.* Indianapolis: Hackett, 1983.

Habermas, Jürgen. *Knowledge and Human Interest.* Trans. J. J. Shapiro. Boston: Beacon Press, 1971.

Harries, Karsten. *The Meaning of Modern Art: A Philosophical Interpretation.* Evanston: Northwestern University Press, 1968.

Harris, H. S. "The Hegel Renaissance in the Anglo-Saxon World Since 1945." *The Owl of Minerva* 51, no. 1 (Fall 1983): 77–106.

Hartmann, Klaus. *Sartre's Ontology.* Evanston: Northwestern University Press, 1966.

Hegel, G. W. F. *Aesthetics: Lectures on Fine Art.* 2 vols. Trans. T. M. Knox. Oxford: Clarendon Press, 1975.

———. *Enzyklopädie der philosophischen Wissenschaften im Grundrisse* (1830). Hamburg: Meiner, 1959.

———. *Hegel's Lectures on the History of Philosophy.* 3 vols. Trans. E. S. Haldane and F. H. Simson. New York: Humanities Press, 1974.

———. *Hegel: The Letters.* Trans. C. Butler and C. Seiler. Bloomington: Indiana University Press, 1984.

———. *Hegel's Logic: Being Part One of the Encyclopaedia of the Philosophical Sciences* (1830). Trans. W. Wallace. Oxford: Clarendon Press, 1975.

———. *Phänomenologie des Geistes.* Hamburg: Meiner, 1952. Translated as *Phenomenology of Spirit* by A. V. Miller. Oxford: Clarendon Press, 1977.

———. *Hegel's Philosophy of Mind: Being Part Three of the Encyclopaedia of the Philosophical Sciences* (1830). Trans. W. Wallace. Oxford: Oxford University Press, 1971.

———. *Wissenschaft der Logik.* Hamburg: Meiner, 1963. Translated as *Science of Logic* by A. V. Miller. New York: Humanities Press, 1969.

Heidegger, Martin. *Being and Time.* Trans. J. MacQuarrie and E. Robinson. New York: Harper and Row, 1962.

———. *Identity and Difference.* Trans. J. Stambaugh. New York: Harper and Row, 1974.

———. *Kant and the Problem of Metaphysics.* Trans. James S. Churchill. Bloomington: Indiana University Press, 1962.

———. *Nietzsche, Volume 1: The Will to Power as Art.* Trans. David Krell. New York: Harper and Row, 1979.

Heine, Heinrich. *Philosophy and Religion in Germany* (1835). Trans. J. Snodgrass. Boston: Beacon Press, 1959.

Heller, Eric. *The Artist's Journey into the Interior.* New York: Random House, 1959.

Heller, Peter. *Dialectics and Nihilism.* Amherst: University of Massachusetts Press, 1966.

Hobbes, Thomas. *Leviathan.* Ed. John Plamenatz. London: Collins, 1971.

Hoffman, Piotr. *The Anatomy of Idealism: Passivity and Activity in Kant, Hegel and Marx.* The Hague: Nijhoff, 1982.

Hofstadter, A., and Kuhns, R., eds. *Philosophies of Art and Beauty*. Chicago: University of Chicago Press, 1976.

Hume, David. *A Treatise of Human Nature*. Ed. L. A. Selby-Bigge. Oxford: Clarendon Press, 1888.

Husserl, E. *Cartesian Meditations*. Trans. D. Cairns. The Hague: Nijhoff, 1970.

———. *The Crisis of the European Sciences and Transcendental Phenomenology*. Trans. D. Carr. Evanston: Northwestern University Press, 1970.

———. *Formal and Transcendental Logic*. Trans. D. Cairns. The Hague: Nijhoff, 1969.

———. *The Idea of Phenomenology*. Trans. W. P. Alston and G. Nakhnikian. The Hague: Nijhoff, 1964.

———. *The Phenomenology of Internal Time-Consciousness*. Trans. J. Churchill. Bloomington: Indiana University Press, 1964.

James, William. *The Principles of Psychology*. New York: Holt, 1890.

Kant, I. *Critique of Judgement*. Trans. with analytical indexes by J. C. Meredith. Oxford: Clarendon Press, 1952.

———. *Critique of Pure Reason*. Trans. N. K. Smith. London: Macmillan, 1929.

Kearney, Richard. *Dialogues with Contemporary Continental Thinkers*. Manchester: Manchester University Press, 1984.

———. *Poétique du Possible*. Paris: Beauchesne, 1984.

———, ed. *The Irish Mind*. Atlantic Highlands, N.J.: Humanities Press, 1985.

Kierkegaard, S. *The Concept of Anxiety*. Trans. R. Thomte. Princeton: Princeton University Press, 1981.

———. *Edifying Discourses*. Trans. D. F. and L. M. Swenson. Ed. P. L. Holmer. London: Collins, 1958.

———. *Either/Or*. Trans. D. F. and L. M. Swenson. Princeton: Princeton University Press, 1971.

Kirk, G. S., and Raven, J. E. *The Presocratic Philosophers*. Cambridge: Cambridge University Press, 1971.

Kockelmans, Joseph, ed. *Phenomenology: The Philosophy of Edmund Husserl and its Interpretation*. New York: Doubleday, 1967.

Kohák, Erazim. *The Embers and the Stars: A Philosophical Inquiry into the Moral Sense of Nature*. Chicago: University of Chicago Press, 1984.

———. *Idea and Experience*. Chicago: University of Chicago Press, 1979.

Kojève, A. *Introduction to the Reading of Hegel*. Trans. J. Nichols and A. Bloom. New York: Basic Books, 1969.

Koyré, A. *From the Closed World to the Infinite Universe*. Baltimore: Johns Hopkins University Press, 1957.

Levinas, E. *Totality and Infinity*. Trans. A. Lingis. Pittsburgh: Duquesne University Press, 1969.

Lifton, Robert Jay. *History and Human Survival*. New York: Random House, 1968.

Lovejoy, A. *The Great Chain of Being*. Cambridge, Mass.: Harvard University Press, 1936.

Löwith, Karl. *From Hegel to Nietzsche*. Trans. D. E. Green. New York: Doubleday, 1967.

MacIntyre, Alasdair. *After Virtue: A Study in Moral Theory*. Notre Dame, Ind.: University of Notre Dame Press, 1981.

Marcel, Gabriel. *Being and Having*. London: Collins, 1965.

————. *The Mystery of Being*. 2 vols. South Bend, Ind.: Gateway Editions, n.d.

————. *Problematic Man*. Trans. B. Thompson. New York: Herder and Herder, 1967.

Martine, Brian. *Individuals and Individuality*. Albany: State University of New York Press, 1984.

Marx, Werner. *Heidegger and the Tradition*. Trans. T. Kisiel and M. Greene. Evanston: Northwestern University Press, 1971.

————. *The Philosophy of F. W. J. Schelling*. Trans. T. Nenon. Bloomington: Indiana University Press, 1984.

Megill, Allan. *Prophets of Extremity: Nietzsche, Heidegger, Foucault, Derrida*. Berkeley: University of California Press, 1985.

Merleau-Ponty, Maurice. *The Phenomenology of Perception*. Trans. Colin Smith. New York: Humanities Press, 1962.

————. *The Structure of Behaviour*. Trans. Alden L. Fisher. Boston: Beacon Press, 1963.

Montefiori, Alan, ed. *Philosophy in France Today*. New York: Cambridge University Press, 1983.

Moravcsik, J., and Teinko, P., eds. *Plato on Beauty, Wisdom and the Arts*. Totowa, N.J.: Rowan and Littlefield, 1982.

Murdoch, Iris. *The Fire and the Sun: Why Plato Banished the Poets*. Oxford: Clarendon Press, 1980.

Nietzsche, F. *Beyond Good and Evil*. Trans. M. Cowan. Chicago: Regnery, 1955.

————. *The Birth of Tragedy from the Spirit of Music*. Trans. C. P. Fadiman. New York: Random House, 1954.

————. *The Gay Science*. Trans. W. Kaufmann. New York: Random House, 1974.

————. *On the Genealogy of Morals*. Trans. W. Kaufmann. New York: Vintage, 1969.

————. *Selected Letters of Friedrich Nietzsche*. Trans. and ed. C. Middleton. Chicago: University of Chicago Press, 1969.

————. *The Will to Power*. Trans. W. Kaufmann and R. J. Hollingdale. New York: Vintage, 1967.

Owen, H. P. *Concepts of Divinity*. London: Macmillan, 1971.

Owens, Joseph. *The Doctrine of Being in the Aristotelian Metaphysics*. 3d rev. ed. Toronto: Pontifical Institute of Medieval Studies, 1978.

Pieper, J. *Leisure: The Basis of Culture*. Trans. A. Dru. New York: Pantheon, 1952.

Plato. *Opera*. Ed. J. Burnet. Oxford: Clarendon Press, 1900–15.

Rank, Otto. *The Don Juan Legend*. Trans. and ed. David G. Winter. Princeton: Princeton University Press, 1975.

Raphael, D. D. *Moral Philosophy*. Oxford: Oxford University Press, 1981.

Ricoeur, Paul. *The Conflict of Interpretations: Essays in Hermeneutics*. Trans. W. Domingo et al. Ed. Don Idhe. Evanston: Northwestern University Press, 1974.

————. *The Philosophy of Paul Ricoeur*. Ed. C. E. Reagan and D. Stewart. Boston: Beacon Press, 1978.

————. *The Rule of Metaphor*. Trans. R. Czerny. Toronto: University of Toronto Press, 1977.

Rist, John M. *Eros and Psyche.* Toronto: Toronto University Press, 1964.

Rockmore, Tom. *Fichte, Marx and the German Philosophical Tradition.* Carbondale: Southern Illinois University Press, 1980.

Rorty, Richard. *Consequences of Pragmatism.* Minneapolis: University of Minnesota Press, 1982.

―――. "Epistemological Behaviorism and the De-Transcendentalization of Analytical Philosophy." In *Hermeneutics and Praxis,* ed. R. Hollinger, chap. 4, pp. 89–121. Notre Dame: University of Notre Dame Press, 1985.

―――. *Philosophy and the Mirror of Nature.* Princeton: Princeton University Press, 1979.

Rosen, Stanley. *G. W. F. Hegel: An Introduction to the Science of Wisdom.* New Haven: Yale University Press, 1974.

―――. *The Limits of Analysis.* New York: Basic Books, 1980.

―――. *Nihilism.* New Haven: Yale University Press, 1968.

―――. *Plato's Sophist: The Drama of Original and Image.* New Haven: Yale University Press, 1984.

―――. *Plato's Symposium.* New Haven: Yale University Press, 1968.

Santayana, George. *Egotism in German Philosophy.* New York: Scribner, 1915.

Sartre, J.-P. *Being and Nothingness.* Trans. H. E. Barnes. New York: Washington Square Press, 1966.

―――. *Existentialism is a Humanism.* Trans. H. E. Barnes. New York: Philosophical Library, 1947.

Scheler, Max. *Ressentiment.* Trans. W. W. Holdheim. Ed. L. A. Coser. New York: Free Press, 1961.

Schelling, F. W. J. *Bruno, or, On the Natural and the Divine Principle of Things.* Trans. and ed. Michael Vater. Albany: State University of New York Press, 1984.

Schnädelbach, Herbert. *Philosophy in Germany 1831–1933.* Trans. Eric Matthews. New York: Cambridge University Press, 1984.

Schopenhauer, Arthur. *The World as Will and Representation.* 2 vols. Trans. E. F. J. Payne. New York: Dover, 1969.

Schwartz, S. P., ed. *Naming, Necessity and Natural Kinds.* Ithaca: Cornell University Press, 1977.

Singer, Irving. *The Nature of Love.* 2 vols. Chicago: University of Chicago Press, 1984.

Spinoza, B. *Opera.* Ed. J. van Vloten and J. P. N. Land. The Hague: Nijhoff, 1914.

Stapleton, Timothy. *Husserl and Heidegger: The Question of a Phenomenological Beginning.* Albany: State University of New York Press, 1983.

Staten, Henry. *Wittgenstein and Derrida.* Lincoln: Nebraska University Press, 1985.

Stepelevich, Lawrence, ed. *The Young Hegelians: An Anthology.* New York: Cambridge University Press, 1983.

Taminiaux, Jacques. *Dialectic and Difference: Finitude in Modern Thought.* Ed. J. Decker and R. Crease. Atlantic Highlands, N.J.: Humanities Press, 1985.

Taylor, Charles. *Hegel.* New York: Cambridge University Press, 1975.

Taylor, Mark C. *Erring: A Postmodern A/theology.* Chicago: University of Chicago Press, 1984.

————. *Kierkegaard's Pseudonymous Authorship*. Princeton: Princeton University Press, 1975.

Toews, John. *Hegelianism: The Path Towards Dialectical Humanism, 1805–1841*. New York: Cambridge University Press, 1980.

Vaught, Carl G. *The Quest for Wholeness*. Albany: State University of New York Press, 1982.

Verene, Donald. *Hegel's Recollection: A Study of Images in the Phenomenology of Spirit*. Albany: State University of New York Press, 1985.

Walker, Ralph. *Kant*. London: Routledge and Kegan Paul, 1978.

Weiss, Paul. *Privacy*. Carbondale: Southern Illinois University Press, 1983.

Welch, Robert. *Irish Poetry from Moore to Yeats*. Totowa, N.J.: Barnes and Noble, 1980.

Westphal, Merold. *History and Truth in Hegel's Phenomenology*. Atlantic Highlands, N.J.: Humanities Press, 1979.

————, ed. *Method and Speculation in Hegel's Phenomenology*. Atlantic Highlands, N.J.: Humanities Press, 1982.

White, Alan. *Absolute Knowledge: Hegel and the Problem of Metaphysics*. Athens: Ohio University Press, 1983.

————. *Schelling: An Introduction to the Science of Freedom*. New Haven: Yale University Press, 1983.

Whitehead, A. N. *Process and Reality*. New York: Macmillan, 1929.

Wittgenstein, L. *Tractatus Logico-Philosophicus*. Trans. D. F. Pears and B. F. McGuinness. London: Routledge and Kegan Paul, 1961.

Index